SPEAK
AND
GROW RICH

SPEAK
AND
GROW RICH

Dottie and Lilly Walters

PRENTICE HALL
Englewood Cliffs, New Jersey 07632

Prentice-Hall International (UK) Limited, *London*
Prentice-Hall of Australia Pty. Limited, *Sydney*
Prentice-Hall Canada, Inc., *Toronto*
Prentice-Hall Hispanoamericana, S.A., *Mexico*
Prentice-Hall of India Private Limited, *New Delhi*
Prentice-Hall of Japan, Inc., *Tokyo*
Simon & Schuster Asia Pte. Ltd., *Singapore*
Editora Prentice-Hall do Brasil, Ltda., *Rio de Janeiro*

© 1989 *by*
Prentice-Hall, Inc.
Englewood Cliffs, NJ

10 9 8 7 6 5 4 3 2

Library of Congress Cataloging-in-Publication Data

Walters, Dottie.
    Speak and grow rich / by Dottie and Lillet Walters.
        p.   cm.
    Includes index.
    ISBN 0-13-824541-X.—ISBN 0-13-825803-1 (pbk.)
    1. Public speaking—Handbooks, manuals, etc.   2. Oral
communication—Handbooks, manuals, etc.   I. Walters, Lillet.
II. Title.
PN4098.W35   1989
808.5'1'023—dc20   89-35781
                                                                          CIP

ISBN   0-13-824541-X

ISBN   0-13-825803-1   (PBK)

PRENTICE HALL
BUSINESS & PROFESSIONAL DIVISION
A division of Simon & Schuster
Englewood Cliffs, New Jersey 07632

Printed in the United States of America

Contents

7 HOW TO SPEAK AND GROW RICH WITH HIGH-PROFIT SEMINARS   145

8 SELLING YOUR PROGRAMS TO MEETING PLANNERS   159

Foreword

Earl Nightingale

Dottie Walters just doesn't quit. She has never quit, even back in the early days when she was pushing a baby stroller with two babies in it, trying to make a living selling advertising. One of the stroller wheels kept coming off. Dottie would watch the wheel and when it was in danger of slipping off the axle . . . she'd kick it! She'd kick it back on again, but she didn't slow down, and I hope to God she never does. We need her.

This is a first-class book for budding speakers. It is also a first-class book for professional speakers who want to know more about the industry, and to see if they're on track when it comes to fees and such.

A speaker is a strange creature. Kipling told the story of a band of primitive Stone-Age men huddled around a campfire. They had engaged in a tremendous battle that day with a wooly mammoth or a sabre-toothed tiger, or perhaps both. And suddenly, one of their number leaped to his feet and began walking up and down, gesticulating and talking, making sounds so graphic everyone around the campfire "saw" the battle all over again. He told them the story of what they had done, and they were filled with awe and frightened all over again, for there was magic in his words. So they took him away and killed him.

Today they would have paid him a fee.

I recall flying home one night after a speech. It was late, I was tired, and it was a long flight. The (wouldn't you know it) little old lady sitting next to me suddenly asked, "Do you mind if I ask you what you do?"

"Not at all," I replied, smiling. "I'm a post-prandial ululator," I said.

Her eyes widened. "You don't say!" she exclaimed. "My! That must be very interesting."

"Yes, it is."

It ended the conversation, and I could imagine her telling the members of her family about sitting on the airplane next to "one of those post-prandial ululators!" I could hear the gasps.

Post-prandial, for the uninformed, means after luncheon or dinner. A ululator, since the word comes from the howling of monkeys, is he who howls. The words simply came to me at the moment and I couldn't resist. But I was wrong when I told her that was what I did. It isn't. I'm a writer/broadcaster who is regularly sought as a speaker. Last Saturday I was in Boston. In a week or so, I'll be in Winston-Salem, then Texas, then Chicago. In about a month I'll be speaking in Munich; last October it was a speaking tour of Australia's principle cities; before that, Guam and Hawaii. Yes, a "speaker" does some traveling. A "speaker" does a lot of waking up in motels with a view of the parking lot; eating restaurant food . . . the interminable airports and the airplanes with their plastic lunches and late arrivals.

But most of the time, I'm doing what I'm doing this minute—sitting at my IBM Selectric II making little black marks on white paper, because writing's my work. A "speaker" in my opinion, should have real, honest-to-God work in the world in addition to his "speaking."

Now a "trainer" is something else. That's his or her business, like my very special good friends, Joel Weldon and Glenna Salsbury. They are experts at training people to be better at what they do, and because they're so good at it, they're asked back to the same companies and organizations again and again, year after year. They earn movie-star incomes and deserve every dollar they get. It's hard, demanding, cerebral work. After a couple of hours in front of several hundred people, they're as tired as they would be after eight hours with a pick and shovel. They're good at what they do, they are experts at what they say, they meet an important need, and they work hard. They are also an important aspect of this book.

A "speaker" is asked to speak because of something he or she does surpassingly well. As Lee Iacocca is asked to speak on management, Dottie Walters is asked to speak on what she does. She has that special talent to put her thoughts into words so that the words go out and move the people. She is an expert with words, and if you have the urge to be a post-prandial ululator, you will need to be an expert with words, too. You'll need to know everything that's in this marvelous, delightful book. This book is as important to a budding speaker as *Chapman's Small Boat Handling* is to the new small boat owner. It's very, very important. For in addition to being a world-class expert on what she does, Dottie Walters is a kind, loving, helpful person who has never for a moment lost her human touch.

By all means read *SPEAK AND GROW RICH* by Dottie and her daughter, Lillet Walters. You'll get to know these remarkable women in the process. They are in every paragraph, and the love comes shining through, clear and bright. I cannot recommend this book too much. I hope it sells a million copies in the first year.

Earl Nightingale has been inducted into the International Speaker's Hall of Fame, and the Radio Hall of Fame. He holds the Napoleon Hill Foundation Gold Medal Award for Literary Excellence. He and his late partner, Lloyd Conant, pioneered the audio-publishing industry, forming the Nightingale-Conant Corp. of Chicago. Earl's famous "The Strangest Secret" has exceeded a million copies and has earned him the only gold record ever achieved for a speaking record. His "Our Changing World" radio show is currently carried in all 50 states, Mexico, Canada, a dozen countries overseas, as well as on Armed Forces Radio Network. Earl wrote the foreword for Dottie Walters' first book, "Never Underestimate the Selling Power of a Woman," published by Prentice Hall Inc. He and his beautiful wife, Diana, live in Arizona.

Introduction

As in any other business, professional speaking takes drive, vision, imagination, determination, inspiration, and hard work. In addition, as the actress Rosalind Russell once said, "If you have a little talent, that is nice."

Speak and Grow Rich shows you how to find your success in the lucrative world of professional speaking, writing, creating products, consulting, and then selling the ancillary rights to your special knowledge over and over again.

Our book highlights and reveals top speakers' techniques, shortcuts, and methods to jump-start your speaking career and keep it moving steadily upward. We show you how, step-by-step. We draw upon our own extensive experience in the professional speaking business to give you clear road maps that can help you see the myriad routes to your golden destination.

Being a professional speaker will lead you in many different exciting directions. As the world of professional speaking expands at an ever-rapid rate, opportunities for all kinds of speaking, training, teaching, writing, and related products are accelerating.

After you study this valuable book, you may decide to focus on the lucrative corporate field, offering in-house training. Or you may want to specialize in the exciting convention world and its many opportunities. The college circuit may also be a perfect speaker target for you. Perhaps you will prefer to perform on cruise ships or at beautiful, worldwide resorts. Or you might decide, as Tony Robbins, the famous "Walk on Hot Coals" seminar leader did, to offer your programs directly to the public in single-day or weekend-retreat formats. There are many ways to offer programs as fund raisers, as well. We show you all of them in *Speak and Grow Rich*. You may even want to combine several types of paid professional speaking into one fulfilling, global, and highly-paid career.

Our book shows you how to become an expert in a topic that will open the door to highly-paid bookings. We help you identify your markets and set fees for your work, and we show you how to offer a smorgasbord of services so that your clients will buy several of them at one time.

Speak and Grow Rich is your handbook of the forms you will need, tips on how to work with many speakers bureaus, how to book yourself, negotiate contracts, work smoothly with meeting planners, create your own five-figure seminars, and design products that will double your income while they instruct and inform your audiences. We reveal secrets of publicity, promotion, and advertising, so that you can become the impresario of your own speaking career.

Most important of all is the rich reward you will receive from your audiences who will write, call, and visit you from around the world, and say you have changed their lives, inspired them, helped them. In our speakers bureau, we know thousands of successful speakers. Many share this thought, I love the business so much, I will never retire. I would do this even if I were not paid a cent. This book shows you how to enter this marvelous world and be paid more money than you have ever dreamed possible. You *will* speak and grow rich.

Endorsements

Standing Ovations

"How does it feel to have blown a handful of inspiration stardust to the world?"—**Napoleon Hill, author of "Think and Grow Rich," on the occasion of Dottie Walters first national television show.**

"There are few other people I would recommend in the speaking and writing field without reservation. What great gifts Dottie and Lilly have given to our profession. Their magazine, *Sharing Ideas,* the organizing of IGAB, the International Association of Agents and Bureaus, are contributions without comparison. Now this great book, SPEAK AND GROW RICH, the Handbook for Professional Speakers. It is a product not only of 25 years experience in speaking and writing but is the combined effort of Dottie and her daughter Lilly Walters, who together built the world renowned Walters International Speakers Bureau. The value to all who read it cannot be overemphasized."—**Cavett Robert, Chairman Emeritus and Founder, National Speakers Association**

"This book is a great help to both beginners and full timers in the speaking business. Dottie and Lilly have written about many subjects that need to be addressed. It will help everyone in or thinking about professional, paid speaking. This book should be on every speaker's desk."—**John Palmer, First President, International Group of Agents and Bureaus; National Speakers Bureau Inc.**

"The lecture industry existed for 100 years with many factions and infighting. Then Dottie and Lilly Walters had the dream of an Association of Speakers Bureaus. Their dream became the reality of IGAB. They pulled the industry together, overcame 100 years of dissent, and started a new era of cooperation."—**Ed Larkin, President, International Group of Agents and Bureaus; Speakers Guild Speakers Bureau**

"Dottie Walters is an excellent exponent of training techniques for professional speakers. I have known and watched Dottie for years. Now she and Lilly have one of the finest bureaus in the world. This book, like their reputation, is excellent."—**John Morley, two term Past-President, International Platform Assoc. (Foreign correspondent)**

"As a professional speaker who has spoken in all 50 U.S. states, and major world capitols, I have observed speakers and bureaus worldwide. Dottie and Lilly Walters know 'where it's at' in the business of professional speaking. They are truly in touch with the industry."—**Somers White, CPAE; Former Arizona State Senator.**

"Lilly and Dottie, I only wish I had read this book 30 years ago. I would be a billionaire now."—**Irwin Zucker, President Southern California Book Publicists Assoc.**

"Dottie and Lilly Walters have shared ideas that have polished many a speaker's mind. Their nurturing, knowledgeable counsel has been the catalyst for a remarkable number of successful professional speaking careers."—**Rudy R. Wright, CMP; Past President, Meeting Planners International. (MPI)**

"There are two sides to this golden coin, the speaker and the professional speakers' bureau. Dottie is the internationally applauded speaker, the creative energy behind the development of our bureau association, IGAB. Lilly is Director of the Walters International Speakers Bureau. Together they truly represent the top professionals on both sides of this coin. What better combination to tell the story of speaking in the 20th century and the great step into the 21st?"—**Barbara L. Kincaide, President Elect, IGAB; Speakers Bureau International, Canada**

"Creative, strategic, practical! Sage advice in this great book that will enable you to achieve your professional speaking dreams."—**Howard Shenson, Advisory Council, American Association of Professional Consultants**

"Dottie and Lilly are tigers! What a wonderful book. Filled with the real, honest information and wisdom of all their years in the professional speaking business. Well done, good friends!"—**John Hammond, President, National Speakers Association**

"Dottie Walters has been one of the most valuable people in America in helping speakers to learn 'the ropes' of the business of speaking. Her newsmagazine, *Sharing Ideas,* seminars and consultations have helped thousands of speakers to find direction. I commend Lilly and Dottie Walters."—**Mike Frank, Past President, National Speakers Association; Speakers Unlimited Bureau**

SPEAK
AND
GROW RICH

1

How to Succeed at Professional Speaking

Karl Wallenda, the famous circus tightrope performer, once re-marked, "Being on the rope is everything. All else is waiting to perform."

Today's professional speakers feel the same way about the thrilling business of appearing before audiences and delivering useful information in an entertaining and beneficial way. Being before the audience—speaking—is everything. All else is waiting to speak.

You, too, can follow this powerful calling. You can educate, inspire, and lead people to take action and make important changes in their lives. By becoming a professional speaker, you can prosper to levels you may have never dreamed were possible in your life. If you have the drive and the dream and can follow our plan, you literally *can* speak and grow rich.

"THE FEAR" VERSUS "THE CALL"

Some surveys show that having to speak before an audience is the number one fear in the world. But professional speakers will tell you that performing is their number-one thrill, biggest challenge, and fondest dream come true.

Many professional speakers say that they were inspired to begin their careers while they sat in an audience, watching and listening to a great performer. Speakers influence, encourage, motivate, and communicate to the spirit. You may have purchased this book because a powerful speaker changed your life. If your heart filled with longing to become a speaker as you listened to a wonderful performance, you have felt that mighty call. The thought of becoming a speaker can galvanize your thoughts. It can hit you like an electric shock. And suddenly, you are certain.

"I can speak like that!" you tell yourself. "Someday, I will be up on that platform. I will touch every heart in the auditorium. I'll inspire audiences in the far parts of the world. They will pick me up at the airport in a stretch limousine. I will perform in the finest, most elegant hotels, resorts, and convention centers. I will become a millionaire. But that is not what is important to me. I want the opportunity to perform. I want to inspire, uplift, help, and teach. I want to be a professional speaker."

Every speaker we have known tells a similar story of hearing this call.

So, who was it for you? Was it Kenneth McFarland of General Motors? Or was it Bruce Barton, the great advertising speaker? Perhaps you heard the gruff and practical Red Motley of Parade Magazine, or leaped to your feet in a standing ovation for Dr. Norman Vincent Peale, Jim Rohn, Zig Ziglar, Ira Hayes, Earl Nightingale, Cavett Robert, or Elmer Wheeler. The professional speaker who inspires you becomes your own personal hero, a source of lifelong inspiration. It has always been so. Every generation has its William Jennings Bryans, Jack Kennedys, and Winston Churchills. Perhaps you were in one of Dottie Walters' audiences when you felt the call. We hope so.

THE TWO INGREDIENTS OF SUCCESS

The call to be a speaker is one of the two ingredients of success that we have observed in all professional speakers we know. The other ingredient is love of the business.

The Call

Kenneth McFarland of General Motors told us a story about his mother. She saved her money for two years to purchase a Victrola and a record of William Jennings Bryan's famous "Cross of Gold" speech. Little Ken listened to that record over and over again. Then, one day, William Jennings Bryan arrived in their town. Ken ran down to the railroad station in his "summer ensemble"—overalls and bare feet—to meet the great man in person. Bryan touched the little boy's shoulder. "What will you be when you grow up?" he asked. "I want to speak like you!" young Ken answered, confident in his vision of his own future.

For Dottie Walters the call came when she heard Bruce Barton speak at an Advertising Association meeting. "I was twenty-one, just starting in the advertising business," she recalls. "It was the first big meeting I had ever attended. I remember thinking as he spoke that I really could do the job I was struggling so hard to do. I had the talent. I had the power. He confirmed my ability. I was so enthralled with his message, that I stayed after his speech and waited until everyone else had left the room. Then I went up to him, wanting to tell him how his message had helped me. I took his hand and said, 'Everyone else came today to listen. But I heard you in my heart.' Bruce Barton put his other hand over mine and said, 'You are the one I came for.'"

Love of the Business

Successful speakers enjoy every aspect and detail of the professional speaking business. A convention of professional speakers is so full of electricity you can feel the hum. The cocktail bars are left empty. Speakers don't need liquor because they are high on their calling.

Great speakers constantly work on ways to improve their performances. They don't think of any of their work as difficult. Every aspect is pleasure because they love speaking so much. Like Wallenda, the tightrope walker, they can't wait to perform again. They don't mind disappointments, rejections, or waiting in airports. They improvise and carry on no matter what happens. They overcome disasters, and turn every experience into material for their programs and products. They never retire, but go on speaking as long as they live. They can hardly wait for the phone to ring with the next booking. They are on fire with the urge to be on the road again to China, Australia, London or wherever there is an audience waiting for them.

WHY AUDIENCES LOVE SPEAKERS

No movie or television program can compare with hearing and seeing a speaker in person. Audiences want to know what a speaker is really like. They often want to ask questions and shake hands. They may press around by the hundreds after a program. People with teary eyes come up to speakers to say, "You have changed my life," or "My son turned his life around after hearing you." They want to touch the speaker's arm, experience the speaker up close.

Humorist Robert Henry tells the story of how a woman in one of his audiences came up and told him about the loss of a family member. She was able to laugh again during his performance for the first time since that loved one's death.

THE BOOMING WORLD MARKET FOR SPEAKERS

Today's market for professional speakers is a thriving, expanding, international business. Convention centers, conference facilities, hotels, and resorts of all kinds are being built from Beijing to Kansas City to Paris. Meeting rooms and auditoriums are booked around the clock to accommodate the burgeoning meeting industry, literally all over the world and on ships at sea.

San Diego, California, for example, has constructed the largest convention center in the world with 2,544,000 square feet of contiguous space under one roof. Cities across the United States and overseas have followed suit with new or expanded meeting and convention facilities.

The Cruise Lines International Association (CLIA), has announced that eighteen huge new vessels are under construction with special decks and facilities to accommodate conventions on board. Cruise ship companies, which once focused their business only on pleasure passengers, now recognize the popularity and enormity of the meeting business and are going after a greater share of it.

The International Association of Convention & Visitors Bureaus reports: The 231 largest cities in the U.S. held 318,643 major meetings in 1989 (up from 126,888 in 1987). The Meeting and Convention Meetings Market study shows 1,006,000 U.S. meetings held in 1989. Projected combined attendance is 93.74 million, up 26% (largest gain in the past 16 years). Of these attendees, 58.43 million were corporate delegates. Association attendance rose from 10.74 million in 1987 to 13.59 million in 1989. A total of $15.01 billion dollars were spent for convention expenses.

In addition, 64,200 U.S. corporate and 5,500 association meetings were held overseas last year. Nine new cruise ships are under construction with larger meeting rooms to accommodate the fast growing number of conferences held on board.

Cities often manage their own convention facilities and earn significant revenues from meetings and convention events. The business of meetings helps create thousands of jobs for airlines, bus companies, hotels, food suppliers, video and film firms, special effects companies, florists, and printers. There is a bull market for professional speakers, morning, noon, and night, all over the world.

Conventions use as many as one hundred paid, professional speakers during their three- to four-day sessions. For example, there may be meal-function speakers, whose programs are humorous and entertaining. Then there are the keynoters, who are inspirational headliners. A convention may also have speakers known as "grand-opening mixers," who help attendees get acquainted, plus health and exercise session leaders, speakers for children's programs, speakers for workshops and seminars where expert techniques are taught, summarizers, and specialists of other kinds. A myriad of speakers, all experts in their various fields, can fill the slots at a major convention.

Often at a convention, ten or more speakers may give concurrent educational programs called "breakout sessions." Attendees at the convention are urged to pick and choose the programs they wish to attend to increase their knowledge and professionalism.

At the same time, speakers may put on special programs for the spouses of the convention registrants. Since women now hold 35 percent of the 12.6 million executive, administrative, and managerial jobs in the U.S., the days of convention programs on "How To Tie Scarves" are long past. At a recent large convention, for example, four buses were reserved to take the spouses on a shopping trip. The spouses, however, refused to leave. The buses stood empty while the spouses crowded in to hear the main luncheon speaker. The latest trend in convention planning, therefore, is to include spouses in the programming. If there are sessions for spouses, they are tagged "Partner Programs" and may feature computer techniques, managerial skills, or other technical information. These are one more example of explosive growth in the marketplace for professional speakers.

Speaking now is such big business that those who do most of the bookings, the professional meeting planners, have formed their own association, Meeting Planners International. Their 9,000 members hold their own meetings and conventions frequently so they can improve their skills. Many magazines now serve the meeting planner profession, on a national and regional basis, as well.

The local meeting business is also booming. Banquets, training sessions, and special-interest groups of all kinds are housed in local conference centers, hotels, and restaurants. The Kiwanis, Soroptimists, Rotary Club, Chambers of Commerce, and many other service clubs meet as often as once a week for regular meetings, then hold large, annual banquets and training sessions. The number of meetings going on at this very moment throughout the United States and the world is astronomical.

Companies and corporations hold local training sessions and awards banquets. Seminar companies and independent seminar producers are constantly on the move, bringing new seminars into major cities each month.

Colleges present star speakers in their auditoriums and offer long lists of seminars through their continuing education divisions. Many colleges and universities also have conference facilities that can be rented by business-users. Churches, hospitals, chambers of commerce, and art galleries are other sources of seminars and programs that require professional speakers.

These growing and worldwide sources of meetings hold tremendous significance to anyone contemplating a professional speaking career. At the front of every auditorium, conference hall, and meeting room is a speaker or panel of speakers. Speakers are the focus, the very reason for the meetings business. Speakers are the heart of a multimillion-dollar industry. There is ample room in this industry for you.

SPEAKING: ONE OF THE WORLD'S OLDEST PROFESSIONS

History does not tell us who started the process of standing up before an audience and presenting knowledge in an entertaining form. But it is not hard to imagine the glowing campfires of ancient peoples and the eager faces gathered around to listen to tales of valor and courage. In certain French caves, you can see drawings on the smoky walls which apparently served as the illustrations for "seminars" on hunting skills thousands of years ago. Much later, in medieval times, minstrels set stories to music and traveled from castle to castle performing in what is today called "the speaker's circuit."

Many of the stories the early speakers told have lasted through time, as new speakers stepped forth to carry on the tales, wisdoms, myths, and truths of previous generations. The most enduring of these stories and teachings are the ones with useful values, such as Aesop's fables, Ulysses' adventures, the 10th-century explorations of Eric the Red, and the wisdom and narrations of the ancient Chinese philosophers Confucius and Lao-Tzu.

Words that inspired centuries ago still inspire today as modern speakers draw upon these legacies. Dottie Walters has used a profound quotation by Lao-Tzu at least a thousand times from the platform. "To see things in the seed. That is genius." The heart jump-starting message handed down by the 2nd-century Roman emperor Marcus Aurelius—"Anything the mind can conceive and believe, it can achieve"—is repeated today by many motivational speakers.

Visualization, incidentally, is often touted as a new way to focus on and achieve goals. But visualization was used in the seminars of Socrates at the Agora, the assembly place and commercial center of ancient Athens, some twenty-five centuries ago.

After hearing Jesus of Nazareth, a Roman soldier declared,

"Never a man so spake." All religions were begun by speakers. Each generation is inspired by its Billy Grahams, Robert Schullers, Amy Semple McPhersons, Martin Luthers, and Charles Spurgeons.

Even in this age of instant electronic communications, the world loves speakers. Perhaps it is because the speaker's human spirit is magnified on the stage and because most members of an audience fantasize about mesmerizing people with their own words, thoughts and ideas.

The most unlikely people can and do become worldwide celebrities through speaking. One of the best examples of this phenomenon is former Marine Lt. Col. Oliver North. After a few days of televised testimony in Washington, D.C., North's sincere speaking and stance on patriotism made this once-obscure, low-profile officer into a high-profile hero. After he left the Marine Corps, Col. North was soon in demand to speak to audiences—for $25,000 per program, according to published reports.

WHAT PROFESSIONAL SPEAKERS ARE PAID

Most beginning professional speakers do not command such high fees, of course, especially in the first years of their career. You will present many speeches for free before you hear those wonderful words from someone in your audience, "What is your fee?" Professional speakers raise their fees at least annually as they improve and become better known.

While successful speakers do say, "I love speaking so much, I would do it even if I wasn't paid," individual profits of over $800,000 a year are not uncommon. What speakers mean by this is that the response of the audience is the highest reward of all.

Speakers are people of influence, power, and prestige who earn very high fees for what they love to do. Professional speaking combines monetary rewards with spiritual ones.

The American Society of Association Executives (ASAE) and the National Speakers Association (NSA) recently teamed up to take a survey of the reasons why ASAE members engage professional speakers. (Remember, associations are made up of individual professionals and companies in the same field. The figures that follow do not include the much higher speaker fees of the corporate world.)

The ASAE members reported using keynote speakers for annual meetings, regional meetings, board meetings, educational meetings, and "other" meetings, with the average fees ranging from a high of $4,910 for an annual meeting down to $1,624 for a local meeting.

For breakout session speakers in the same category of local meetings, the average fees ranged from $1,750 down to $439.

The three main groups that pay speakers to perform are associations, corporations, and colleges. The fees for speakers who appear at local banquets or luncheons start at around $500 to $750. These speakers are able to raise their fees to $1,000 as they continue to build their skills, expertise, and renown. Many business speakers, meanwhile, are paid $2,000 to $7,000 or more for a one-hour keynote address at a convention. The professional keynoters booked by our Walters International Speakers Bureau command fees that range from $1,500 to $15,000 for a 60-minute keynote. Celebrities earn fees that start at $10,000 and range as high as $50,000 per program.

When we interviewed Dr. Tony Alessandra, a successful sales and marketing speaker, he told us his estimated annual combined gross for speaking, consulting, and product sales, totaled $800,000. This figure can be broken down to about $400,000 in speaking fees, and $400,000 in consulting fees and product sales. His products are the books, audio and video cassettes, and workbooks he has created that are related to his topic. Tony works from an office in his beautiful home overlooking the Pacific Ocean.

OTHER WAYS PROFESSIONAL SPEAKERS EARN MONEY

Seminars for special audiences can be another lucrative way for speakers to profit. Weekend seminars, for example, often are marketed at $1,500 per attendee, which is paid by the attendees' corporations. Multiply that figure by 40 participants and you get a gross income of $60,000 for a two-day educational weekend retreat. It is easy to see why speakers add special seminars to their fee speaking schedules.

Successful public speakers not only offer keynote speeches, but also highly paid training sessions, consulting, public and private seminars, product sales, and various other services on their fee menu. All speaker fees on contract are plus travel and hotel expenses, paid by the client, and often include additional fees for printed handout materials, consulting, books, cassettes, or other educational materials produced by the speaker and purchased by the meeting planner for each attendee.

THE EIGHT PILLARS OF SUCCESS

When you sit in an audience and watch and listen to a star keynote speaker, or take part in a fact-filled, smoothly flowing seminar presented by a professional, the business of speaking looks easy, like a circus trapeze artist performing flawlessly.

The trapeze artist, however, has spent many months outside of the public eye, practicing and perfecting his daring flights above a safety net. Before they can succeed, professional speakers must also perfect their programs and their delivery.

The eight pillars listed below are vital to every professional speaker's success. As you go through the list, compare your own background and knowledge against the requirements for each pillar. This process will enable you to see where you stand now and which of the pillars must be strengthened to support your career. Our book will show you the steps you must take.

Pillar #1. The successful professional speaker is a passionate expert in the topic. The way to begin building your own Pillar #1 is to list the business subjects you know and approach with enthusiasm. Then ask yourself, in each of these subjects, what do I know that other people need or want to know and will pay to hear?

Pillar #2. The successful speaker specializes in delivering information of particular interest and help to a specific group. To create your own Pillar #2, you must develop expertise in your chosen topic and constantly keep working to improve your knowledge to stay on the cutting edge.

Pillar #3. Successful speakers carefully research the needs and likes of the target audience they wish to reach. To build your own Pillar #3, focus on a particular audience and deliver the information that group is seeking.

Pillar #4.   The successful speaker creates the image and tools necessary to be a professional. To create your own Pillar #4, you must learn how to promote yourself and your topic and develop an array of sales tools. (We explain how in Chapter 3.)

Pillar #5.   The successful speaker presents the right professional image to buyers in the target market. To build Pillar #5, cultivate a "you" attitude. Make everything you produce serve your clients' needs.

Pillar #6.   The successful speaker learns how to negotiate booking and speaker product contracts with buyers and speakers bureaus. Follow the ideas and suggestions in this book, a compilation of many speakers' great ideas, to give full measure and value-packed deals to clients.

Pillar #7.   The successful speaker has a polished program with a sincere, eloquent speaking style, and constantly strives to be even better by improving delivery, content, and knowledge. To build your own Pillar #7 requires concentration. Everything you read, listen to, and study will be of use to you if you focus on your market. Carefully monitor other speakers, not to copy but to learn better ways to present your own material.

Pillar #8.   The successful speaker follows up all booking leads and sales in an immediate, business-like, concerned, friendly, and consistent manner. The best source of new bookings is an enthusiastic referral and recommendation from today's presentation.

As you succeed in setting up these eight pillars you will keep working on them, shoring them up and making them stronger, throughout your professional speaking career. The business of gathering and trying new material, learning, improving, rehearsing, and marketing never stops. The reason why can be seen in the following true story. A reporter asked a famous manufacturer of a very successful product, "Why do you continue to spend so much money advertising to the public? Can't you just ride on your reputation now?" The manufacturer pointed to a jet plane flying overhead. "Business is like that plane," he explained. "Flight would terminate in a hurry if we shut off the engine."

To sustain the flight of your speaking business, you must keep its engine running, continue to hone your talent, improve your subject, add new topics as times change, develop new products for your speaker product line, and keep the powers of publicity turned on full throttle.

TIME AND MONEY: HOW MUCH SHOULD YOU INVEST IN YOUR PROFESSIONAL SPEAKING CAREER?

At our seminars for beginning speakers, the question we are asked most often is: How much time and money should a novice invest to begin a professional speaking business?

The answer is to invest not money, but your own burning desire, determination, and enthusiasm. These three items are far more important than cash and cannot be purchased from anyone else. Our passionate purpose in this book is to show you how to begin, step-by-step, so that you can purchase the materials that cost money as you earn, and thus constantly improve.

Most speakers start their careers as a part-time operation. You will develop your materials, marketing, and expertise as you progress. Begin with the minimum of materials, but choose the colors and type styles for these carefully, so that you can add other items later and make them match.

We advise you to invest in yourself by taking as many speaking classes, seminars, and coaching sessions as you can. If you do not have the money for these, you might offer to help a speaker with back-of-the-room product sales or do office work in trade for what you need. If you can work in the office of a successful speaker, you can learn a great deal about the business in a short time.

Purchase books, cassette and video albums, and tickets to hear the best speakers you can find. Take a recorder and a notebook. Watch and listen as a great football coach would. Ask yourself what this speaker is doing right and wrong. Ask the personal coach in your own head how you could do it better. Concentrate on it.

As Sir Isaac Newton said in his old age, "I have stood on the shores of time picking up a beautiful seashell here and there. While all before me lies the great sea of life. Undiscovered." Never stop learning. Never stop getting better or thinking of ways to give more to your audiences.

TEN STEPS TO YOUR FAME AND FORTUNE

As soon as you have found the inner conviction to believe you will become a great speaker, you must identify your market. Look for one that is big enough to give you many opportunities for bookings over your lifetime. If there is no such market for your subject, re-think it. You do not want to prepare a speech for which there is no audience. Identify the audience first, then prepare a speech that this particular group needs desperately. For example, employers need to know how to deal with foreign-born employees. Manufacturers need to know how to negotiate contracts with Pacific Rim countries. Sales managers need to know how to recruit and inspire top sales teams. Single parents need to know how to cope with all of the trials and tribulations of handling difficult teen-agers.

In Chapter 2 of *Speak and Grow Rich,* we teach you the second step: How to pick hot current topics and create smashing titles that will attract audiences like a magnet. The very sound of the words in a title is important. Many titles have implied meanings. We show you the secrets of "hooking" your buyers with words. We show you how to tie your topic to individual groups.

Chapter 3 zeroes in on the public relations skills and self-promotional techniques you will need to build your professional image and attract ever more buyers for your expanding programs. We show you how to start with simple, basic materials, then develop more elaborate ones as you progress. We explain the importance of letters of recommendation, and reprints of articles you have written and of stories published about you for your press kit. We also show you how to coordinate attractive matching stationery, business cards, shipping labels, and other image-building items. We list many simple ways to publicize yourself with very little money, but with tremendous impact. We have gleaned these techniques from the thousands of speakers we work with in our speakers bureau.

Chapter 4 explains the business of closing paid speaking engagements, negotiating multiple fees, finding new prospects, making sure of your payment, and even how to be paid far in advance. We show you how to move from free practice speeches to higher and higher fees, as you steadily climb toward your goal of becoming an internationally prominent professional speaker.

Chapter 5 presents valuable and proven tips for overcoming stage fright, handling hecklers, and using the famous Dottie Walters' "Scheherazade technique" to give your audiences just enough excellent material so you leave them cheering for more. No speaker is successful on a hit-and-run basis. We show you how to be booked again and again with the same client.

Chapter 6 features practical ideas and examples of how to set up an efficient office that will serve as the headquarters for your growing speaking career. The text includes (1) how to involve and train your family members and employees; and (2) how to use successful business techniques in either a professional building or, as is more common among speakers, in your office at home.

Chapter 7 introduces you to ways you can cash in on the $3.1 billion seminar industry, both here and abroad, on land or at sea. We cover how to work with seminar companies and find sponsors who will pay all the costs of your seminars, then split the gate with you. We explain how to create and market seminars to the public and to special groups, for high profit and visibility.

Chapter 8 reveals the all-important steps for selling your keynotes and other convention and conference programs to meeting planners. Meeting planners are the buyers in the corporate and association markets. Each one books many speakers every year. We show you all the ways to reach the meeting planners in your focused market and how to work with them successfully.

Chapter 9 shows you the many advantages of being booked by an agent if you are a celebrity or by many non-exclusive speakers bureaus if you are not. We teach you how to identify which bureaus fit your topic and fee and how to woo them and build lasting and lucrative working relationships. We show you how to see the speaking business through their eyes. They are the "professional sales representatives" of the business. We explain the risks they take when they book you with one of their clients. We list the usual requirements of bureaus, along with ways to get in step with bureaus and become a team player. We give you an insider's view of speakers bureaus, what they charge, how they work, and how you can get their attention once you are professional enough to command fees of at least $1,000 per engagement. We show what they do and what they do not do, so that you will not stumble and stammer when you approach bureaus.

Chapter 10 shows you how to increase your gross speaking income through the creation of many helpful and lucrative products which your audiences need. We explain the many ways to sell and promote your own products, which can be books, audio cassette albums, videos, posters, workbooks, and many other educational items that you can develop from your topic. We show you several ways to sell these items. Products can double your income from your speaking fees.

Speak and Grow Rich also gives you two advantages that have never before been offered in other books about the professional speaking business: a complete glossary and a list of speaker resources. The glossary is important because, as in every profession and business, there are "inside" phrases and words that separate the experienced practitioners from the beginners. By studying these phrases and words, you can gain an understanding of what the pros in the speaking field are talking about. Our glossary can save you the potentially costly embarrassment of using the wrong terms at the wrong time, which could shake the confidence of any meeting planner or speakers bureau.

Our first-in-the-world list of speaker resources has been gathered over the years to include the finest sources of the things speakers need. We list many names and addresses of people and organizations who offer important services, products, and help for speakers at every step of their development.

Our ultimate goal in *Speak and Grow Rich* is to give your speaking career a head start if you are a beginner and a quantum leap forward if you yearn to move higher in the world of paid, professional speaking.

2

Topics and Titles That Attract Paid Bookings

To profit from speaking, you must be able to attract paid bookings. To land speaking engagements that pay, you must offer topics that meet a need in the marketplace, with titles that promise benefits while they capture the attention and curiosity of buyers. This chapter focuses on how to do just that.

Speakers often come to us and ask for help in finding markets for their subjects. Frequently, their subjects are similar to these: "How to Find and Marry Your Ideal Mate," "How to Predict Your Love Life Through Numerology," "How to Dress to Attract the Opposite Sex." They ask us to help them obtain bookings in the corporate world. While the corporate world is a well-paying market, it is not the right place for their subjects.

We explain the market to them this way. Visualize a fork in a road. One path leads to seminars sold to the public. On that path, the people who pay for the seminar also benefit from the subject. For example, the topic of how to find your ideal mate belongs on this route, as do all of the topics involving personal improvement. Pursuing this path leads to seminars given independently, or through the sponsorship of colleges, hospitals, or churches, but not to seminars given to businesses. Still, there is a big market down this path, and many speakers do very well in it.

The second route that leads from the fork goes to the business market. Topics there benefit the corporate world. The business pays for the seminar. The employees and managers do a better job because of it, so the business benefits.

What kinds of topics are offered on this route? The five most popular at a recent National Management Association showcase of speakers were as follows: (1) how to get employees to listen; (2) how to work with foreign-born employees; (3) how to keep your company out of court for wrongful firing; (4) how to negotiate with Pacific Rim countries; and (5) sexual harassment in the office. Note that each addresses a specific business problem.

It is possible to adapt a personal-interest topic so that it can be brought into the business world. For example, "Dressing to Attract the Opposite Sex" could be converted to "Dressing to Close More Real Estate Sales." Instead of, "How to Find and Marry Your Ideal Mate," the business side of the coin would be, "How to Find, Hire, and Keep Great Salespeople" (or telemarketers, office workers, computer operators, etc.).

HOW TO PICK GOOD TOPICS

All booking, marketing, advertising, and promotion begin with your topic. You cannot find an audience that needs your topic until you identify your specialty. Your background, business experience, family, education (either in the academic or business world), will be the foundation on which you stand as a speaker.

Begin With Who You Are and What You Know

Always begin your search for a topic with who you are and what you know. Will Rogers usually presented himself as a simple cowboy who had a wry, homespun wit and some canny remarks about politicians. His famous line was, "I only know what I read in the papers." What he didn't say, however, was that he regularly read every major news publication in the country. To be a success as a political humorist, he worked hard at becoming a leading current events expert. His humor was built on public amazement that a rope twirling "bumpkin" had such "smarts." He did indeed have such smarts. Will Rogers was the highest-paid speaker of his day.

Many other speakers have succeeded by relying on who they are and what they know. An old gentleman who sold balloons in a park had two sons who decided to do something new with balloons. These two young men conceived the idea of making balloon bouquets for special occasions. Later, they went into the manufacturing and franchising business. They took their own specialty and developed it.

Another example is Paul Hogan who became "Mr. Australia" with his Crocodile Dundee character by portraying a heroic bush ranger of the outback. Hogan knows "Dundee" inside out, so he plays the part of the hero Australian and makes that part bigger than life.

A young sales and customer relations speaker came from a family who operated an independent automobile garage. One day as he visited his father, he overheard a mechanic fighting with a woman customer. Later, he told his father, "That was handled badly, Dad. Don't you have any cassette tapes or books to help this employee? Could you send him to a training seminar on customer relations for the automobile repair business?" The father replied, "I've never heard of any such services in our field." The son had a flash of inspiration. He decided to take his sales and customer relations knowledge and apply it to the problems of the auto repair business he knew so well. Today, he is the authority in this field. He offers seminars, tapes, videos, a newsletter, in-house training, and keynote presentations to many automotive repair companies and associations. He found his topic niche in his own back yard.

Develop a Personal Focus

Developing a clear focus on your topic helps you become an expert in your own field. Meeting planners book experts, not speakers who are eloquent on any subject. The fact is, meeting planners book speakers by topic and celebrity standing. Focusing on a topic and becoming an expert on a subject allows meeting planners to book engagements with you based on your expertise and skill in a specific field.

Our speakers bureau receives as many as twenty calls a day from fledgling speakers wanting us to book them with our meeting-planner clients. The 7,000 speakers listed by our bureau are categorized by topic, fee, and speaker's home location, so our first question to a caller is, "What is your topic?" An inexperienced speaker often replies, "Oh, you just name it. I can speak on anything!"

Beginning speakers like these have no focus. They are not experts in any field. Meeting planners want content as well as eloquence. No bureau gets a request for the topic of "anything." That is simply not the way things work in the world of paid speaking. Can you imagine an author writing a book with no subject, or an architect constructing a building with no idea of what it is to be used for?

Your topic is the beginning of all of your speaking materials, and most importantly, it will tie into your marketing. As an expert in your niche, you gain confidence. Immersing yourself in your subject allows you to speak with power. Ernest Bevin, an English speaker, stuttered as a young man. He worked in the British coal mines where he became deeply interested in improving bad working conditions. He joined the union, worked hard, and eventually brought about the changes of which he had dreamed. In his passion and research for his subject, his stuttering disappeared. His speaking eventually helped him become Britain's Foreign Minister.

When you hear beginning speakers stumble, stutter, and use "ah-ah-ah" over and over, it is because they are not completely knowledgeable and comfortable with their topic.

Demosthenes, a well-known speaker in ancient Greece, also had a stutter. He practiced his speech with pebbles in his mouth. He became such a dynamic speaker that Greek listeners commented: "When other speakers present he applaud. But when Demosthenes speaks, we arise and go to war."

Becoming an expert on the topic of your interest—a topic specific groups need—will give you the confidence, passion, and power essential to becoming a successful speaker.

Choose Topics with Broad Interest

A topic, while specific, should be broad enough in interest so that it is appealing to a large population. If you choose an obscure subject which no association or corporation wishes to book, you will waste your time and money trying to find buyers.

A good business practice is to find the audience first. Don't be a speaker who can't find an audience. Locate your target market or audience, then prepare your material.

Follow these two simple rules when picking out a topic:

1. Business people must need your topic; and
2. You must have a background that makes you so knowledgeable that an audience will want to listen to you on this topic.

A new speaker once called to suggest that our bureau book him on the topic, "Is God a Woman?" We asked what kind of audiences had booked him on that subject so far, and at what fee. "Oh, no one," he replied. "What market is the material aimed at?" we asked. "Everyone wants to know this subject," he answered. "Why don't you start by booking me to the atheists?"

We explained that we had never had a group of atheists call our bureau to book a speaker. In the speaking world, they are simply not a hot market. The speaker's topic was not so hot, either. You may think your topic is interesting, but if no one else does, then there is no one to whom you can market.

Customize Your Topic to Your Audiences

After selecting a suitable topic that is broad enough in its appeal to supply you with numerous audiences, you should customize the topic to suit a smaller or related group. Recently, a meeting planner in a large medical test facility called to ask us to supply a speaker on the subject of "How to Handle Difficult Professionals." A speaker with this topic could spend a lifetime delivering programs to the medical supply field. The next move would be to offer the same material customized for dental, legal, and other professionals. "Handling Difficult or Irascible Professionals" is a subject needed by many groups. It can be focused, aimed, and expanded.

Twelve Steps to Becoming an Expert

1. Go to your local and county libraries. Ask the reference librarian to help you find every book on your subject.
2. Haunt used book stores. Search for out-of-print books and magazines in your field.

3. Get a list of pertinent current trade publications, magazines, and newsletters in your chosen field from the library. Subscribe to all those on your topic area. A subscription to one periodical normally puts you on the mailing lists of others in your field. Remember, libraries have back issues that you can read, too.

4. Collect books of quotations and proverbs. These will be a wonderful help when you prepare special material for your clients.

5. Subscribe to "Dialog" or other computer search systems that find all articles written in your area of expertise on a continuing basis, to locate new material.

6. Join associations in the areas of business you intend to address. Attend their meetings. Meet people. Make contacts. Ask which speakers and subjects booked recently were the most successful.

7. Continue going to seminars and lectures regularly to hear other speakers. Learn what is in the marketplace. If you use or adapt other speakers' material, give them credit. (Note: In the front row of every great speaker's audience is a row of new speakers watching, listening, and learning.)

8. Offer to assist other speakers and experts in your field with setting up, back-of-room sales, or slide projection. You will learn invaluable information by working with a pro, and will make a business friend at the same time. Speakers recommend each other to clients and often team up for advertising and seminars.

9. Be so familiar with your subject that no one can stump you with a question.

10. Develop a passion for your topic.

11. Stay on the leading edge by creating new and innovative ideas.

12. Develop a unique viewpoint on your topic.

Research Your Topics for Uniqueness

Once you have found a suitable topic to market and customize to individual groups within your market, you must find a new approach to its presentation. Although you may think you know a great deal about your subject when you begin, you undoubtedly will find there is much more information to learn.

You might start your research by contacting the nearest college or university and asking them if they subscribe to "Dialog" or another computer search system which locates articles on a particular subject. If they do, ask if they will search your topic for you.

Study all the material you find available on your subject in books, magazines, and newsletters. Listen to tapes and watch videos. Take academic courses, attend seminars, and go to lectures on your subject, as well as related ones.

As you study and re-study your topic, you will gain a perspective on the material that is uniquely your own. Through your passion for your subject, you will find your own views and opinions taking form. Your special slant will send you beyond what has been said and thought on your topic to this point. You become like Captain Kirk on the bridge of the starship *Enterprise,* boldly going where others have not dared to go before.

Abraham Lincoln emphasized the importance of learning all there is to know, then going beyond it. "Towering genius disdains a beaten path. It seeks regions hitherto unexplored," he said.

Uniqueness is what makes you unforgettable. Plato called it the opening of the "flood of ideas." Intense study opens up the flood gates of the genius river. You will be booked again and again if you are an expert with a unique slant on your topic.

After you've developed your unique slant, your research should not end. Take a professional approach to learning everything available on your subject. Merchants shop their competitors. Restaurant owners dine at each new eating place that opens, checking out the menu, the decor, and the service. Do the same by attending the programs of other speakers on your topic. Whether these speakers are good, bad, or indifferent, you will learn from all of them. Take notes. Listen to their material, and watch their style.

Appoint yourself to be the imaginary stage director. What did you think of the opening? How many points did they use? Was their humor appropriate and well done? Did they customize their material to this particular audience?

Your aim is never to copy what other speakers are doing, but to see all the facets and possibilities of the topic and presentation skills. Then develop your own uniqueness. There is no better way to determine your own individual slant at a presentation than to watch your competition. You will get hundreds of new ideas while watching others. Your mind will be triggered to use material from your own experience that you previously had not thought about. Speaker studying falls into two categories:

1. The first group includes speakers who are not as good or experienced as you are. Pretend you are his or her coach. Note the things you would do to improve the presentation. At what point in the speech was the audience lost? And why? How would you deliver the same speech to make it better. Where would you add different material? How did the speaker close? Was it effective? Was the audience bored, or did they want more?

   Your reason for monitoring the speaker is not to become his or her critic. Keep your thoughts to yourself and remember that people rarely, if ever, want unasked-for advice. Use this information to learn from even the weakest of speakers how to improve your own presentation.

2. The second group of speakers includes those who are better or more experienced than you are. Note exactly what they do that gives them star quality. Write down your thoughts. List every great move, delightful story, connection with the audience, use of voice levels, and/or physical movement.

Learn from top speakers how to upgrade your own presentations. If you are not able to see them first-hand, borrow a video from the library or purchase tapes and films of famous speakers.

Study the masters. Begin to take instructions from your secret, inner "director." Your mind's eye manager can be a means of constant improvement. You are your own best teacher and critic. Listen to your inner voice.

Use Surveys to Find New Topics

If there is one "most valuable" piece of information that you gain from this book, it should be: take a survey.

Sound simple? In fact, it is—profoundly so. Decide which market your topic is best suited for, then write a survey of five or six easy-to-answer target questions. Go directly to the people you want to speak for and ask them your questions. Find out what these particular people want and where they have problems. Search for the answer to, "What hurts?" This is the IBM sales method of Probe, Verify, Empathize, and Close.

Mattel's inventor, Jack Ryan, of Barbie Doll® and Hot Wheels® fame, says, "Don't invent a solution until you know the problem." His wisdom is just as applicable to speaking as it is to inventing. Don't construct a speech until you figure out what your audience needs. A survey is the way to find out.

Once you have compiled the results of your survey, you are on the road to becoming a "leading expert" on your topic. Napoleon Hill, John Nesbitt, and Tom Peters became famous speakers through the use of surveys.

The material you gather in your survey can be used in speeches, seminars, articles, interviews, audio and video cassette albums, and books. Your topic is a specific cure for "what hurts" businesses in your market. Make up charts and graphs of your target group's problems, and your solutions.

Give your audience what they want to hear by making use of the survey information to focus your topic. Before taking a survey, Lee Boyan spoke on sales topics in general. After taking a survey of the salespeople in his audiences, he became more focused. Here is how he did it.

He asked salespeople, "What bothers you most about your work?" (What hurts?) There were a number of answers, but the majority replied that they hated knocking on new doors. They feared rejection.

Although this was not a new idea, it focused on "what hurts?" Lee decided to zero in on how salespeople can find new customers without rejection. In the Great Depression, a famous radio comedian did a door-to-door salesman character who knocked and said, "I hope there is nobody at home. I hope, I hope, I hope!"

When Lee changed his topic title to "Conquering the Cold Call," it was a hit. His new topic title is very successful. He has since written books, prepared videos, and even has other people offering his seminars all across the country.

Lee's secret was to focus his topic. But first, he created a survey to show him what his audiences wanted.

The Twelve Most-Requested Topics

In a recent survey sponsored jointly by the National Speakers Association (NSA) and American Society of Association Executives (ASAE), association meeting planners were asked to pick from the twelve topics listed below the three most requested topics for their speakers. (The totals shown below do not add up to 100 percent, since the planners were allowed to pick more than one topic.)

Most Requested Topics	Percentage
1. Business and economy	42.2
2. Management development and communication	38.8
3. New technologies	33.3
4. Legislative issues	32.1
5. Self Development/Motivation	26.6
6. Future projections	21.5
7. New products and services	16.5
8. Legal issues	16.0
9. National affairs/politics	13.1
10. National affairs/policies	11.8
11. Health, fitness, and lifestyles	10.1
12. Others	11.4

Use this survey to check out the percentage of speakers who are needed in your field of expertise. Whatever your niche is, you need sharp focus on your target audience's problems. Find a unique part of their problem and address it. Think of yourself as a doctor, or other specialist, who offers healing for specific problems. (Specialists in any field are paid higher fees.)

Profiting from the Flip Side of Topics

Many successful seminars have been held on assertiveness during the past ten years. The other side of the coin of assertiveness is the plight of those being stressed by the assertiveness of others. "How to Handle Cranky Customers" and "Calming the Exploding Phone Caller" are examples of how some speakers have taken advantage of the flip side. There are even management seminars on "How to Handle Employees So They Will Not Quit When They Must Cope With Assertive Customers!"

Many speakers can turn their topic around and make use of a new market. One speaker, who teaches seminars to people employed by the government and large companies, attended our speaker seminar. His seminar title was: "How to Be Successful at Interviews Pertaining to Job Raises and Promotions." The attendees at his seminars are the interviewees, who pay for his course themselves. When we spoke of the other side of the coin, he got a great idea. He began another series of seminars for those on the other side of the table, the interviewers. In many companies, the interviewers have no special training on "How to Conduct Job Raise and Promotion Interviews."

He found an even larger and more lucrative market waiting for him with interviewers. Companies pay for his expert training, because he's already proven himself to be an expert in his field.

One speaker came to our bureau for advice on how to expand his market. At the time, he was presenting seminars at colleges as a dog-psychoanalyst. Audiences enrolled in his seminars because they love and want to train dogs. Although he is a leader in his field, it is not a high-profit market. So we suggested that he look at the other side of the coin. Current attendees loved dogs. We asked him, "What businesses and professionals hate dogs?" Together we made out a list:

1. Post office mail carriers;
2. All kinds of delivery people;
3. Municipal and utility meter readers;
4. Real estate people;
5. Police officers; and
6. Firefighters.

From that list, he developed a new topic entitled "How to Stop Dog Attack!" Its bookings have been sensational. His title states a benefit for those who attend. He focuses on one problem. He's an experienced expert in his field. Since millions of dollars in medical benefits and sick leave are lost yearly due to vicious dogs, employers are willing to spend big money to keep their employees informed on the subject, and therefore, out of the hospital and on the job. He found a new target market waiting for him on the flip side of his topic.

Four More Ways to Get New Topic Ideas

Topics for speeches are all around you. Here are four more ways to get new topic ideas.

1. Listen to people when they say "I need . . ."; "I have a problem . . ."; and "I wish I could find . . ."
2. Take notes when people talk. You may hear the seed of a seminar or speech topic.
3. Think through each idea thoroughly and check out which population segments, industries, businesses, or groups might want a speech on this problem.
4. Attend meetings related to your field and listen for topic ideas.

CREATING TITLES THAT GRAB ATTENTION

One speaker had a long and slightly obscure title on her promotional material. Then, she heard a corporate employer say, "If only I could get an honest day's work for an honest day's pay." This comment inspired her to add the words "How To" at the front of this phrase and create her new title: "How Employers Can Get An Honest Day's Work for An Honest Day's Pay." Her programs are now selling briskly to business associations.

Why Good Titles Draw Good Fees

People often judge the quality of books, speeches, or seminars by their title. When Ken Blanchard researched his book, *The One-Minute Manager,* he probably asked managers what they wanted and needed. The managers no doubt replied, "A quick, simple method that works for managing people, in order to get the work done easily and with the cooperation of my employees." Ken Blanchard's title, *The One-Minute Manager,* suggests that by reading the book and implementing the formulas, managers can become successful at handling many problems in only one minute.

The title implies there is a magic formula, which will make things right almost with a snap of the fingers and the word, "Abracadabra!" This idea appealed to managers, who are constantly stressed and strained. *The One-Minute Manager* took the essence of managers' problems and created a top-selling title targeted right at them. Therefore managers were willing to spend their money based on this title. *The One-Minute Manager* book and speeches are best-sellers. A number of follow-up titles have since come forth, including the *One-Minute Salesperson, . . . Father, . . . Mother,* and *. . . Lover.* Recently we heard of the *Fifty-Nine Second Employee (How to Stay Just Ahead of the One-Minute Manager).*

Ten Tips for Producing "Grabber" Titles

1. Think of your topic as a movie marquee or the jacket of a book. Use simple, easy-to-understand words that will intrigue people and make them want to hear you.

2. Avoid titles that are long, boring, or obscure.

3. Create titles that produce the image of "sleeves rolled up and ready to go to work," not "cute," complicated, or hard to understand. Titles aimed at the business world in particular should be straightforward and indicate a level of expertise.

4. Write out the entire title, then take away all of the unnecessary words. Pare the title down to the very essence of the idea.

5. Add pizzazz to your topic titles.

6. Use alliteration to make your title memorable. Titles such as "Sales Secrets," "Marvelous Mentors," "Power of Positive Thinking," "Living Legends," "Invention Convention," and "Broadway Bound" stay in one's mind. Choose same-sounding letters and rhythms because people remember titles with alliteration. Dr. Robert Schuller is a master at this. One of his titles is: "Turn Scars into Stars."

7. Make use of rhyming words. Nursery rhymes have been used for centuries to teach children. Notice the names of

books and movies. See how many of them rhyme. Dr. Schuller's latest advice is entitled, "Sift, Don't Drift; Lift, and Remember the Gift."

8. Use contrasting ideas to make interesting titles. Titles such as "The Rise and Fall," "The Agony and the Ecstasy," or "Up the Down Staircase" make use of this concept. Remember, music and art are studies in contrast. Without contrast, music would be monotone and art would be a wall painted a single color. Contrast makes life fascinating. Think of titles with contrast, and you will catch the interest of the buyer.

9. State the benefits to the buyer in the title. "Increasing Productivity," "Memory Made Simple," and "Conquering the Cold Call" are all examples of this concept.

10. Combine several of these tips to make sensational titles, such as "Conquering the Cold Call." Before pruning, this title might have been: "How You Salespeople Can Conquer Your Fear of Calling On Prospects You Do Not Know Who May Treat You Coldly and Reject You, and Make a Sale Anyway."

How to Avoid Bad Titles

Titles that suggest something negative are always considered bad titles. For example, Lee Shapiro, a judge who left the courtroom because he felt it was depressing, wanted to talk about love and caring. He chose the title: "The Happy Hugger."

He came to us for advice. Our feeling was that the title "Happy Hugger" might have an unpleasant connotation for some people, because it sounds too much like "Happy Hooker." We've discussed that who you are, and your experience and accomplishments comprise your basic pedestal or platform. Judges are prestigious. The "Happy Hugger" did not project that advantage. We made the following suggestions to Lee.

1. Change the topic title to: "The Hugging Judge."

2. Use a gavel on all of his business cards, stationery, brochures, and press kits.

3. Take a real gavel for the introducer of his speeches to use at the lectern.

4. Use "Oyez, Oyez, Oyez! The Court of Love is now in session. Judge Lee Shapiro presiding!" as his written introduction. Have the announcer bang the gavel after reading it.

5. Begin his bio with: "He put away his Judge's robes forever . . ."

The contrast suggested and used by Judge Shapiro has been sensational. The very first time he used these ideas in a press release, the wire services picked it up. Lee received calls for radio interviews from across the country. The difference in the two titles was contrast. People wanted to hear more about a stern judge, who now hugs people instead of "hanging" them. Now, as promotional gifts, he gives out bumperstickers that say, "Don't Bug Me! Hug me! Lee Shapiro, The Hugging Judge."

Using contrast to paint the picture is not a new idea. But you have to be careful not to contrast to the negative. Art, music, plots, and creative advertising are all made interesting with light and dark contrasts. William Shakespeare places Juliet on her balcony, dressed in a white robe, with Romeo speaking below. "She hangs upon the cheek of night, like a pearl in an Ethiope's ear." Light and dark create the appealing picture. Contrast is the "hook" used by the master word painter.

The Walters Title Formula and How it Can Work for You

Your material and your speaking performance must both deliver what your title promises. They must be first rate, of course, or you will never be booked again. However, if your title doesn't attract the buyer's attention, you will not have the opportunity to show what you can do. Titles are very important. Publishers have purchased titles without a book. Movie producers have done the same with scripts.

A great title is like an advertising headline in a newspaper. It attracts the attention of the buyers, because it features something of interest to them. Have you ever seen the title of a book or a movie that "grabbed" you? You say to the person next to you, "That is what I need! I have to have that."

The title of your presentations must have this same sense of urgency—make the public want it *now*. The way to accomplish this effect is to highlight the buyers' benefits in the title of your topic.

Use the Walters' Magic Topic Title Formula. No matter what your title, it should say plainly, or simply, the following:

"HOW TO _____ SO THAT YOU CAN _____."

The title points out the problem and implies that your material contains the answers that the audience members can't find, or don't have the time to find, for themselves. This is called a "benefit title."

In the title, "Solid Gold Customer Relations," speaker Carol Sapin Gold says the methods she teaches are "solid," the results will be *customers*—the "golden," profitable reward every business desires. If you have a business dealing with the public, this is an enticing title. The title also reinforces the speaker's name, Carol Sapin Gold. It is an ideal choice. Buyers remember her name *and* her topic because of her excellent title.

Why Speech Titles Should Offer a Benefit to Your Audience

A gentleman called our office for advice on why his mailings to various Chambers of Commerce had generated no response. "What topic did you offer them?" we asked. He very proudly told us his topic title was, "How to Take This Job and Shove It. Get into Business for Yourself!"

No wonder he had no response! Chambers of Commerce are composed of bosses. What employer would want to sponsor a seminar for his employees which gave them advice on how to quit?

This speaker's material might be fine for a general seminar with tickets sold to the public. It might be of special interest if he held the seminars on weekends when employees who might be considering a job change are not usually at work. The "Quit!" topic, however, was sadly mistargeted to Chamber of Commerce employers. But these same people might have jumped at the chance to book him on topics concerning advertising, direct mail, time management, how to avoid taking bad checks, customer relations or a hundred other topics that would stimulate their business or make their employees more productive. Your topic title must be of interest and offer help to the one who pays your fee.

How to Get Your Topic Titles to the Right Markets

Your title can be focused to the exact audience you wish to reach. If you are a sales expert and you wish to speak to the auto industry, use titles for that specialized audience like "Closing Contracts For Car Salespeople," "Telephone Qualifying for Greater Insurance Sales," etc. You might use "Bank Customers: Bring 'Em Back Alive!" as a title for a program on how to bring in repeat bank customers.

Take a big piece of paper and write "Who Cares" at the top. Now list your targeted audience. If your topic is "How to Get Along With Difficult People," change it to how to get along with difficult neighbors, employees, sales people, customers, clients, patients, doctors, retired people, foreign-born employees, managers, nurses, spouses, bosses, computer operators, suppliers, and so forth.

Now list the businesses or organizations who need help in these fields. Your "Difficult People" title is an umbrella which can be switched to assist dentists with difficult patients, banks with difficult customers, managers with difficult employees. Whatever else any business does, it also deals with people. Topics that address specifics on how to manage people and their problems will evoke immediate interest and response.

Every group is special. Its problems are unique. Each group wants to book an expert speaker who knows how to "fix" its problems. Put benefits and solutions into your title by adding their name to the benefit.

In our bureau we receive many calls and letters from people who say they are "motivational" speakers. Our clients, however, don't buy such a broad subject. They want to book programs aimed at their particular audiences. They want speeches that are crammed with ideas of benefits for their particular group. They want titles that pique their interest. Give them such topics and titles, and you will have little trouble speaking and growing rich.

3

Using Public Relations, Promotion, and Advertising to Obtain Bookings

Once you develop your topic and polish your presentation, you are ready to sell yourself as an expert and a speaker.

We will make the following point several times in our book. Do not be put off by the word "sell." Fame and fortune almost never single you out. If you truly wish to succeed and prosper as a professional speaker, you must be willing to learn and apply the rules of public relations, promotion, sales, and advertising. Remember and heed the words of playwright George Bernard Shaw, "The people who get on in this world are the ones who get up and look for the circumstances they want, and if they can't find them, make them." Ex-astronaut and now U.S. Senator John Glenn states, "My view is that to sit back and let fate play its hand and never influence it, is not the way we are meant to operate."

Public relations (commonly known as "PR"), promotion, and advertising are effective ways to make good things happen to your speaking career. They are an extension of your constant awareness of golden opportunities all around you. You will network, make deals and trades, and cooperate with other speakers and the media to advance your career. Promotion, PR, and advertising do not happen by themselves. You must make them happen, watching for every opportunity to do so. You will generate news releases about the surveys you take, new information in your field, inventions and creative ideas, always listing yourself as an authority in the area of your specialization. The articles you read and the stories you see and hear on the media do not appear there by accident.

1. PR includes your appearances on radio and television interview shows, and being interviewed by appropriate newspapers, magazines, trade journals, newsletters, etc.

2. Promotion includes the gifts you present to your introducer, and the meeting planner and/or bureau who obtained the booking for you. Promotion also consists of personal thank-you notes for every referral, and to every person who helps you. Promotion is also the look of your printed materials, your personal appearance, and your clothes. You must look the part of the successful speaker, as well as be the expert in your field.

3. Advertising is purchasing or trading for ad space in appropriate publications or media in creative and unusual ways. It also includes the beautiful one-sheets, flyers, and press kits you use to advertise your programs to prospective clients and bureaus.

Let's describe promotion further. Promotion involves working with other speakers, exchanging ideas and materials. It is joining the associations in your field, and participating in their activities in a positive way. It is also doing everything you can to help the bureaus who obtain bookings for you by handing out their materials at your performances.

Promotion is also going the extra mile to assist the meeting planner you work for. Most of all, promotion is your attitude. When we take the word and separate it into its parts, "pro" and "motion," it obviously means a positive move ahead. Make every single thing you do, from the way you answer the telephone to the speed with which you return a phone call (and always keep a warm smiling quality in your voice), give "pro-motion" to your speaking business.

Giants of the speaking world use all three techniques—PR, promotion, and advertising—to their advantage. None of the methods are new. For example, you might not think of President Abraham Lincoln as an effective speaker or a promoter, but he was both. When it was time for him to run for his second presidential term, be bought a small newspaper. He had the editor set a front-page headline that read, "Draft Lincoln." Then he had his supporters march on the White House brandishing the newspapers, to demand that he run again.

Your goal in the use of PR, promotion, and advertising is to generate the image of yourself as the expert in your field. Celebrities earn the highest fees, some as much as $75,000 per program including product sales. The more you are known in your field, and the better the job you do for your clients, the higher you can raise your speaking fees. Instigate news of interest to your specific audience. Just as President Lincoln instigated his own "Draft Lincoln" march, you must be always behind the scenes, creating new publicity ideas, promotion, and advertising copy.

BUILDING YOUR SPEAKING CAREER WITH GOOD PUBLIC RELATIONS

Many new speakers tell us, "I have no time for PR. I only want to make big fees immediately." This reminds us of someone who says, "I want to lose weight, but I won't change my eating habits." Successful speakers are also successful PR people. The two go hand-in-hand.

We use the following story in our speaking seminars to explain the importance of developing PR and getting the "you" attitude into every idea you use:

There once were some speakers who did not want to work at their own public relations. Instead, they decided to ask the Lord for fast action. They requested beauty, power, and money.

The Lord answered, "My children, there is beauty in every atom of your body. I have already given it to you. All you need to do is express it. There is power in the life force I gave you the moment you were conceived. It is switched on and running. All you need to do is use it. As for money, I am sorry, but there is none here in heaven. I have only great creative ideas to help people. All you need to do is catch them."

Effective PR takes consistent time and effort. It is not something you can do once and stop. Successful speakers continually work on new PR ideas. You may want to hire a professional public relations firm to handle your public relations, or perhaps you will want to do your own PR work. Many speakers and speakers bureaus such as ours often do both.

HOW YOU CAN BENEFIT FROM THE POWER OF FREE PUBLICITY

Getting free publicity in the media is an effective way to build your image as an expert and attract paid bookings. However, keep the following in mind about newspapers, magazines, and radio and television stations. They do not want to promote you. They want to deliver fascinating, helpful material to their readers or audiences, so their circulation or ratings will increase and enable them to profit by charging higher rates for advertising. If you view the media business from their side, you will quickly see that if you help them get such information to their readers, listeners, or viewers, the publicity for you and your topic will naturally follow. You will be identified as a fascinating source, and that will heighten your image as an expert on your topic.

One of the best ways to be called by radio- and TV-talk show interviewers and major publications is to be listed in the <u>Directory of Experts, Authorities, and Spokespersons,</u> which reaches 82 percent of the leading U.S. talk shows and media. It is published by Mitchell P. Davis, 2233 Wisconsin Ave., N.W., #406, Washington, DC 20007-4104.

Attract the media's attention by getting the "you" attitude into your public relations, self-promotion, and advertising efforts. This means creating and publicizing presentations that have "How You Can. . ." in their titles and sending appropriate packets of information and news releases to editors and news directors. Soon, representatives of the media will call you to ask, "Okay, how can you . . . ?" If you are well-prepared and knowledgeable in your topic, you will find yourself appearing in print and on the air—and receiving offers for bookings.

Remember the advice we gave you for finding your topic and title—"Take a survey." The same idea can work for your public relations and self-promotion efforts.

For instance, a PR expert wanted to promote her business, but did not have much money. She decided to use her unlimited skills instead. She took a survey of the businesses in her own downtown office building. "What bothers you? What hurts?" she asked. They answered, "Being robbed—in our offices, stores, and on the way to the bank."

She concentrated on this problem and soon thought of a simple, inexpensive way to help them. She called her printer and had a few thousand stickers made up to be used on building and car windows. The stickers said "NO MONEY ON PREMISES." Her design featured a large "$" inside a red circle with a diagonal line through it.

Next, she called the media and reported the results of her survey. She offered to give the stickers away free to any business that had the problem of being robbed. Of course, this meant she had to give out the address and telephone number of her business, as well. Her offer was well received. She was booked for radio, TV, newspaper, and magazine interviews, and soon, businesses from all over the state called to congratulate her on her unique idea and ask for the stickers. She asked each one about their other problems. They asked her for quotes on PR work. She had spent only $200 on the stickers. If she had paid for the airtime and publications space with advertising dollars, her cost would have exceeded $20,000. Instead, she got free publicity because she had created a helpful solution to a problem, and featured a free offer.

Remember that your own subject is your hook or angle. Publicity positions you as an expert in your field. Get your own publicity bandwagon going by writing articles, sending out press releases, authoring books, creating audio and video products for sale on your subject, and appearing on radio and television shows or in print interviews.

Whenever possible, offer something printed on paper as a free gift. We suggest this because paper is the lightest, least expensive promotional item you can offer. Yet, what is printed on that paper, such as "Ten Rules," "Eight Tips," "Five Secrets," etc., will make it valuable to the recipient.

SIX WAYS TO BECOME FAMOUS

Speaking fees are paid according to how good you are as a speaker, how unique, interesting, and informative your material is, and how well known you are. Your fees will increase dramatically once your clients recognize your name. To speak and grow rich, you must set a simple goal for yourself—Become famous. Here is how:

1. Begin by getting your own business cards, stationery, envelopes, and labels, all printed with your name, address, logo—your unique and recognizable symbol—and your photograph.

2. Take the most interesting, controversial aspect of your material and write an article on it. Contact the magazines and newspapers who reach the clients for whom you would like to speak. Offer the article free. Be sure to drop the Scheherazade hint in the article that you are THE speaker on this subject, and that there is much more information about it in your speech.

3. Offer meeting planners your free "Ten Rules," "Eight Tips," or "Five Secrets" information if they will write to you. Those who do are "hot" prospects for bookings.

4. Call the local radio and TV stations. Ask to speak to the programming or news director. Grab those first few seconds on the phone and ask, "Would your viewers like to learn how to. . . ? Would your listeners like to know the answer to. . . ?"

5. Watch the mail, the media, everything that comes to your hand. And ask yourself these two questions:

   a. Is there a possibility here for a story or interview?

   b. How can I be of service to these people?

6. Set publicity and PR goals for yourself. Make up your mind how many articles you will write and how many

shows you will appear on each month. The world stands aside to let those pass who know where they are going.

STEPS TO EFFECTIVE DO-IT-YOURSELF PR

To gain publicity and sell yourself to those who pay for speeches and seminars, you must have the right tools of the professional speaker's trade. These tools are the items speakers produce in order to engage in the paid speaking business. The steps we describe show you exactly what you will need. In the beginning, you may not need them all, but they are all valuable tools in constructing your career.

The first promotional item you should have printed for your speaking career is an attractive flyer. It should be one sheet that lists your topic title, the points you cover, your photograph, a few endorsements and a very short biography at the bottom. This material can be printed on one or both sides of the paper.

Next, choose a color scheme for your business materials, so your flyers, demo tapes, business cards, envelopes, stationery, and related materials will all match. Here are two ideas to help you make the right choices for color selections and designs.

Idea #1: Take a walk through your neighborhood supermarket. Forget what is in the packages on the shelves. Look only at the colors and designs. Let your eyes roam. When you see packages that attract your eye, buy them. It does not matter what is in them. Now study those packages. Especially note the titles, the benefits listed, and the attractive picture of what is inside. "What you see is what you get" is the theory that this exercise illustrates. These packages are designed and tested by marketing experts at great expense, to catch the eye of the buyer. (They caught your eye, didn't they?) Note the colors. Likely, they will all be in the warm "action" spectrum—reds or yellows. If cool spectrum colors are used—green, blue, black—they are used with a warm spectrum "color surprise" as contrast. Take several packages you like to your printer and graphic artist for suggestions and ideas on color combinations and type styles. Do not copy the ones you like. Adapt their techniques to your needs. Acquire inspiration and knowledge by studying the packages closely. Beware of printing your photograph in pastel or bright colors. Use black or very dark brown tones only for photos.

Idea #2: Go to the biggest magazine stand you can find. Again, let your eyes roam over the rack. Never mind what the magazine is about. Just buy the ones that grab your attention. Note how, frequently, there is a picture of one person on the cover. Notice how that person's eyes and hair are lighted. Then note the benefits (article titles) which are listed on the cover. Take these magazines to your photographer for ideas on poses and lighting. There is a current trend among star speakers to have the cover of their press kits suggest the cover of a sophisticated fashion, news, or sports magazine. They do not copy the magazine, but use its familiar appearance merely as a suggestion. If you have ever heard a medley of music, and remember that the audience involved burst into applause when they recognized one favorite tune, you will understand the effect of a design that reminds the viewer of something familiar. Remember, your materials may be considered on the desks of the buyers along with the materials of many others. You must do everything in your power to make your materials eyecatching and attractive so the speakers bureau representative or meeting planner will reach for yours first.

The following items should be added to your promotional efforts as your professional speaking business grows:

1. Press kit
2. Publicity releases
3. Articles written by you on your topic
4. Articles written about you by others
5. Your own newsletter

The remainder of this chapter focuses on each of these important promotional materials.

HOW TO CREATE YOUR PRESS KIT

A speaker's press kit is a large promotional package that is used in two ways. First, it is sent to prospective clients to show them who you are and what subjects you cover in your presentation. In this instance, the press kit is an invaluable asset in helping you find and close bookings. Second, press kits are sent to media personnel to interest them in considering you for publicity interviews on TV, radio, or for magazine and newspaper articles.

Press kits often are printed in full color and sometimes have foil accents or elaborate die-cuts. These high-quality types of press kits are both beautiful and expensive. Do not send them out unless a client or bureau is negotiating with you to book a speaking date. They contain the contract for the performance, and are designed to be "closers."

Press kits are also called promo kits, promo packages, marketing kits, or marketing packages. We caution you to remember the use of color. We receive many speakers' press kits which have been printed in all-black or "penitentiary grey." These are dull and uninviting and not likely to draw many bookings. A press kit is meant to sell you and reflect your talent and presentation.

Good press kits usually contain the following items:

- Your brochure or one-sheet flyer;
- Your topic title and speech outline;
- A video demo tape of your live presentation;
- An audio demo tape of your live presentation;
- Copies of letters of recommendation;
- Lists of clients for whom you have spoken;
- Reprints of articles you have written on this topic;
- A menu of the services you offer;
- Your fee schedule;
- Newspaper and magazine story reprints about you and your work (written by others);
- Biography information, often referred to as a "bio";
- Black-and-white glossy photos of you, taken both posed and while you are in action before an audience;
- Your letter to the potential buyer or speakers' bureau or publicity source; and
- A copy of your contract (not needed when you send press kits to the media).

How Speakers Use Press Kits

Although these important packages are called "press" kits, they are not just sent to the media. You will send out your press kits when you are working to book yourself. Speakers bureaus also will use them when they work on your behalf.

Good professional press kits cost from $5 to $15 each to produce, with $10 as an average. For every twenty press kits you send out to qualified prospective clients, only one typically will lead to an actual booking. (Actors tell us a similar tale. They generally have to try out for twenty parts to get one!) Including postage, the twenty kits will cost a total of approximately $300 to mail out. If your fee is $2,000 or $3,000, you must figure that the mailing expense is money well spent. Never ask a meeting planner or bureau to send back your kit if you are not booked. Sometimes, another speaker who is chosen may not work out as well as they had expected. Your press kit in their file will serve as an instant reminder of your ability and may bring you a booking for their next program.

The most popular press kit design is a folder printed on good quality glossy cardstock with pockets on the bottom of the inside sections. Without the inside lip, your items fall out on the floor. It is a good idea to have a tab along the long side, which extends to display your name and topic title when the kit is placed in a file cabinet. As you improve your performance and raise your fees, you will want to use the services of a professional brochure designer, such as Nat Starr, who is listed in the back of our book in the Speaker Resources appendix. His press kits have won top honors and results.

Sometimes, press kit flaps are created with a die-cut in the shape of the speaker. A photo of you is printed on this shape. This gives the effect of a "pop-out" as the kit is opened. A demo tape slot can be cut on the other flap, or small crosscuts can be added to hold a business card.

Remember—your press kit is your silent salesperson. Be sure your design and colors transmit the idea, "Let's book this one!" Don't let the copy and colors suggest, "Let's go to sleep!" Your competition won't. Use the K.I.S.S. system: Keep It Sweet and Simply elegant. When you work on your own bookings always include a mail-back card for replies, requests for more information, and other matters. As F. W. Woolworth often urged, "Make it easy for them to buy."

Custom-packing Your Press Kits

You should fill the pockets of your press kit individually for each prospect, to be sure that you send only the most appropriate materials.

In most cases, however, the following items should be included in every press kit that is sent to a potential client: (1) letters of recommendation and testimonials from those in the field; (2) copies of articles you have written and published in related publications; (3) high-quality publicity photos; (4) an audio demonstration tape; (5) your speaker's "bio" sheet; and (6) your fee schedule. These six items are discussed in more detail in the pages that follow.

How to Use Letters of Recommendation and Testimonials

Buyers will only give your materials a few minutes' time before they put them aside to look at someone else's press kit. So always custom pack your materials specifically for each buyer's needs, including a cover letter on your matching letterhead and copies of letters of recommendation and testimonials you have received. Your cover letter should be the first item in the right-hand pocket and should state that you are eager to serve the group and will work hard for them. If this potential client is likely to be interested in your program on leadership, for example, add to your press kit some copies of your most impressive, complimentary letters from other groups who have heard you speak on this subject. Highlight the word "leadership" in the letters of recommendation. This backs you up as an expert on the topic.

Next, choose some letters from the prospective buyers' own industry. Make it easy for them to see you are exactly right for them. Highlight the portions of the letters where your clients mentioned other benefits the prospective buyer is looking for, such as problem-solving. For the buyer looking for plenty of humor, highlight sentences such as, "Kept us all laughing." For the buyer who wants substance, highlight sentences such as: "Your methods and techniques have increased our productivity by 25 percent."

Another idea, used by Alan Climberg, is to pull out the most important line from a letter and print it across the top of the page in large type, underlined in red. For example: "You've done it again. Even better than the last three times you spoke for our group!"

When you have the letters reprinted, store them by category: bankers, sales, manufacturers, etc. Then you can easily pull the ones that apply to your prospect's field. The letters will help make the prospect feel you are especially keyed in to their problems. Send the bankers letters from other bankers, or related institutions, such as escrow companies. Cross-file other letters in your files by "sales points" such as humor, motivation, etc.

Letters from celebrities or leaders in the industry you speak for should go into every press kit. You are fortunate if you have a testimonial from someone who is very well known, such as Dr. Norman Vincent Peale, Lee Iacocca, or Ross Perot. They are respected celebrities. Be careful not to include material from controversial people. Your circle of friends might think this person is wonderful, but the CEO of a large company can take one look at such material and reject your program. So why take that chance?

Getting letters of recommendation and testimonials takes planning and purpose. A speaker once called us to complain that he was having trouble obtaining letters of recommendation from clients who had booked him. When we asked what method he was using, he explained that he had prepared six-page sets of extensive questions with rating totals at the bottom of each page.

It's no wonder no one mailed them back. He was asking his clients to spend too much time. Make it easy for people to give you testimonials or letters of recommendation. Here are six ideas and tips to help you get started.

1. Make it a habit to discuss a letter of recommendation with the meeting planner before each program. Explain that the letter is very important to your career and that you will especially appreciate the effort and thoughtfulness of the planner in giving it to you.

2. Get the right letters. Your first letters of recommendation may come from the local Kiwanis, Lions, or Soroptomists clubs, where you have presented your practice talks. Soon,

however, you will want to begin to charge a fee. If your letters of recommendation are all on service club stationery, experienced meeting planners will know all of your previous talks are "freebies." What you need are testimonials from business people. Fortunately, they are the very people who make up the audiences in the clubs. So ask them to give you a letter on their own bank, business, or service company letterhead. This way, instead of 20 letters from Kiwanis clubs, you can have 20 separate endorsements from business people.

3. Use current letters, no more than two years old. If you get a particularly good letter, perhaps from a famous or high-ranking person or prestigious company, white out the date before you reprint the letter for use in your press kits. (A letter is "old" tomorrow.)

4. Help your buyers write the letter of recommendation. When you have finished a program, ask the meeting planner or the president who praises you to please be so kind as to dictate those very words to their secretary so that you can have a letter of recommendation. Jot down their praise. (Some speakers use recorders for this, asking first if they may record their comments.) Call the secretary and ask her to put the letter together, for the president's signature. Make a letter easy for them to do. Follow up, and always send a note of thanks.

5. Here is another way to use letters of recommendation. Keep in mind that most business persons belong to several organizations. When you receive an especially positive letter of recommendation, call and ask the sender if he or she could help you again by letting you know if they belong to a group that you might call for another engagement. Ask if you may use their name. If they like you, they may even call and arrange the date for you. If you do not ask, they may think that you do not want any more speaking dates. Successful speakers obtain at least five new speaking engagements each time they use this method of referral. Don't forget to send a note of thanks.

6. Use audience rating sheets each time you speak. We have provided a form in this book which gives you one extraordi-

narily successful example. A speaker recently wrote that he obtained 28 speaking leads, plus 15 top testimonials from one performance through the use of our rating sheets. Remember to offer a reward to the audience for filling them out. Hold a drawing, and give a prize. We always give a full set of the completed sheets to the meeting planner. The letter of recommendation will usually use the audiences' ideas for comments in your letter.

Testimonials and letters of recommendation are very valuable to your career. Some will come to you unsolicited, but most require time, effort, and planning on your part. They are well worth it.

Heighten Your Image as an Expert with Copies of Your Articles

When you send press kits to prospective clients, enclose copies of the articles you have written on the same topic. Highlight those sections in the articles where you discuss the issues and problems in which your buyer expressed an interest.

One of the best ways to be seen and have your views heard by potential clients is to write and publish articles related to your topic. These articles not only will keep you in the public eye but will keep you in front of buyers in the markets you want to reach, as well. While it may be awhile before you become an international, household name, you can start quickly to be a celebrity expert within your defined market.

When you are asked to speak for any organization, also see if you can write an article on your topic for their company publication or newsletter. Being published gives you credibility. You can also reprint your published articles and include them in your press kit. When you are ready to have your own book published, you will already be well-known in your field.

There literally are hundreds of publications in every field. A reference librarian can help you locate copies of the most appropriate media for your target market. Call each editor, ask for a sample issue and their author's guidelines. Some may charge you for the sample copy. Pay it gladly. Most magazines are on the lookout for good material of interest to their particular readers. Study the style and length of the articles and the angles from which they are written.

You also can obtain the address of newspapers and magazines, as well as radio and television stations, from visitors and convention bureaus, the Chamber of Commerce, and the phone book. As you are booked to speak, ask each client which trade journals they read. Make it a point to locate and contact those publications with an article offer to develop more bookings in your field.

When you write for a specific company publication or association newsletter, put the name of their group in your headline. For example, the topic "How C.P.A.'s Can Handle Irate Phone Calls," would be ideal for an accounting publication. It is often much easier to get started writing for trade journals than for major publications.

Once you begin writing articles, be patient for the payoff. Do not expect to be paid in money for your articles. You will be highly paid in other ways. Writing increases your visibility and attracts paid booking clients who are interested in your field and expertise. The value of inquiries from your articles for speaking, training, consulting, and product sales is tremendous. With such added recognition, you will be able to raise your fees, as well.

Small publications and newsletters frequently will be delighted to print your articles, if your material offers benefits to their readers and is the right length and style. There are special publications for everything you can imagine, from people who jump out of airplanes with parachutes, to people who are single parents.

To find these publications, go to the library and find a directory of newsletters. It should list thousands of publications on every topic. Call and talk to the editors of the appropriate ones. Offer to write articles for their newsletters. If you have established a newsletter of your own to send to clients and prospects, you can exchange plugs with other newsletter publishers. Offer something free if their readers write to you. You can often use almost the same article for different fields by rearranging and changing the material to fit each publication. Newsletters for dentists, for example, are not in competition with those for bankers. Use this same method when writing for magazines and newspapers, as well.

If you have been faithfully taking surveys, you already have valuable information. Call business magazines and tell the editors you have, for example, a story about the results of your survey of top business managers in their field. You have discovered exciting new material on these executives' best techniques for "Getting the Job Done," or "Handling the #1 Managerial Distress: Interruptions."

Very often, the editor will be interested. You have news to offer. Ask for a copy of their writer's guidelines. This will enable you to send a story of the right length and style. We have had speakers send a 40-page story for publication in our 40-page speakers newsmagazine, *Sharing Ideas,* including a note which says we may be "free to edit." This means the editor has to spend a great deal of time and effort just to be able to use the story. Instead, send in your material as requested—the right length and with the angle the editor has suggested to you. Address the material to the editor you spoke to, and get your story in promptly, ahead of schedule. You will have a much better chance of having it accepted. Also send a short bio and a glossy black-and-white photo of yourself with the story. Don't forget to mention the free gift for readers who write in, thus your address is listed.

NOTE: Give only first-time publication rights for your articles. This means a magazine has permission to print your article once, but the article itself belongs to you. Then you can rework your articles for non-competing publications, gather them into books or booklets, and reuse and rearrange their text for audio cassettes and video programs.

When you have an article published, ask for or buy copies of the publication. Dottie was asked to write a story for *Success Opportunities* magazine. She sent it in and then booked a speaking date in the city where the magazine has its main office. She called and invited their publisher and editor to come and hear her, as her guests, making sure this was agreeable to her client. The magazine people were impressed with the audience interest and with Dottie's presentation. They decided that day to use her picture in full color on the cover of their issue with her article. When the magazine came out, she asked if she might have some copies of that issue. They gave her several cartons full, a fantastic addition to Dottie's press kits.

THE IMPORTANCE OF HIGH-QUALITY PUBLICITY PHOTOGRAPHS

You will need hundreds of copies of your black-and-white glossy publicity photos. Most press kits contain at least two. Speakers also use their photos on book jackets, album covers, brochures, business cards, and their letterhead, as well as with their magazine articles.

The publicity photographs you will send to the media and potential clients must help convey the image of a competent, polished speaker and expert. Therefore, the quality of your publicity photographs must be top-notch. Hire a photographer who has a studio or a complete set of portable lights and is familiar with the process of shooting good business or fashion photos. Do not choose an "artsy," soft focus, or outdoor-shot specialist.

Lighting is the key to good photography. Be sure the background is light if your skin tone is dark, and that the background is dark if you are fair. A brunette against a dark background gives the effect of a face peeking out of a black bag. Contrast makes an interesting picture. Tell the photographer you want pictures with sharp contrast for media reproduction.

Your eyes should be lit so that your expression snaps out of the picture. A good photographer will "capture your spirit." Take along to the photographer's studio the props you use on stage—such as a telephone, a sign, or a microphone. Your apparel for the session should include a sports outfit, some formal attire, and several business costumes. The photographer may take as many as 100 shots of you with the different costumes and props showing you in a variety of business poses and action shots. Suggest that color pictures be shot at the same time as the black and white ones. Be prepared to pay extra for this service, which saves you the time of a separate shooting session.

The most popular size of publicity photos for speakers is the 5 in. by 7 in. When you order photos, ask that your name, topic, address, and phone number be printed at the bottom, in the margin of the photo, for your own promotional use. This costs just a few cents more and is printed right along with the picture. Have some of these photos printed with your name only for bureau use.

We have listed at the back of this book, a top wholesale producer of black-and-white glossies who can supply prints in quantity.

Quality action photos of you speaking are wonderful for your promotional materials. However, they are the hardest to obtain. Carry a 35mm camera with you to your speaking engagements, loaded with black and white film. If you cannot afford to hire a professional photographer to cover your speeches, ask the meeting planner if anyone in their group is an amateur photographer and willing to take pictures of you. Give this person a gift, perhaps one of your books, to thank them for their efforts.

Often, the group you will address already has hired a photographer for the event. Ask the photographer if he or she can take some shots of you while you work. Offer to pay for the pictures. Ask the photographer to capture the crowd response and you speaking, in the same shot if possible. This works very well if you work with a hands-free or long-cord microphone and go down into the audience.

Another inexpensive idea is to call a camera shop near the venue or a college close by that has a photography class. Ask for someone to come and shoot two 36-exposure rolls of black and white film. Then have them developed yourself. Any one-hour photo shop can do a good, quick job of processing your photos. You pay only for the time the student or freelancer uses taking pictures.

If there is a celebrity or well-known speaker on the program with you, arrange for a shot of them shaking your hand or looking at your book. These pictures are great for publicity. Another good photo is you with the meeting planner or president of the group that booked you. Send a copy of this picture with the articles you write for them in the future, or use the photo to help illustrate their testimonial letter or letter of recommendation.

INCREASE YOUR COMPETITIVE EDGE WITH A TOP AUDIO DEMONSTRATION TAPE

Good-quality audio demonstration tapes are something you simply must have to compete for paid speaking engagements. Meeting planners ask for them, speakers' bureaus request them for their clients. Since all the best, constantly booked speakers have demo tapes, there is no choice for you but to have one too, if you plan to compete. This is not our opinion as a bureau, but the opinion of our meeting planner clients.

A bureau already has many speakers to choose from who have great demos at the ready. So to get good bookings, you must produce a solid audio demo tape. Video is coming in fast, but having a video demo is not yet mandatory until your fee tops $5,000 for a keynote. So start with audio, then add video once your career is off and running.

We have received some very sad examples of audio demo tapes over the years. One was from a man who billed himself as a humorist. His material was not funny, but his tape did have laughs at all the wrong times! When he called for our reaction, we asked him how the strange placement of the laughter happened.

"Oh, those laughs were from the audience next door. They were laughing at their speaker. My audience didn't laugh," he explained.

How could any bureau suggest that their client buy a speaker like that? The moral of this story . . . never send a bureau an unsatisfactory or unflattering tape. Bureaus do not edit or cut tapes. That is not their job. It is yours. Send the most smashing, elegant, wonderful tape you can create, one that a bureau will be proud to send to their clients.

A demo tape may also be an audio tape you have developed for resale, but only if you have prepared a good, dynamic presentation. Just be sure it has a fast start, with some of your best material in the first two minutes.

Another good PR idea that you can use with audio demos is to have the recording studio leave ninety seconds blank at the beginning of your audio demo tape. Put the tape into your own cassette machine and record a custom message for the client on it before you send it out. Use their name. Mention the things you discussed over the telephone. Customizing the tape takes just a minute, costs nothing extra, and can be a very powerful PR tool.

The latest speaker demo idea is a WATS 800-number telephone service such as Vox Populi. You give out their number, and your client can call and listen to your demo tape instantly, then leave a recorded message for you. Later, you can call in and pick up your messages.

One enduring rule in the speaking industry is that demo tapes must never be more than ten minutes long. A planner might listen to thirty demo tapes before making a decision. To give you a scenario, let's say your tape is thirty minutes long. You call the planner and ask, "How did you like my demo?"

"Oh, your topic wasn't quite what we were looking for. We wanted more on leadership styles," the planner replies.

"But I do a whole section on that. It is twenty minutes into the tape!" you protest. Of course, it would do little good. The busy planner must pick speakers on the basis of ten-minute reviews of their demo tapes, so be sure your tape covers your topic in that precious ten minutes.

When they hear a speaker they like, meeting planners usually listen to an entire ten-minute demo tape at least once, then ask for the whole keynote program the speaker has produced. Then they may want to hear the speaker in-person at another performance. How long does it take you to decide you *don't* like a car when you test drive it? Five minutes, ten?

Therefore, you have about 60 seconds to prove to the buyer, in order of importance, that:

1. The audience liked you;
2. You speak well; and
3. You are an expert on the topic the buyer wants.

These points should not be made by an announcer in those first sixty seconds, but through your live examples. As the poet Edgar Guest once put it, "Fine counsel is confusing, but example is always clear." Arrange a demo tape that begins with your best segment. Then speak to the buyer on the tape, explaining what you do. Invite them to listen to the whole program, which follows. Despite the tendency to do short demo tapes, we like demo tapes that lead with a top ten minutes, then go on with a whole program, at least forty-five minutes long.

Meeting planners tell our bureau they want your audio demo to be live, recorded in front of an audience as you perform a speech on your particular topic. Meeting planners do not like to listen to television and radio interviews. If you don't have any paid engagements coming up, offer to do one free for a local service club and pay to have it taped. Then edit it carefully. A rousing audience reaction, with you at your very best, is one of the most effective sales tools you can use.

Get a taping system that will tape audience response, in addition to your speech. The potential buyer listens to your tape not only to hear if you are a good speaker, but to listen to the audience reaction. The buyer's first concern is that other audiences loved you.

The following five tips are very important to the process of creating an effective demo tape.

1. In the first few seconds, the buyer should hear you being loved by the audience, coming across as expert, and speaking well. Edit a section of the speech at its highest point for this first section.

2. At the point where the applause fades out, have the announcer or yourself come in with a very brief sentence or two on who the speaker is and what this tape is about.

3. Fade in with audience background noise to the speaker giving a brilliant point in the speech.

4. When the applause fades out again, the announcer should fade back in with more brief credits about the speaker.

5. Repeat the above process for anywhere from three to ten minutes. Then have the announcer come in with major credits and conclude with, "Now, listen to _____ with a full thirty-minute speech as performed for the _____ audience."

How many demo tapes should you prepare? If you have four very separate topics, you must have four separate demo tapes. It does not work to tell a meeting planner or potential client, "I really speak on leadership, but this tape on time management will give you a sample of my style!" They will assume that you are really a time management person who is experimenting with leadership as a new topic, and they will reject you. They want experts. It is much more effective to have separate tapes for different topics.

You will need to keep at least fifty to one hundred tapes on hand at all times. But do not prepare many more than that unless you anticipate a large resale market, as well. You will constantly be improving as a speaker, and you will want to re-do your demo tapes on a regular basis. If you print thousands of tapes at the outset, you will be tempted to keep second-rate tapes on hand instead of remaking and improving them every six months to a year.

Be sure your demo tapes are attractively packaged with foil, your picture, appealing type, in colors that match your press kit. Add these items to a top performance, and your demo tape will become a powerful sales closer.

HOW TO PREPARE YOUR "BIO" SHEET

Your "bio" of speaking credits should also be included in every press kit. Speakers often send our bureau a vita, thinking it will suffice as a bio. The two are quite different. A vita lists the educational background of the speaker and may be several pages long. A bio is one sheet. It lists the reasons this speaker is an authority on this subject.

We once had a speaker send us a bio that began with her birth weight. While we did get a sense of massive conscientiousness from it, we could not send it on to our meeting planners. Your bio is not your life history. The meeting planner just wants facts about your qualifications to speak on your topic. If you have written articles or books, spoken for major companies or been presented with honors, these are the things you should list in your bio. Put speaking credits first, then other publicity, such as media appearances. Your picture and topic title should go at the top of the page.

PROJECT THE IMAGE OF EXCELLENCE

As you become more professional and your fees increase, the image your promotional materials project must take on a higher-quality and more expensive image as well. You and your materials must "look the part of excellence." Like the clothes you wear on the platform, your press kit must express you. A little foil on the front will look elegant and gain attention. Foil comes in many shades, and can make your lettering come to life. For example, speaker Maxine McIntyre has beautiful, coppery-red hair. Her press kit and demo tapes feature foil in the same shade. The impact is stunning!

When you design press kits for use by speakers bureaus, remember that many bureaus will insist that you do not have your own phone number, address, or city printed anywhere on the materials. However, when you send material to clients who are booking you directly, you will always need to have these items listed. A solution to this dilemma is to have part of your material printed with your contact information, and part printed without it. Leave a blank space instead for the phone number, address, and city for the use of each bureau you work with. The bureaus will affix their own stickers in the reserved space.

Another idea is to leave a small space blank on all of your printed materials. Then have a classy foil sticker designed and printed. This sticker can be affixed to the kits you send out yourself or left off of kits that are sent to speakers bureaus. When this technique is used, your material has to be printed only one way, and that can save you some money.

Always keep in mind that it is not possible for you, or your bureaus, to obtain bookings with high fees, such as $3,000 or $4,000, if your press kit projects your image as a $500 beginning speaker. Like a beautiful business suit and a great hair cut, your promotional materials make a first and lasting impression.

Of course, excellent promotional materials can never take the place of top talent and superb presentation content. But the materials can have a powerful impact on your career. They are an essential part of your professional image.

THE POWER OF PUBLICITY RELEASES

Publicity releases are short news accounts that should be sent out to the news media when you receive an honor, are elected to an office, have a book published, take a survey, name or make a list of "ten best," or launch any other PR project you want to promote. Copies of the releases and any mentions they have generated in the media then should be added to your press kit.

If you follow these sixteen rules, the media will pay closer attention to your news release and work with you:

> 1. Put the source of the release in the upper left-hand corner of your paper. This is the name, address, and phone number of the person to contact for further information. The contact person may be you, or someone at your PR service.

2. Put the release date, typed in capital letters, slightly below the source information and on the opposite (right-hand) side of the page.

3. Sum up the most important thrust of the release in the headline in capital letters.

4. Use standard 8 ½ in.-by-11 in. sheets of paper for your releases. Smaller or larger sizes are hard for media people to store. Use only one side of the paper. Keep the length of the release to one page, whenever possible. If you must use more, type "(MORE)" at the bottom. Staple all pages on top left. On the last page, type "###" or "-30-" or "END."

5. Your releases should be typed double-spaced. Leave a three-inch margin on the top of the first page and leave margins on each side that are wide enough for editing.

6. Dottie Walters' journalism teacher wrote the following poem by Rudyard Kipling on the blackboard the first day Dottie was in her class. It has since helped us in every business enterprise.

> "I keep six honest serving men,
> They taught me all I knew.
> Their names were What and Where and When,
> And How and Why and Who."

Be sure to get all of your "serving men" in the first paragraph of your news releases. Put the most important and exciting one at the head of the story.

7. Use a fine grade of paper. A color other than white may help you stand out in the crowd. But stay in the warm spectrum.

8. Don't send out news releases that have a "copy machine" look.

9. Avoid highly technical language unless the release is for a technical audience.

10. Find out how far in advance each contact wants your information. Send it out when they want it.

11. Don't pass off non-original material as exclusive.

12. Don't try to make an advertisement for yourself out of an article or release. Make it fascinating news for readers instead.

13. Give a source for additional information (name, address, phone number). Make sure your source knows all the details and does not have to check with someone else for answers if a reporter calls for additional information. This source could be an association or company mentioned in the article.

14. Find a way to make your news noteworthy! Give it a twist that is specific to the audience who will read it. A dog expert working with plumbers might come up with a topic such as "Plumbers Use Dogs to Sniff Out Deadly Gas" to catch the attention of a plumbers' publication. Other news media outlets, however, might also find that topic worthy of attention.

15. Releases should be the minimum length necessary to present the facts of interest to this audience.

16. Keep your news release mailing list up-to-date. Post changes as you receive them. Media people like to see releases addressed to them rather than to their predecessors.

HOW TO WRITE COPY THAT SELLS YOU AS A SPEAKER

Inexperienced speakers sometimes send us introductory materials that are covered with sea gulls or wild designs unrelated to their topic. They print their materials in expensive full color. Their front page copy reads, "I am a wonderful, wonderful, wonderful, WONDERFUL speaker." This is somewhat like a restaurant menu with one word printed on it—FOOD.

Being "wonderful" does not create interest, because everyone in this business is expected to be a "wonderful speaker." We also see numerous variations of the "I'm wonderful" theme. Sometimes the adjective claims the speaker is "unique" or "charismatic" but the point is the same. The buyers are not nearly as interested in your opinion of yourself as they are in what you can do for their audience. Benefits are what they are after!

When we find no topic title, benefits, or name on the front of any of a speaker's materials, we feel pity. The new speaker has spent a great deal of money and time on ineffective promotional printing. Our meeting planner clients tell us repeatedly that they do not like materials that make them wonder who the speaker is, or what the subject is about. They say, "Don't ask me to play 'guess what?' I am too busy. Put it out in front where I can see it." Beginners often mistakenly list the benefits of their program at the end of the last page.

The front page of everything you print must include three items:

1. Your picture;
2. Your topic area and its benefits to the audience; and
3. Your name.

The title of your presentation should follow the formula we discussed in Chapter 2, with how-to's and benefits clearly stated. Design your materials with the thought that the buyer may never look inside. Make the title "grab" them!

HOW TO TRADE YOUR SPEAKING FOR PUBLICITY

There are times when it will be beneficial to your career to exchange your fee for advertising space or time. In return for performing, you get to advertise your services as a speaker, or promote your seminars and products in the client's publications or media.

A good example of such an arrangement is the sales trainer who gave a series of sales seminars for radio time-representatives. He took his payment out in radio-time for himself. Then he made his own commercials and used the radio-time he received in trade to promote his public seminars. He thus earned in seminar sales many times the fee he would have earned as a trainer for the radio station. He included a plug for his other speaking and training services in his seminar commercials and was called by businesses to do additional training sessions, as well as conference and convention speeches.

There was a side benefit, as well. His commercials were so good, the station asked him to do several commercials for other companies, for good fees. He now often works in the TV and radio commercial field, and enjoys residual payments for his advertising speaking.

His willingness to trade out his commercials for radio time opened the door to many other pieces of good business. We find that business often begets business. The more you are heard and seen, the more you will be called for additional business.

USING DIRECTORIES AND ADVERTISING EFFECTIVELY

Several radio and television talent directories are published and can list you and your area of expertise. These directories often are used by radio and television stations when they need someone to interview on a particular topic. For example, when the Challenger disaster occurred, Paul Hanover, whose topic is "Living in Space," was called by many stations across the country because he was listed under "Space" in the directories. Try to be listed in as many categories as practical. Be sure your title for each is a "grabber."

Regional as well as national directories of speakers are published. Some require membership in their group before a speaker is listed, while others sell listings and display advertising space to any speaker. Here are some ideas to help you maximize your advertising efforts:

1. Team up to buy a joint ad. Since advertising is often expensive, consider sharing a full-page ad with other speakers in your field. For example, we know four humorists who buy full-page ads that show them all together. These humorists are all outstanding performers. Since a full page usually costs less than four quarter-page ads, the "team-up" idea works well and saves advertising money. Each one only pays a fourth of the full-page rate.

   Another reason to team-up is that meeting planners usually want a new humorist for each booking. If they like one of the partners, they are likely to be pleased with the others, as well.

An extra advantage to the teaming arrangement can be the shared use of a toll-free, wide-area telephone number (800-number, also known as a WATS line). Team members can share the line and costs so that clients can call them easily.

2. Attend trade shows. There are trade shows of all kinds and sizes aimed in every market. Many trade shows look for professional speakers who will trade a presentation aimed at their particular group in exchange for a free booth, and/or a display ad in the trade show program or directory. This is a good bargain. You have the opportunity to speak to an ideal audience of prospects and to sell your speaking services and products at a booth. When selecting trade shows for speaking and selling your products, be sure you choose those that tie in with your subject.

3. Advertise in speakers bureau directories. Often, bureaus publish speaker directories. The bureau pays for publishing and mailing the directory to thousands of meeting planner clients and prospects. There is no opportunity for teaming-up in these directories, however. All speakers must buy their own ads, but this is still an inexpensive and good way to advertise. The speaker's advertisement, picture, and topic are sent directly to the bureau's buyers. A typical directory ad costing $300 reaches 10,000 meeting planner prospects. A speaker could not pay for printing, postage, labor, and "rent" for a mailing list to produce such a large mailing for that low price. Bureau directories are an excellent way to advertise, because meeting planners keep them and use them all year. Only the address and phone number of the sponsoring bureau appear on this type of directory. All bookings go through the bureau.

HOW TO GET WRITERS TO WRITE ABOUT YOU

You will write many articles yourself, but it is also desirable to be written about. Here is an easy way to accomplish this. Bylines are the name-credit lines given to the author of articles. This is the person who found the subject, conducted the interview, and had the article accepted for publication. Watch for these bylines on articles which are the same type story you would like to see written about you and your topic. For example, call the publication and ask for the writer of a specific story. The person may be on staff or work on speculation. In either case, when you reach the writer, say how much you enjoyed the article. Then explain that you have a story you think he or she might like. Tell the writer about the unique work you do. The writer's business is looking for interesting people and topics for feature stories. We have had many publicity stories published in this way, some of them a full page in the Sunday edition of a daily newspaper, with several pictures. By asking for the writer by name, you go right to the person who may want to write a story about you.

As your career grows, you will be interviewed by business magazines, newspapers, and hosts of radio and television shows. Not only will you enjoy the pleasure of an interesting interview, but you will gain many other benefits for your speaking career, as well. Here are five ideas for getting maximum value from your publicity interviews:

1. Know the media before you approach them. Listen to and read the media in which you want exposure. Call the producer or editor of the programs or articles pertaining to your topic. For example, if your topic is money, you should not call the beauty editor of a magazine or newspaper, or the host of a beauty show on television or radio, unless you can slant your topic effectively to their subject. For example, you could offer articles or interviews on "How to Look Better When You Ask for a Raise" or "How to Borrow More Money at a Lower Rate by Looking Successful."

   For your regular money topic, call the editor of the newspaper's or magazine's financial or business pages or the producer of a money program on radio or television. Study each publication and program well in advance of your call. Notice the kinds of topics and guests that appear. Some hosts want controversy, while others look for adventure. The same goes for publications.

2. Match the interviewer's pace. When you are interviewed for radio, television, or the print media, keep your eyes and

attention on the host or writer. Being interviewed is like engaging in ballroom dancing. Follow their lead; respond to them. Do not look at the camera or around the room. Concentrate on, and react to, the person who is speaking.

Watch and listen, How fast does the interviewer walk? Talk? In both cases, get in step. Off-camera or when the tape recorder is turned off and the notebook is closed, ask the host or writer about his or her own plans, dreams, goals. It always helps to be interested.

Dale Carnegie, author of *How to Win Friends and Influence People,* once said, "You can make more friends in two months by becoming interested in other people than you can in two years by trying to get other people interested in you."

Another example. . . when Dottie was to be interviewed on a major television show, the hostess asked off-camera for suggestions on how to help her sister, who was having difficulty finding work. On camera, Dottie concentrated on positive ideas people can do to create jobs, using her topic as a subtle sideline. The hostess was so pleased, she asked Dottie to stay so that they could record a second one-hour program to be used on another date.

3. Motivate interviewers to do a great job. Use the power of visualization. See the interviewer in your mind as a person who is the best he or she wants to be. If you visualize them this way, you will soon find yourself adding such phrases as "A wise person like you. . . " or "Someone with your pep and enthusiasm. . . " during the interview.

The reason why this technique is effective has been summed up by Vince Lombardi, the legendary coach of the Green Bay Packers. He once said: "In each player's heart is a dream and a hurt. When I concentrate on the injury, a synergy takes place and the hurt grows. Pretty soon, the player can think of nothing else and drops out. When I think and speak of the positive dreams, a different synergy takes place. It blazes. It sparkles. Soon the hurt is forgotten. The life-force of the player is called up. Therefore, I only talk of dreams."

For outstanding interviews, think and speak in terms of other peoples' dreams. Interviewers are people, too.

They will respond to your interest in them and their needs.

4. Get media referrals. People who work in radio or television or for publications often know people in the same field who may be interested in your topic. Don't be afraid to ask them for a referral to a non-competitive show or publication. Follow it up. Thank them.

   Speakers, it is often said, are divided into three types:

   a. those who are immovable and who don't grow or change with the times;

   b. those who are movable but who are influenced by what others tell them to do; and

   c. the speakers who are also great self-publicists. They know how to move on their own. Be a mover.

5. Prepare properly for telephone interviews. Each radio host works in a different manner. Some want you to send them questions in advance. They may want your press kit, tapes, or books. Some prefer the spontaneity of not knowing about the guest in advance. Whatever their method is, get in step with their program.

You might also initiate a radio interview by calling a station with an appropriate show, or the station might call you when your topic is listed in the radio directories. We have appeared in-person in the studios of radio stations all over the world. However, many radio interviews are now conducted by telephone. The station calls you in advance to set up the time and to discuss the questions they will ask. Here are five tips to help you give more effective interviews by telephone.

1. The person who makes the arrangements with you is the producer of the show. He or she will call you again when it is time be on the air. Your interview may be as short as 10 minutes, or could run up to several hours on a call-in talk show.

2. Ask in advance for the emergency studio telephone number in case you are cut off during the show. Get the name of the host, and call the host by name during the interview. Write that name in large letters and put it up in

front of you during the show. Send a thank-you letter afterward.

3. At your end of the line, have a glass of water, a box of tissues, and something to eat handy if you expect to be on for a long period of time.

4. Take the interview phone call in a room where you can shut the door and keep out unwanted noise. Arrange for someone to be in your office or home with you to take care of anyone who comes to the door while you are on the air. Turn off the bells on your phone so that any other incoming calls will not be heard.

5. Before the interview begins, you should write several key words and phrases from your topic on a big piece of paper and have it in front of you. This will serve as a reminder of the things you want to get on the air. Subjects you should list are benefits to the listeners, the host's name, the studio's emergency telephone number, and how listeners can reach you.

The booking benefits of a radio interview to your speaking career include the mentioning of your topic, the fact that you are a speaker and are available, and any telephone numbers, books, album prices, and ordering information you can give out during the show. Arrange with the producer in advance for the opportunity to offer these things. Some show producers prefer to have the host plug your free gift and products.

About 90 percent of the benefits of a good show go to the radio station. The remaining 10 percent, however, are there for you. Having these things written out in front of you will remind you to stick to your material. Sometimes a host will go off on a tangent, on a subject that has nothing to do with you or your topic. Be funny and warm, but pull the conversation back to your topic.

MORE WAYS TO GET NOTICED BY THOSE WHO PUBLICIZE AND THOSE WHO BUY

Your biggest PR job in your speaking career is to help people remember you. Here is a baker's dozen of good ideas you can adapt to your speaking career for little or no money:

1. Decide to be unique. Movie actress Kim Novak always wore shades of lavender. She became famous for that color. Some speakers always wear a hat. Think of ways to look unusual and to help people to remember your name and your topic. Use a special color in your business stationery, business cards, or press kit.

2. Work with an unusual prop. Gene Harrison tells a very funny story about coon dogs, and he imitates their baying in his stories until the audience laughs and laughs. Naturally, he uses a coon dog on everything he prints. Some speakers use puppets, monkeys, signs, or other props. Zig Ziglar became famous by using an old-fashioned kitchen hand pump on stage to demonstrate his point of putting some action into your life by priming your pump. Props help your audience enjoy and remember you.

3. Be alert to everything. *Webster's Dictionary* says, "Promote is the opposite of demote." Promotion constantly goes up, just as demotion heads down and out. Ask yourself "How can positive things be done to use things up, cut down on waste, and raise the value of this effort?" An example is the leftover flyers your client used to promote your speaking program. Rather than let them be thrown away, ask if you may have the leftovers after the show. Box them up and arrange for them to be shipped to your office. (Be sure to send a thank-you note.) Then use them in your press kits.

4. Look for "jewels" in your junk mail. Your mail box is filled each day with what some people call "junk mail." Don't you believe that it is junk. Many business opportunities are there. As you pick up each piece, ask yourself, "How can I be of service to these people?"

   For example, we once received a flyer in the mail from SMI of Waco, Texas. They produce talking programs on business subjects. Dottie called them at once, offering to do a tape on "Seven Secrets of Selling to Women." By a strange coincidence, they told her that someone else had promised to do a recording for them on that very topic, but had let them down. If Dottie had not studied her "junk mail" that day, she would not have made the call.

They requested her manuscript. After receiving it, they called to tell her that they would have a man on their staff read and record her script. They planned a geometric design for the cover. Dottie didn't want them to do that. She realized that the recording would promote her speaking career if her picture was on the cover, and if her voice delivered the program. Besides, she felt the "Seven Secrets of Selling to Women" could best be presented by a woman.

We have a sign in our office that says, "Make no little plans. They have no magic to stir our souls. Make big plans. Aim high in hope and work." Dottie looked at that sign and reached for the phone. She hired a recording studio, and cut the master herself. Then she had a photographer shoot a unique picture for the cover. Dottie had a man facing away from the camera, and she leaned forward with her hand beside her mouth, telling him the "Seven Secrets." Within a week, she sent the entire package to SMI ready to go. They bought it all. That program has since been translated into Spanish and French and is sold all over the world. The same mailbox that brought us SMI's "junk mail" now delivers their royalty checks to Dottie on a regular basis.

Your mail box is the bazaar of the world, full of ideas.

5. Watch the stories that appear in the media. Ask yourself, "How can I tie in with that and help these people?" Benjamin Franklin's most frequent words in all of his letters to the movers and shakers of his day were, "I observed." By capitalizing on your observations, you will be able to find a sponsor for a seminar, do a joint venture in advertising, or find a client who needs a training session. Study the news and advertisements, as well. They are full of prospects.

6. Make your business card unusual and unique. Use bright, warm colors. Have your printer print your card as a Rolodex card with a colored tab extension indicating your topic title in reverse letters. Some speakers give out two cards. One has their name on the tab, and the other

has their subject for cross reference. This way they appear twice in their clients' cardholder. Remember to put your picture on your business card, as well. You are the main product you are promoting.

7. Ask everyone you meet for their business card. We have suggested that you always ask for a second card, as well. Read it carefully and let them see you put it into your wallet. Tell them you want to pass their second card on to someone who might be especially interested in them. Write a note on the card you will keep for yourself, so that you will remember what you said you would do for this person. Then do it. Be a promise-keeper. You will help two people. If you must choose between giving your card and getting theirs, get theirs. Then send them yours.

8. Develop a "promotional outlook" by looking at every business card with these questions in mind: "How can I help these people? How can these people help me?" or "How can I get these people together with someone who needs them?"

9. Give a PR gift. It is fascinating to watch extremely successful speakers practice personal PR. Somers White, for example, once called us to ask our bureau for some information. We gladly found what he wanted and sent it to him. The next day, a beautiful wallet and a thank-you note arrived in the mail. It is hard to forget someone who constantly gives appreciation.

Wally "Famous" Amos, the cookie man, uses a small but very effective gift. It is his business card with a plastic bag attached that contains two cookies. Wally was formerly a New York PR man before he opened his cookie business and began speaking.

When we took him to dinner, we watched him give one of these little gifts to the restaurant's maitre d', then to the busboy at our table. The people at the next table came over, then the bartender. Before we left, almost the whole restaurant had found us, including the chef from the kitchen. Wally Amos shook hands, grinned at everybody, and said, "I want you to have some of my Famous Amos cookies!" each time he gave out his cookie card. He always carries a box of these small gifts with him. After dinner, we asked him, "Wally, what does it cost to give these cookie gifts? How many do you disburse per week? Month? Year?"

Wally smiled and told us, "You know, I never count them. I just keep planting seeds."

10. Remember that you can't say "thank you" too many times. When you are on the road, you may think you don't have time for the thank-yous you should send, but you do. There is that endless wait at the airport. Or the time on board the flight. Use those times constructively by catching up on your thank-yous.

11. Print custom postcards. Put your picture and your name on the same side as the message. Keep a small notebook with you to jot down names and addresses of people you want to thank, such as your introducer, meeting planner, the company secretary, others on the panel, and so forth. Carry the cards with you and send them out while you are on the road. Use a pen with a complimentary color ink. People will be impressed with your promptness and thoughtfulness. Take plenty of stamps with you when you travel. There will be no doubt about the note being personalized. It will stand out among the printed and standardized form letters we all receive. In this computer age, a handwritten note can be one of the only items that is not tossed out. We have seen our cards posted on company bulletin boards, and over the desks of hundreds of our clients. They cherished our personal thank you. That is PR in action.

12. Smile! Your voice is different when you pull back your lips. Smiling is the most inexpensive PR, and the most effective cosmetic on earth. When your eyes are interested in someone, your ears are listening, and your hand is taking notes as that person talks, you are irresistible.

13. Reward referrals. This is a marvelous PR tool. Joe Girard once was featured in the Guinness Book of World Records as the record holder for the most cars sold by one man. All he did, he said, was ask customers for referrals and rewarded those who gave them to him.

In our bureau, we reward speakers who call in leads for bookings that they cannot fulfill. These may be jobs they are not qualified for, or dates they cannot accept because they are already booked. We work on the booking lead, find the perfect speaker for the client, then share the commission with the speaker who gave us the lead. Everybody wins.

Think about ways you can reward people who give you business. It can be very powerful PR.

HOW TO USE THE "HANSEL AND GRETEL" PR SYSTEM

Always leave a trail of paper that leads back to your headquarters or to your agent or speakers bureau. When you write an article, ask for permission to reprint it with the logo of the magazine or newspaper. Use these reprints in your press kit, as well as one sheet give-aways at your programs, or as gifts offered through media interviews. List other topics you speak on.

Print your essay, poem, or "Ten Rules" on fine-quality paper stock so that people who receive it will want to hang it on their wall. These become constant, positive affirmations for them and continuing advertisements for you. We have had many requests for additional copies of our essays, articles, and poems from other publications because of this reprint technique.

Leave a trail of good feeling. Look at every situation from the viewpoint of those with whom you might work, and work to make friends. Comedienne Phyllis Diller has said, "The reason I've lasted so long is that I've never closed a door behind me. I've never caused management any trouble. I've never been anything but straight. Also, I've always wanted to make sure the house made money on me. I work as if I own the joint."

Leave a trail of gifts. Have some of your short essays, poems, or articles printed and decoupaged on plaques. They can be excellent gifts for your client, meeting planner, television or radio host.

Finally, leave a trail of awards. You might follow Suzy Mallery's example. She is the president of the Manwatchers' Association. Each year she chooses the "Ten Most Watchable Men" (all of them celebrities) and prepares plaques for them. Then she calls and invites each one to plan a press party for the presentation. Of course, she is the one who makes the presentation. Some of the gentlemen who have received her awards include astronomer Carl Sagan and actor Henry "The Fonz" Winkler. She sends out press releases on the awards that result in articles in publications all over the world.

THE ADVANTAGES OF PUBLISHING YOUR OWN NEWSLETTER

One of the best ways to become known quickly and to promote your speaking topic is to publish your own newsletter. You can mail your newsletter (which might be one legal-size sheet printed on both sides) to past, present, and future clients. Writing a newsletter on your topic promotes you as an expert.

Begin with an annual newsletter. Then expand it to quarterly, bi-monthly, or more-frequent schedules. Keeping yourself and your topic on clients' and bureaus' minds is excellent PR and is one of the many benefits of publishing and distributing a newsletter. You can even publish several versions of each newsletter. One can be sent to clients you work with directly. Another can be sent to the speakers' bureaus who book you. A third can be sent to clients or speakers' bureaus you hope you will work with soon.

ALWAYS USE SPEAKING ENGAGEMENTS AS PR OPPORTUNITIES

We stress this point repeatedly in our book and in our seminars for speakers. Wherever you speak, invite people to come and hear you—editors, producers, bureau representatives, potential clients. Call ahead and make arrangements. Watch for opportunities to do good business. Inviting people to preview you is excellent PR.

At every performance, always think of a way to do more than you are asked to do. Give other people credit. Be cheerful and helpful. Your personal PR will zoom. You will be asked back again and again. If you plant good PR seeds, soon you will have a profusion of blossoms and fruit. Recently, when Dottie accepted a series of speaking dates, she closed the conversation to the client with, "I'll work hard for you. You can count on me." The client replied,

"We know you will, Dottie. That's why we called you." Get the reputation of being a "Go-Giver." PR is not just being interviewed on the media, or being published. Most of all, PR is how you treat people. Be a good personal publicist for yourself. The world is watching.

OTHER WAYS TO PROMOTE YOUR SPEAKING CAREER

While you watch and search for articles published on your subject for your research file, use the opportunity to help others as well. Follow these tips:

1. Watch for articles to send to customers and colleagues on topics they are interested in. Cut these out and mail them with your business card and a note.

2. Look for articles written by another speaker, a bureau owner, or a client in your field. Write a card of congratulations. Tell them how much the article helped you.

3. Watch for interviews, articles, and mentions of companies and clients in your field of expertise. Clip out the articles and send them to the company in the story. Attach a note of congratulations. Your note could pave your entry into a whole new market. Include your own material each time you use this method of direct PR. It is called "leaving a trail of goodwill." We believe in actively practicing this ancient and good advice:

> "Do all the good you can,
> By all the means you can,
> In all the ways you can,
> In all the places you can,
> At all the times you can,
> To everyone you can."

You will find these methods are like casting bread upon the water. You will be rewarded. For example, we once sent a card of congratulations to a friend who had been interviewed in a major publication. We mentioned its gigantic circulation and told him how proud we were of him. The letter took about three sentences. He later called us to say we were the only ones who knew him personally who had congratulated him in any way. He was very appreciative. Then he asked, "What can I do for you?"

We thought a moment, then replied, "Would you give us the name, address, and phone number of the writer who interviewed you for the article?" Our friend gave it to us. We called the writer and congratulated him on the excellent story. At last count, that writer has written fifteen stories about us and our clients for major publications.

KEEP THE MOMENTUM GOING

Remember always that public relations literally means your relationship with other people. The way to find friends is to be friends. Actively showing appreciation raises value. Criticism **and deprecation** lowers it. So be delighted with other people's success. Show it. Send appreciative comments. Mean it. Public relations, promotion, and advertising can all bear abundant fruit for your successful speaking career and your life.

4

From Free to Shining Fee: Getting Bookings That Pay

A "booking" is an engagement where you will speak for compensation. Usually, this compensation is a fee—money paid in exchange for the speaker's service. Speakers can also be paid in a variety of ways besides money—in additional paid engagements, in business leads for their profession or business, or in trade for the client's services or products, for example. This chapter shows you the steps you can follow to move forward from free to high-fee speaking engagements.

SEVEN WAYS TO SPEAK FOR FREE NOW AND GAIN HIGH PROFITS LATER

No one begins as a virtuoso in any field. We all need practice. To illustrate that point, Abraham Lincoln often used a story about a wood chopper who said, "If I had eight hours to chop down a tree, I'd spend six sharpening my ax."

A good way to sharpen up your speaking for the world of paid bookings is to practice your topic material at no charge before live audiences. Many successful professional speakers have prepared themselves for paid speaking by first speaking for free at local service clubs. You can do this in your own city. Your local library, Chamber of Commerce, or local newspaper should be able to supply you with lists of the types and names of service clubs in your area. These organizations, which hold meetings morning, noon, or night, seven days a week, need free speakers who can deliver 20- to 30-minute talks. Here are seven ways you can get the practice you need and gain lucrative benefits by speaking free:

1. Offer to do free community speaking. Speaking for service clubs lets you develop and improve delivery and timing, and allows you to try out new ideas and material. By speaking for service clubs, you also serve your community and make excellent contacts. We suggest that you concentrate on the topic you want to sell so that you can polish it. Do not offer a different topic each time, but instead concentrate on one area. You will develop your reputation as an expert.

2. Work to gain publicity. Most speakers begin by speaking free, sometimes for their own professional meetings. Many companies, hospitals, and legal firms train executives to do this kind of speaking. The payoff is prestige, publicity, and fine public relations for the parent organization.

3. Obtain prospective clients who pay. However, you may begin your professional speaking career by speaking free to promote your business or profession.

    For example, an attorney might speak to wealthy, mature audiences about "How To Avoid Probate." A plastic surgeon, using "before and after" slides as examples, might speak about new surgical techniques to improve appearance.

    These free seminars and speeches, given as a means to attract new clients, do produce new business.

    One very successful financial planner we know gives only one program a month, since he needs the rest of the month to follow up on all of the leads the program provides for him. He is paid in prospects. Dottie's advertising business began when she spoke to service clubs. Her title was "What Does Your Customer Want?" Dottie's pay was the business cards she picked up from the audience. She called upon those people the next day for advertising sales. This method of promoting business is extremely successful.

4. Practice and try out new materials. Local service clubs are anxious for speakers. Their meetings provide a marvelous opportunity for you to practice your material. Most Chambers of Commerce, or local newspapers, can give you a list of service club presidents. These leaders can direct you to the program chairpersons. Your free talk at such functions should last about twenty- to thirty-minutes.

5. Learn to correct your own performance problems. Purchase a small tape recorder with a clip-on mike. Fasten the recorder to your belt, then attach the mike to your lapel. Record every speech you give so you can listen carefully to the audience's reaction to every story and every point. The Roman orator Cicero once counseled, "Nobody can give you wiser advice than yourself." So you should honestly analyze the response to your material. Even top comedians such as Robin Williams and Joan Rivers try out new material at comedy clubs to test audience reaction. If the audience does not laugh, perhaps a word was not understood and you must re-work the material.

   After you have concentrated on the audience's reaction to your speech, ask a friend, another speaker, or hire a speakers bureau or speech coach to listen to your tapes with you and help analyze your performance. This is an excellent way to improve your material and your delivery.

6. Speak for the opportunity to sell your products. In Los Angeles, an organization called Round Table West features famous speaker/authors at luncheon programs who autograph and sell their books after the program. Speakers sell so many of their products at these functions that they are willing to speak free in return for the opportunity to make the product sales.

7. Strive to meet the right buyers. If you are invited to speak free to a group which hires many speakers, such as Meeting Planners International (MPI), the American Society of Association Executives (ASAE), or the International Group of Agents and Bureaus (IGAB), jump at the chance. The competition is keen for these slots. Many speakers have been

launched into highly paid speaking careers by such an opportunity, because the audience consists of top buyers who are looking for good speakers.

8. Be ready to handle opportunities for paid bookings. Most speakers become professional when someone in their "free" audience comes up to them and asks what their fee would be to speak. Be prepared for this to happen by having a printed fee schedule ready which lists the programs you offer. The basic types of paid speaking bookings fit into the following categories: one-time keynotes; break-out sessions of various lengths; breakfast, luncheon, banquet, and panel performances; and custom sessions for special convention groups.

TWO WAYS TO OBTAIN PAYING CLIENTS

Here are two methods speakers use to find new buyers. The best method for you will depend on your topic. Study each one carefully.

Method #1: Speaker Showcases

There are many showcases offered to speakers which are sponsored by speakers bureaus, speakers associations, the National Association of Campus Activities (NACA), the National Management Association, and others. A showcase allows buyers to audition several speakers. Speakers pay a fee for their slot on the showcase program, which is a little like a Paris fashion show. Buyers come to look, listen, and book. When a bureau sponsors a showcase of speakers, all business is booked through the presenting bureau.

Showcases are an excellent way to get started and are well worth the fee. Before you pick a showcase, however, ask presenters exactly which buyers will attend. That way you will know if the meeting planners coming to the showcase are interested in your type of topic.

For example, if you are a sales speaker, you would be a perfect fit for the Sales and Marketing Executives group, but you would not fit in with engineering and management audiences of the National Management Association (NMA).

Most showcases allow each speaker to present a ten- to fifteen-minute excerpt from their program. If you have two or three suitable topics, you may want to purchase more than one slot. You are usually allowed to bring demo tapes and flyers, and have them available to the buyers. Speakers sometimes receive a list of the meeting planners who attend the showcase, so be sure to ask for one.

The National Association of Campus Activities' meeting planners review the programs of professional speakers in regional districts and book speakers for multiple college circuits and/or big auditorium events. Sometimes a speakers bureau sponsors some of its speakers at these large showcases.

Method #2: Speaker Card Packs

Several groups offer direct mail advertising card packs of speakers. They are mailed to association, corporation, and Chamber of Commerce meeting planners. Each speaker has an ad on one side of the postcard and his or her return address on the back. The meeting planner fills in the card and mails it back to the speaker as an inquiry. When the card pack approach is taken, the important thing to watch out for is that the card pack is mailed to appropriate target contacts in your field.

HOW SPEAKERS SET FEES

Speakers' fees are set according to the stature of the speaker (for example, a celebrity vs. expert business speaker) and the type of speaking session (for example, a main room or breakout session, a custom session for a specific group, a panel session, or a meal speech).

Meal programs are usually the shortest time slots, running thirty- to forty-five-minutes. Keynotes range from thirty- to ninety-minutes. Seminars and workshops can run for two hours, a half-day, full-day, or even several days for technical seminars.

You and other speakers may each be booked to present ten-minute speeches on a panel. Afterwards, each panelist must be ready to answer questions from the audience. Set your fee for being a panel participant at less than you charge for being a panel moderator.

Convention keynote speakers have the highest visibility of all speakers because they appear before the entire assemblage. When most people think of a "speaker," they think of the "keynoter," the person who delivers the main address to the entire gathering. The full assembly may be called the general assembly, the opening session, or the closing session. Usually, keynote speakers are more motivational and entertaining than others. They are often big-name celebrities and are paid the highest fees.

Seminar and workshop speakers educate as well as entertain. You may be asked to address the entire group or to speak to break-out sessions where attendees are divided into interest groups. The breakout speech may be repeated several times in the day to different audiences, so you might present the same workshop four times in one day, for a larger fee than a one-time performance. All speakers are paid by contract, a set fee for each segment, by the client organization.

OTHER SOURCES OF FEES: CONSULTING AND TRAINING

Often, companies need special help with a problem. They don't want a pre-established training course, but look instead for an expert, a consultant from the outside, to evaluate their problems and offer concrete suggestions for improvement. Consulting might mean going out in the field with the client's sales people, or monitoring incoming calls, then preparing a presentation. Speaker Bob Popyk, for example, does this type of consulting work. He calls hundreds of car dealers by phone, acting the part of a buyer who wants to purchase a new car. The dealers' responses are recorded. His programs for those same dealers use the recorded phone calls as examples of how to, and how not to, handle buyer inquiries.

Zig Ziglar and Nido Qubein are examples of speakers who have been invited to become members of large client companies' boards of directors, so they can provide continual consulting and professional advice.

Once a company or association has used you as a speaker, you have an excellent opportunity to be hired again for consulting, writing workbooks, or conducting training sessions. The training field is one of the largest areas of opportunity for professional speakers. Many companies buy the services of a professional trainer or seminar leader for a few hours a week rather than keep one trainer on staff full-time. Trainers and seminar leaders also develop books, and audio and video materials. These may be custom products created for a particular client, or generic ones which can be used by any client. Training can be at one location within the facility of the client, or around the world, at differing locations. A training session can be booked for one day, several days, a month, or for whatever length of time the client needs. The astute speaker seeking a training booking will ask the potential client well-focused questions about needs, set a consultation time, then offer a proposal to fill those needs.

When you approach a company with hopes of being booked for keynotes, seminars, and training, be sure to make your initial approach to the right person. The company's personnel department or the head of training and development may contract with you. Or it may be a meeting "manager" or meeting planner. Usually, however, someone higher up will make the final decision on whether or not to bring in an outside seminar leader.

Your complete contract might include a keynote for the client's banquet, consultations to obtain information, writing and production of custom workbooks, audios and videos for continuous training, a series of twelve in-person training sessions, and a series of twelve articles for the client's monthly publication, plus your books and tape products. Many speakers earn at least $80,000 for such a contract.

The largest organization for trainers is the American Society for Training & Development (ASTD). The society provides excellent opportunities for advancing your training skills.

FEES AND YOUR OWN WORTH

The question asked most frequently by beginners in the professional speaking business is, "How and when do I set fees?" Novices ask this with fear and trepidation. "How can I be worth real money?" is their unstated question. We use this story in our seminars to help them begin to set fees.

"Visualize a meeting of 300 well-dressed people. They have arrived at a glamorous hotel for a banquet. You are the featured speaker. Before the meal is served, the attendees gather in the cocktail lounge for the happy hour. What do you estimate they spend per person for drinks?"

Our students typically give all sorts of answers. But the Hotel Association gives as the correct answer an average of $10 per head, plus tips. Then we ask our speaker students to see a scale in their minds. On one side is the bar bill for this banquet. It is easily over $3,000. On the other side is the program to be offered.

Next we say, "Now ask yourself, 'Is one more important to the success of the banquet than the other?'"

We know the answer to this, because we all have had the experience of attending a meeting at a beautiful site, where we enjoyed the before-dinner cocktails and the delicious food, then were bored by a terrible speaker. We have watched people walk out before the program was over. What will be remembered about this evening?

We believe that when you set your fees, you should consider this point. If you are a good speaker with a message a group is vitally interested in, *you are worth the price of the liquor.*

You will implant your worth in your own mind if you post your fees above your telephone where you can see them as you speak to clients. We also suggest you put up a copy of the following poem by Jessie Rittenhouse. It has helped many beginning speakers:

> I bargained with Life for a penny,
> And Life would pay no more
> However I begged at evening
> When I counted my scanty store;
> For Life is a just employer,
> He gives you what you ask,
> But once you have set your wages,
> Why you must bear the task.
> I worked for a menial's hire,
> Only to learn dismayed
> That any wage I had asked of Life
> Life would have paid.

You should start charging for your speeches:

1. When you have become an expert;
2. When you have given 50 to 100 free speeches and you have learned to be a good, reliable, exciting, informative, professional presenter who can handle any emergency; and
3. When you have a passion for your subject and your career of professional speaking.

THE PITFALLS OF NEGOTIATING FEES

There are times when it is appropriate to negotiate your fees, but be careful when you accept a fee lower than usual. Have good justification for charging one client more or less than another for the identical program. When clients say they need to negotiate and reduce your fee, do not give them a bargain price for no viable reason. Dr. Tony Alessandra says, "Find a way to exchange value for value." When you do this, the meeting planner and group will have respect for you and the quality of services you offer.

ELEVEN REASONS TO ACCEPT A
LOWER FEE

You might be willing to accept a lower fee under the following circumstances:

1. If presenting the speech for this client has marketing opportunities for other speaking, consulting, or product sales. Audiences of speakers bureau representatives, meeting planners, and association or corporate executives fall into this group. If your talk is a showcase for future business, you will be expected to speak free. You will pay your own expenses for the opportunity which is well worth your time and effort. It is considered quite a "plum" to be asked.
2. If the client has a service or product that is of real value to you. Barter part or all of your fee in exchange. Speakers

have traded speeches and seminars for new automobiles, fur coats, long-distance dialing credits, and boats!

3. If the audience might prove a good market for your books, cassettes, products, and other services. Exchange part of your fee for an ad in a national company or association magazine or event program brochure. These ads can bring you cash sales. An ad is a concrete value which has a price for which you can negotiate.

   Note: Trade should be taken at least in full dollar-to-dollar retail value of the item, or even more. The mark-up on items the client barters is often 75 percent over the wholesale cost. Exchange your normal "listed" full fee, for double the value in retail list price on their items. Both the client and the speaker receive a bargain. (Be sure to talk to the Internal Revenue Service about how to report trade deals on your tax forms.)

4. If the buyer purchases a large number of your products as training materials or gifts for attendees. Offer a volume discount. For example, if your regular fee is $1,000, and the client needs 1,000 cassette albums which retail for $80 each, you might offer them for 50 percent off with your full speaking fee. Or discount your speaking fee to $700 and offer 45 percent off the retail album price.

5. If you are skilled at several topics. Visualize the twenty to thirty open slots the meeting planner must fill for a convention and offer to do one of your other topics at a lower fee, at the same conference, if they buy the first one at full price. They get the advantage of paying only one set of expenses and gain an additional quality program at a bargain price.

6. If they need a speaker to create and tailor a second performance for the spouses, children, managers, presidents, etc., who attend the conference. Offer a combined fee for your keynote speech and these services to create a package deal.

7. If the client needs several speakers during the year for differing audiences. Offer to do a series of performances at a lesser fee. You might be told, "Cut your fee on this talk, and then we may use you in a series." In which case

you may reply, "This program will cost full price, but I might consider adding a clause such as the following: 'If a series contract is signed within one year of this date, a credit of $_____ will be deducted from the series price.'" This is a much more business-like approach than accepting pie-in-the-sky promises.

Don't be afraid to ask for bottom-line promises. An alternate to the offer above is to write all of the dates of the series on the original contract, with a deposit due on all of them, including the first one. The balance on each contract date would be paid on each program day.

While it may seem tempting, accepting a cut rate on the date at hand with the hope of a future contract is not a good idea. This offer might be made only to reduce your fee, with no real intention of offering a future series. In addition, you might pass up other bookings because you are holding a series of dates. Without a contract, they could decide to cancel. If they are sincere in their promises, however, they will not hesitate to sign a firm contract for a series at the lower rate. If the dates are not set, just write into the contract, "four programs within _____ [their time frame]." The deposit should apply to all four dates.

8. If the buyer needs specially designed training materials, and you will be delivering speeches and/or seminars as a package deal. Offer to design the training materials and forward them to the buyer for approval after a contract has been signed and a deposit has been accepted for them as well as for the speech.

9. If you offer to include a set of twelve monthly articles for your client's own publication. Discount your regular price for the articles, but charge full price for the keynote presentation.

10. If the buyer is willing to pay you in full at the time the booking is made, instead of half with the contract and the balance on the date of the presentation (see more on cash discounts later in this chapter).

11. If the company will pay for transportation, hotel, and meals for both you and your spouse which extend beyond the dates of the meeting so that you can have a vacation.

Often, a large convention has complimentary rooms and discounts on airfares.

HOW TO ESTABLISH A FEE SCHEDULE

Your fee schedule is a kind of menu which lists all of the things you offer your clients: consulting, panels, seminars, workshops, keynotes, media publicity days, special programs for groups at conventions, such as managers, presidents, children, spouses, etc. Also, be sure to list your products. If you do not list these things, the client may not know that you offer them.

Great material, outstanding delivery, plus celebrity status all combine to determine your fee. You may have begun with a modest $250 per talk. But once you are established, you can begin raising your rates. Recently, the starting non-celebrity business speaker's average was $1,000. An experienced speaker may increase that fee each year to a high of $7,000 per talk. A speaker at this level, working two times a week, will earn a gross of $728,000 annually in fees. Remember that these figures do not include product sales, which usually double a speaker's income.

Speakers typically set fees using two criteria: the duration of the program and the amount of travel time involved. Local engagements (no overnight, within driving range, or a short plane ride from home) are set at a lower fee than out-of-area dates. Fees often are scaled according to the length and type of presentation—for example, thirty minutes to two hours, two- to four-hours, four-hours to full-day (usually six hours). Some speakers charge by the day. If they speak overseas, the fee often is per-day from the day they leave home until they return.

It is imperative that you establish a fee schedule and stick to it. Meeting planners and bureaus know each other. People at one bureau know people at other bureaus. If you charge one client $500 and the next client $2,000 for the same program in the same geographical area, the discrepancy will become known. The meeting planners and bureaus will not think simply that the client who hired you for $500 got a great deal. Instead, they will assume that you overcharged the one who had to pay more. They will always believe that the lower fee reflects what you are really worth.

The box shown is a sample fee schedule. Be sure it is dated, and posted in your office by your phone.

Sample Fee Schedule

Dottie Walters, C.S.P.
Certified Speaking Professional:
National Speakers Association Designation

Keynote, Seminar Topics: (Custom topics also available upon request)
- 101 Ways to Promote Your Business
- Hiring & Training Great Salespeople
- Selling to the New Woman Buyer
- The Selling Power of a Woman
- Finding the Pearls of Potentiality (business opportunities)
- How To Enter the World of Professional Speaking

	In So. California	Outside So. Calif
Breakfast or Luncheon	$1,500	$2,000
½-Day Seminar/ Keynote/Banquet	$2,000	$2,500
Full-Day Seminar	$2,500	$3,500
Panel Participant	$1,000	$1,200
(in addition to any of the above)		
Panel Moderator	$1,200	$1,500
*Publicity Day	$1,000	$1,500

*Client arranges media celebrity interviews. Dottie Walters speaks about her subject and publicizes the client.

Professional Consultation (Per hour $150)	$1,000 per day	$1,500 per day

(All fees are plus hotel and travel expenses.)

Listed fees are for Dottie's standard programs. If you require extra research and customization for your group, Dottie will be glad to quote you a special fee, which will include consultation and preparation time.

Discounts

Dear Bureau and Meeting Planner:

Need any other programs for your event? If any of Dottie's other topics are appropriate for another slot, she offers the second and third program at the same event at 3/4 the regular price! Of course, you will have already paid her expenses for the first program, so you will also save on hotel and airfare.

Wholesale volume prices are also available on Dottie's books and albums for all your attendees. Or if you prefer to let your people invest in themselves, Dottie would like to donate ten percent of all back-of-room product sales at this event to your favorite charity. She will need four assistants to help her at the autograph table in this event. Dottie will present a gift to each of these helpers.

If you choose to have Dottie donate to your favorite charity, how shall we make this check payable?

All travel expenses will be prorated if Dottie is on the road at a time when we can co-ordinate her schedule in conjunction with your presentation.

WHEN TO RAISE FEES TO MATCH YOUR EXPERTISE

Experienced speakers say the moment to raise fees is when your calendar is full of bookings. Name value, popularity of topic, and professional delivery, are three important factors to justify a fee increase, plus availability.

Another way to determine when to raise your fee is to check with fellow speakers, bureaus, and your potential buyers. Determine the fee range being charged for the same type of presentation and services you offer. Start lower. Raise your fee as your abilities grow and your name becomes known.

Remember, household-name speakers receive $10,000 to $50,000. These celebrities are used to draw the crowd of convention attendees or rally participants. Most non-celebrity business speakers who are experts present for the $1,000 to $7,000 fees we discussed previously.

Changes in fees can also be made to adjust for the difference between a standard presentation and one which you must customize. The increase should cover the extra research, study, consultation, field trips, and other work necessary to develop the customized material.

The famous law of supply and demand applies to fees. When your appointment book becomes filled to the point that you are uncomfortably busy, it is time to raise your fees. Raise your fees each six months to a year as your calendar dictates. Establish a date for the fee hike to go into effect, then put out a letter to all of your bureau's clients, announcing your new fee schedule. It is considerate to give six months' notice and to honor all past proposals at the old fee.

When a prospective client asks a speaker to quote his or her fee, some speakers counter with, "What is your budget for this slot in your program?" If you close with your fee menu, you might also negotiate additional slots or product sales. However, if you have been charging $500, and the meeting planner tells you he or she has $5,000 to spend, DO NOT reply that your fee is $5,000 when you have never earned that amount for a performance. The word will get around. If you have been working for $500, it is because you have not improved to the point that you are worth $5,000. You will not live up to the meeting planner's expectations, and will make him or her look very bad with the company or association.

FEES AND CHARITY PRESENTATIONS

One of our most frequently booked speakers, Col. Charles Scott, a hero of the incident when the American Embassy was taken over by militant Iranians in Teheran, once received a booking call from a large military school. When they heard his standard fee, they offered him half. He told them, "No, that wouldn't be fair to my other clients. However, I have a personal interest in your school, so I will donate my time."

The school officials felt slightly embarrassed, so one of their high-ranking generals on the school board called Col. Scott and said, "You know, we really do have the amount we originally told you. Let us at least pay you what we can afford."

Col. Scott replied, "General, it's all right if you can't afford my level of professional speaker. I will donate my program to your group." This way Col. Scott maintained his high fee scale and made a charitable donation at the same time.

If you want to do a speech, but you know the client who has offered $200 just can't come up with your (let's say) $1,000 fee, you might try the following. Tell the client you will do it for the lower fee, but you want the check made out to your favorite charity and mailed directly to the charity. This keeps you straight with your meeting planner clients who pay your full fee.

Remember, people tend to appreciate what they pay for. When they ask you to accept less, explain that the way you earn your living is by speaking. Ask for your fee again. You may be surprised by the response, "Oh, okay. I just wanted to see if your price was firm."

One meeting planner told us recently that she always offers a speaker half the regular fee. If that offer is accepted, she is ahead, but the speaker's eagerness tells her she may not have a top speaker. If she hears "No," she gladly pays full price, knowing she has an excellent, in-demand speaker.

Unfortunately, there are numerous stories of speakers who have arrived to speak free for a worthy cause, only to learn that one of the other speakers on the program was receiving his or her full fee. As Eleanor Roosevelt once said, "No one can insult us unless we let them." Don't let this happen to you.

Here is a way to handle the situation if you receive too many low-fee or charitable invitations to speak. Explain that you give one free charity talk per month, and that you will be pleased to put them on your waiting list (which is two years ahead). This lets people know that you do give of yourself to charity, but that you are in demand. You will be astounded by those who will then offer to pay your full price after all.

SEVENTEEN MARKETING TIPS THAT WILL HELP YOU LAND PAID BOOKINGS

1. Use service clubs as coaching sessions. By speaking often at service clubs, you can work constantly to improve every facet of your presentation, from your appearance and

elocution, to your voice and content of your program. A good idea is to invite other speakers further along than you are to attend. They can listen to you and give you suggestions for improvement. You might return the favor by coming along as a back-of-the-room product sales helper for one of their next programs.

Professional coaches are also available who can help speakers. Use them. They are the fast track to improvement. After all, stars of all kinds take lessons. Some speakers hire speech coaches, drama teachers, or speakers bureau owners to come and watch them give practice talks, then review the program with them line by line to improve movement, content, and pronunciation.

2. Listen to the coach in your head. You can coach yourself to make many improvements. Record every talk you make. As you listen to yourself later, note the audience reaction to your opening, your important points, your illustrations, your humor, and your closing. Ask yourself, "How can I make this talk better the next time I speak?" Take careful notes. Rearrange and improve material and delivery. Make up your mind to be better every time. The greatest speakers say, "I am still learning."

Often, you can use some of these practice talk recordings as your first demo tapes. Remember, you can edit them, using the best sequences from several programs. Add explanations to them in a recording studio. If the sound is sharp enough, you might also use them for your first audio album. It is perfectly all right to use part live and part studio performance on the same album or demo tape.

3. Locate groups who need and want your topic. When preparing your material, you must keep in mind the key words "target group," which are associations, corporations, and colleges—any gathering for professional or business purposes. A target group is one which will naturally be interested in your topic. Focus on your primary marketing targets. These are the people for whom you prepare your material. Get to know them well.

4. Don't spend time preparing a subject that is only appropriate for people who do not gather together in meetings. Find the associations and corporations which need and want your topic. Current popular subjects include competition, customer satisfaction, productivity, change, innovation, business ethics, and the future, according to a recent survey by the National Speakers Association.

5. As you prepare your subject material, make a list of every group which would be willing to pay to hear someone speak on your topic. Address their specific needs in your presentation. For example, Susan Sarfati, Director of Education of the American Society for Association Executives (ASAE) reports their seminar participants want substance versus general information. Such audiences have very high expectations and are impatient if the speaker does not deliver as promised. Every minute must fill needs. Therefore, your material must be carefully aimed at the audience.

6. Market to your best bets first. As Benjamin Franklin once said, "Go first to those you are sure will buy." Then take your materials to those whom you think might buy and show it to them. They will very likely become buyers, too, if the material is aimed at their particular needs.

7. Also try marketing to those with whom you think you have no chance. Influence this market with the list of all those who do buy your service. Your less likely markets may become your best bets.

8. If you receive a call for a date that is already booked, tell the client you are sorry, then add: "Let's nail down your program for next year, so that this will not happen again." If the client agrees, send the contract out at once with your usual deposit clause. You will find next year's calendar fills quickly with contracts if you use this method. Also, tell the client you will have your speakers bureau find them a suitable speaker for this year. This will please your bureau and encourage them to remember you for other paid dates.

9. Increase your bookings at the same event. When a meeting planner calls to book you for one session at a conference or convention, visualize that meeting planner working with a big chart with at least thirty speaker slots to fill. You should ask, "Is it possible that there are other slots still open? Perhaps I might be able to do two programs for you and save your association some dollars on airfare and hotel accommodations. If you could use me for both programs, I'll present the second one for half price. My only requirement is that you place me on the same day as my first program." This technique will help you cash in on the advantages of simultaneous bookings. Your $2,000 booking becomes $3,000, you increase the dollar value of your speaking day, and your meeting planner has another slot filled at a bargain price by a good speaker. Everybody wins.

10. Remember that "prophet" can mean "profit." A wonderful marketing idea is to target your efforts to those groups coming to your home town to hold meetings, conferences, and conventions. You are a good investment for out-of-town meeting planners, because they can save air fare and hotel bills if they use you. Some speakers offer a lower local-only fee because they do not have to spend time getting to and from the engagement. They list these lower local fees on their fee schedule. Meeting planners like to gain this double discount.

11. Take advantage of your locale. Work up a second talk about your own area in which you cover local history, customers, shopping opportunities, and so forth. For example, one San Diego speaker wears a Mexican costume to present a second program on eating and cooking Mexican food. Conventions coming in from outside the San Diego area pay her for a regular business program, plus a second fee for a fun session about native cuisine.

    Another San Diego speaker, whose regular business topic is negotiation, also offers a talk about what can be bought when shopping in Tijuana, the Mexican city across the border. Using props of beautiful Mexican leather, glass, and paper flower items, she teaches attendees how to negotiate for the best price.

Ralph Archbold, who lives in Philadelphia, portrays Benjamin Franklin at many local conventions. He never steps out of character as he shows he loves his audience and his city, as Ben. "What is a meeting in Philadelphia without Ben?" asks Archbold in the copy he sends to every convention scheduled for his area.

He offers longer programs, as well as an appearance to welcome the convention to Philadelphia, and invites everyone to bring cameras. He often does several programs in one day and is so successful at bringing Benjamin Franklin to life that he was chosen to appear in Philadelphia's full page ads in major media for the Constitution celebrations. In addition, he was sent across the country to appear on television to publicize the event.

Many local speakers create wonderful programs about their areas. They are profitable *prophets* in their own home towns.

12. Don't ignore the appeal of the foreign. One of the strange facets of hiring speakers is that meeting planners sometimes think the speaker on the other side of the country is automatically better than the hometown one. On the other hand, those associations that are located somewhere else and come to your town for a meeting might think you are a much more interesting speaker than those they left back home. This is especially so if you can offer a "destination" program like the ones we have outlined.

13. Consider sending meeting planners who are coming into your area a small newsletter with news of your community and your topic. Offer to be of service and help in advance. Repeat the fact that by using you, they can save hotel bills and air fare.

14. Obtain the roster of a group's members, or other related groups for the purpose of soliciting new markets. If it is

not available, you can still make contact, but it usually is available for the asking.

For example, the sales association you speak for can supply you a list of other chapters of the same association. The branch of the bank where you perform has a list of its branches and of financial associations they belong to. Then, ask for a letter of recommendation from the initial group. This letter will open the door to related groups. Be sure to send a thank you note to each person who helps you with lists or referrals.

Call first, then send a letter of inquiry to the new group, mentioning the names of the key people in the first group, with copies of your letters of recommendation. These "lateral" referrals are an excellent method of increasing your bookings, because the new group will see you were well-liked as a speaker by others in their industry. Compile some of the best comments from the rating sheets and include these in the mailing. Follow up with another phone call to interested prospects. Remember, the odds are one in five that you will be booked, so do not expect every call or letter to produce immediate results.

15. After any speech, delivered for free or fee, send a thank you note and ask again for referrals. When inquiry calls come in, always be sure to ask, "How did you learn about me/us?" We send out a personal thank you note to the referring person that very day.

16. When you are successful with one type of client, market laterally to similar associations and businesses. For example, after you have done a good job for the local bank, market to other banks in the same city, then the county, then across the state and country, and eventually internationally. All of your materials, literature, and letters of recommendation from your past buyers should show you as an expert on your topic for the banking industry.

17. Next, approach clients whose interests are associated with those of the associations or businesses for which

you have worked. For example, if your first successes are in banking, then try savings and loans, escrow companies, credit associations, real estate brokers, which might lead to building contractors and plumbers. Each group has similar and related problems and needs. You will be just as successful with them as you were for the first group. Each, in turn, will recommend you to others if you ask them to—and if you have done a great job.

Pam Lontos' experience shows how this works. Pam speaks on advertising sales. She began her career at a radio station giving in-house sales seminars for her employer. The radio station promoted her to sales manager, then to general sales manager for their seven other stations. Next, Pam went into business for herself, offering sales seminars and keynotes, first for radio stations, then for other advertising media. She began locally, then went statewide, then nationally and, eventually, internationally. She branched out laterally, one step at a time, to related industries.

FIVE WAYS THAT RATING SHEETS CAN HELP YOU GET NEW BOOKINGS

The best, most constant, and least expensive source of new bookings is from your most recent audience. Since most people belong to several organizations and associations, they can provide many contacts.

When you look out at your audience, picture each person as a door leading to future business. Rating sheets are a simple key to open those doors and unlock business. It is possible to obtain three, five, or nine new engagements from the present one by using rating sheets in all cases, whether you also have products at the back of the room or not. We have two ways of handling rating sheets: with and without an autograph table. If you do have an autograph table, you may print a product order form on the back of the rating sheet, and the rating sheets may be deposited there with payments. You can modify this idea to fit your own situation.

Rating sheets are great tools for helping you promote your business because:

1. They gather feedback which will help you enhance future presentations and development of your material.
2. They supply written testimonials to your effectiveness as a speaker.
3. They pinpoint markets by letting you know who else might be interested in your presentation.
4. They give you direct booking leads.
5. They put an order form right into the hands of the audience.

How to Create a Useful Rating Sheet

In the past, many speakers have depended on numerical rating sheets that looked something like this:

On a scale of 1 to 10, with 10 being best, please rate my:

appearance   _____
delivery style _____
material   _____
voice quality _____

Speakers, companies, and associations have used this numerical rating sheet. Such a sheet is not really very helpful to a speaker, however. When you study the results after your performance, you are left with nothing but numbers. We believe a "10" rating depends too much on each listener's mood. Critical people in the group give you a low rating because they never give anyone positive feedback. Others may give you a ten because they give everybody a ten.

Since we found the "numbers game" did not help us to improve, grow, and to get into the minds of our audience, we redesigned the traditional numerical rating sheets. We developed a new idea based on what all speakers need and want from each audience: valuable information and additional bookings. Here are the types of rating sheet questions we found are most helpful in attaining these goals:

1. What basic message did you hear that you could use tomorrow? (Purpose)

2. How will you use what you heard to increase your profits and/or productivity? (Practical application)

3. Is there something else about my subject that you would like to know that I did not have time to give you in this presentation? (New topics)

4. Do you know of others (businesses, associations, etc.) that would benefit from the material presented today? Who are they? (Referrals)

5. What is your opinion of my presentation? (Testimonials—make sure there is a permission check-off, so you can use their comments.)

Here is a sample of the new rating sheet we developed which includes these five items. It has brought about thousands of paid dates for our speakers. You can change it, improve it, and make it fit your own unique material.

Eight Tips for Getting Your Rating Sheets Returned

Here is a system that will ensure that your rating sheets will be filled out and returned. You don't want to find them blank and left on the seats or floor after the program.

1. Include instructions about filling out the rating sheets as part of the printed introduction you have given your introducer. Have the introducer mention that the rating sheets will either be picked up or else where they are to be turned in. Always bring the introduction typed, double-spaced, and ready.

   For example, the introduction might say, "We care about your opinion. We especially want to know if we gave you ideas which will help you. If you know of

Sample Walters Rating Sheet

Rating Sheet
for Dottie Walters - Date _____

Please help us to constantly increase the VALUE of our material to you.
We appreciate your filling out this form and handing it in at the end of the program.

Your   name_____Company_____
Address_____City_____
State_____Zip_____   Phone_____

What is the BEST, usable IDEA you gained from this program?_____
_____

How do you plan to apply this idea?_____
_____

What do you wish there had been more time for?_____
_____

Opinion   of   today's   program:_____
_____
May we quote you? Yes! ❏

What is your most urgent professional need from us?_____
Personal Speaking Consultation?   ❏   Paid Speaking Seminar?   ❏
Speaking Training Materials?   ❏   Sales Training Materials?   ❏
Chapter in Speaker Anthology Book? ❏   Subject of your chapter?_____
Anthology Speakers Album?   ❏   Subject 1 hr tape for album?_____

ORDER FORM REVERSE SIDE WITH TODAY'S SPECIAL OFFER

Do you have a friend or business associate who would benefit from THIS
PROGRAM? Please give us their names. We will send them publications and
program information. Thank you!
Name_____Company_____
Address_____City_____
State _____   Zip_____ Phone_____

Name_____Company_____
Address_____City_____
State _____   Zip_____ Phone_____

Do you belong to a group looking for a speaker? (Our Bureau will assist you)
Name of group _____ Date Speaker Needed_____
Subject_____Person in charge:_____ Phone_____

someone else who could also benefit from our work, we would appreciate that information." Rehearse with the introducer in advance and give the introducer a small gift.

2. Reward the audience for filling out the rating sheets. Hold a drawing. Have the announcer say, "There will be a drawing. One of the completed rating sheets will be drawn for this special gift provided for the lucky winner by our speaker." The prize is your album or your book. This also gives the introducer the opportunity to hold up the prize, show it, and give a brief description, which will increase your back-of-the-room product sales.

3. The introducer explains there will be a pause at the end of your presentation, so that the audience will have time to fill out the rating sheets. Then the introducer and the introducer's assistants will pick up the sheets. Rehearse the introducer in a conclusion. (This will give you an opportunity to take your bows and still get to the autograph book table in time.)

4. If you have an autograph table, instruct and rehearse your assistants. Ask them to smile and say, "Thank you, we appreciate your helping us by filling out the rating sheets."

5. After the rating sheets are picked up, and the winning sheet has been drawn, go to work at your autograph table at the back of the room. This break enables you to sign autographs, talk with attendees, and sell your products.

6. After the break, pick up the rating sheets in your hands, and stand in the traffic pattern by the coffee and refreshment area to read them. Anne Boe does this after every talk. She says she never fails to have at least five members walk up to her, hand her their business cards, and say, "Please contact us. We want to book you."

7. When the meeting is over, sit down with the meeting planner and review the rating sheet results together. Especially, go over the things the audience wanted to know more about. Planners usually only hear from the two percent of the audience that is always critical. If the results are 98 percent favorable, you may be rebooked on the spot. Positive, hand-written comments are very

impressive. This is a good time to present a small gift to the meeting planner.

8. When you get back to your office, copy the rating sheets and send a set to the meeting planner. The meeting planner will be sure that the boss or committee sees them. This is a good place to enclose a request for their letter of recommendation, and a proposal to speak on another topic. Enclose a self-addressed, stamped envelope.

Follow up on the leads your audience provides on the rating sheets. The odds are that one in five participants will give you specific booking leads. With good follow up, one in five of those will book you. If there are one hundred in the audience, eighty will fill out the sheets. Of those, sixteen will give you multiple leads. This means you will gain about thirty-two referral leads for additional bookings. Thus, your rating sheets may net you six additional paid engagements from the original program.

Knowing how to use rating sheets can make you successful. Once, a man who had spoken for five years but who had never been paid for a talk, attended our seminar. He wondered how he might go from free to shining fee. We taught him, as we always do, the use of the "Walters Rating Sheets" to obtain new bookings. We were delighted when he called the following week to tell us he used our technique as the key to obtaining leads at his next free talk. He carefully completed each step and booked nine paid speeches from one free one. The potential had been there all along, but he had not known about this simple key or how to turn it to unlock opportunities.

THE DIRECT MAIL APPROACH TO PAID BOOKINGS

Speakers disagree about the best way to market themselves. Some use only telemarketing, others send out blanket direct mail pieces. Our bureau uses a combination of methods. We advertise heavily, attend meeting planner meetings and events to meet buyers, attend showcases, use selective direct mail to new and old clients, and constantly call prospects by phone. Our computer system tracks the dates when our clients will be planning their next event.

In advertising, repetition is the key to success. Most people do not remember the name of any product or service until they have seen or heard it five times. This is why we see successful speaker's ads repeated in every speaker catalog and magazine. To gain valuable knowledge about advertising, ask speakers in non-competitive areas about their experience in marketing. You might also arrange joint-venture mailing and marketing with these other speakers.

Learn from the best teachers you can find. Go to a direct mail expert such as Bill Steinhardt, or telephone marketing wizards such as George Walther or David Yoho. Hire them and their expertise. As Benjamin Franklin said, "Your own experience keeps an expensive school. A fool will learn in no other." Learning from other people's experience is a shortcut to success.

Direct mail refers to sending out promotional material to mass-mailing lists you have gathered or rented. Since each speaker's subject and market are different, you will need to experiment with trial runs. Remember, direct mail—at best—produces about one percent return. So expect approximately fifty inquiries from a 5,000 mailing. When you follow up those fifty leads, you can expect to close about ten bookings, providing you had good copy and mailed to the right prospects.

We recommend a careful study of the prospect list. Make a phone call first, then mail only to the person who is truly a prospect. In this way, you save postage and printing, learn about your market, and find out about the prospect's specific needs. You may be able to get the exact dates when a program is needed, the name of last year's speaker, and the theme of the next conference. Send the "right person" a full press kit, personal letter, and contract. Then follow up later with another call and close the deal.

Don't be discouraged when you do not succeed with all of the prospects you approach. The greatest sales person who ever lived does not connect every time.

HOW TO TURN COLD CANVASS INTO HOT CASH

You will not be able to turn every call you make into a booking. Only those inexperienced in sales expect to sell every "suspect," which is someone who might be interested in booking your presentation. Your job is to turn suspects into prospects, and then prospects into closed sales.

People in all fields do a lot of preliminary work before they win a job or a contract. Roger Dawson, a famous negotiation speaker, has his inside marketing person make fifty "cold" calls on brand new suspects daily. From these fifty calls they find fifteen prospects who are interested in receiving Roger's press kit. They close booking contracts with one in five of those who have received the kit. The balance of the original fifty remain on his mailing list and are slotted for future follow-up calls.

The final odds are fifty prospect phone calls to three bookings. If you want to present three paid programs a week, you will need to call fifty new prospects a week. This may not seem like a genius idea, but genius goes around disguised as intelligent persistence. Remember—Don't give up, follow up.

FOUR OTHER WAYS TO OBTAIN BOOKINGS

1. Paint your own professional image. An audience may assume that you have been asked to speak this one time "just for fun." Entertaining your audience is important, because what is learned with pleasure is remembered. But you also need to take positive action to be booked again. In the body of your program, plant the thought that you are a professional and would be a delightful and valuable speaker for other groups. Unless you do this, the idea that you could be booked for other appearances will never occur to the audience.

2. Include in your introduction the following announcement: "[Your name] is available for other presentations. Your suggestions on the rating sheets identifying other groups who might be interested in this speaker are appreciated." Having the introducer read this announcement makes it seem "official."

3. Two or three times during your speech, use phrases such as, "My audiences love this story" or "As I was on my way to speak in Chicago." This plants the thought that you are

a professional speaker who is in demand. "Nothing succeeds like success." So speak, think, and act the part of the successful speaker, and you will be one.

4. Always refer to yourself as a professional speaker. Your business cards, letterhead, envelopes, and everything you print should feature your title as the "[your field] expert" and "professional speaker, trainer, and consultant."

HOW TO KEEP TRACK OF INQUIRIES

Marketing by tracking is an extremely useful practice. Make up a form to keep by your phone to remind you to ask all callers how they heard about you and to record their answers. This will help you establish which of your advertising, direct mail, and publicity projects is the most effective and should be repeated. Also, your records will enable you to thank those who refer clients to you.

It is imperative that you track incoming inquiries not only for your own benefit, but also to maximize the use of multiple non-exclusive bureaus which obtain bookings for you. If the caller heard you at a program, ask which program. Check your records. How was that program booked? If it was booked for you by a bureau, get all the information first, then call the lead to your bureau. The bureau will appreciate your honesty about the client and will work for you enthusiastically on many new bookings.

If the lead came from a fellow speaker or business client, send out a thank you letter the same day.

HARVESTING PROSPECTS FROM OLD BOOKINGS

There are two kinds of clients: new ones and old ones. Repeat business to old ones is often overlooked in speaker marketing, but it should not be. Here are more tricks of the trade that will help you obtain return engagements.

1. First, last, and always, be so good that they can't wait to have you back again. One way to do this is to always customize your material for them.

2. Don't be a "crazy maker," demanding all kinds of extra service and concessions from your meeting planner. Such speakers are rarely invited back.

3. Be a team player, a trouper, willing to help out in a pinch for the client's success.

4. Be pleasant to work with, flexible, and cooperative. Do not argue with anyone.

5. Give as much information as you can, whether your program is a condensed version or the expanded one, in the time allotted to you. But always make it clear that there is more to be said on your topic.

6. Let your audiences know that you have other topics that will also be of value for them. Refer to your other topics by saying something like this, "Just last week that question came up in my seminar on that subject. Here is one of the many ideas I gave them . . . ."

7. It never hurts to glance at your watch and say regretfully, "I wish we had more time to go further into this point, but we don't. However, I would love to come back and work with you again!" Show that you enjoyed being with them and can't wait to come back.

8. When you are booked again, your return speech must give as much honest new substance for the money as you gave the first time, preferably more. Keep careful notes of each speech's content so that you can avoid repeating yourself in encore sessions.

9. Love your audience. Let them know you care about them. Let it show in every gesture, every story, every inflection of your voice.

THE ART OF CONTRACTING AND COLLECTING

A few speakers use a formal, written letter to the client, with all the details of their agreement spelled out instead of a contract. The client signs the letter and returns it to the speaker.

A contract is better than a letter, however. Companies and associations are accustomed to working with contracts for hotel, catering, and all other services needed for the convention.

A non-refundable deposit of 25- to 50-percent is standard to hold the date, with the balance made payable on the date of the presentation. You take the date off the market with the receipt of the contract and deposit. You cannot sell that date to anyone else.

Discounts offer a way to entice early payment. Somers White offers his clients a discount if the entire fee is paid in advance. Thus his speaking dates are paid ahead for as long as two years. If you offer this option to your clients, you will have the advantage of the money in your own bank account. However, the client may ask for an agreement that you will provide a back-up speaker on your same subject if you can't make the date. (You must make an arrangement with another speaker that you will stand in for each other.)

If your contract asked for a deposit, then the balance at the event be sure to send out a reminder just before the event, along with an invoice and a copy of the contract, stating: "We appreciate your having the check ready for us on the _____ (date). In case you need an invoice or another copy of the contract, they are enclosed. We will bill you for the miscellaneous expenses after the event."

Put everything you have agreed to do for your buyer, or they have agreed to do for you, in your contract. The buyer may contract for your services six months to a year ahead of the date. Since buyers work so far ahead, it is possible that not even intending to mislead you, they simply forget what they have agreed to, such as expenses for two in exchange for a lesser fee, ten extra banquet tickets for a family that lives in the area of the event, and so forth. Put these things in writing, and there will not be any hard feelings later. This will also serve to remind you, many months down the line, of your side of the bargain.

If an agent or bureau obtained the assignment for you, the negotiations, contract, and billing will be handled for you.

Shown is a sample contract with a buyer, a sample engagement reminder, and a sample invoice. Use this form to create your own customized versions.

Engagement Reminder

Todays Date: 05/18/88

Mister   **Planner**
Executive Director
Professional Performance Group
601 Spadina Crescent East
Saskatoon, Sask.   **S7K3G8**

Dear Mister

Just a reminder of the agreement we have made for you with your upcoming speaker: **Jeff Speaker**

Date/s of engagement: Location:
Wednesday, June 1, 1988   Saskatoon, Canada, Marriot Hotel on Main St.
                               303-555-1212

Time of presentation: **10:00AM-12:00 & 1:00PM-3:00**

Fees and expenses:

$1,750   speaking fee, plus expenses. Full expenses for **one**
including round trip airfare (if required) from **Redding, CA (coach)**
to place of presentation. Plus all other normal, out of pocket expenses, such
as; ground transportation (taxi, car rental, limo service, etc.), hotel, food and
gratuities. Your speaker will be as fair and reasonable as possible on expenses.
Please remember that "coach" expenses are not the same as "super-saver"
fares. Speakers are rarely able to confirm travel plans far enough in advance to
be able to use the lowest fares.

Did you make hotel reservations at Mr. Speaker prefers to arrange himself at
                                        the hotel of your choice . . . Bill to be
                                        submitted after the event.

A non-refundable deposit of   **$437.00**   was paid on   **4/1/88**

The balance: **$1,313.00** made payable to **Jeff Speaker, Inc., Soc. Security # 000-00-0000**

Is to be waiting for your speaker upon arrival at your venue on **Wednesday, June 1, 1988**

Let me know how else I can be of service!   Lillet Walters, Executive Director

cc: Jeff Speaker

Special Arrangements:
Cordless mike preferred, neck hanging type lavaliere with long cord
acceptable. 35mm carousel slide projector (tested) with remote control,
extension cord and screen. **PLEASE NOTE:** extension cord for slide projector
remote device must reach from the projector to the podium (standard cords
are usually too short).

*Return to: **Walters International Speakers Bureau***
PO Box 1120, Glendora, CA 91740
If we can assist you in any way, 24 hours a day, call
818-335-8069 or 335-5127

Invoice for Payment & Agreement to Engage

as a speaker for

Prepared and sent to you on:

Correspondence, billing, etc., shall be directed thru:

Description or Title of the Event:

Theme of Event:

Speaker Phone, if you need to call your speaker direct:

Date/s of engagement: Location:

Time and duration of presentation:

Presentation title:

The audience is ...

further agrees to pay the following fees and expenses: speaking fee, plus expenses. Full expenses for
                    including round trip airfare and/or mileage (if required) from
to place of presentation. Plus all other, out of pocket expenses, such as: ground transportation, meals before and after, etc.
Speakers schedules change frequently, they are rarely able to use super saver air fares.

A non-refundable deposit of _____ is needed to secure this date. The speaker will give us a firm hold on this date when this contract and the deposit are on hold with Walters International Bureau.
Deposit payable to Royal CBS Publishing, Inc., Tax I.D., 95-3899721, upon receipt of this invoice/agreement to engage.

The balance: _____ made payable to
that amount is to be paid by _____
Because of the potential loss of income to the speaker, cancellation of this date, less than 90 days before the event, carries an penalty of _____ in addition to the deposit, plus, all expenses incured by the speaker in preparing for this date.

Special Arrangements: _____

Other Material enclosed with this contract and invoice:
_____

shall arrive at: _____ on _____

Your speaker needs to be available in a timely & refreshed manner for your group. Make reservations on appropriate nights for your speaker at:
_____

Speaker shall be transported from the airport by:
Speaker shall be transported from the hotel to the meeting site by:
How long does it take to get from the airport to the meeting site?

If questions arise, speaker should contact:
Phone: _____
An alternate contact:

Through disaster, if the chosen speaker/s is unable to appear, Walters' International Speakers Bureau will send a suitable and equally qualified speaker.
IN ADDITION: NO RECORDING DEVICES OF ANY KIND UNLESS APPROVED BY THE SPEAKER.
Approved by _____ Title _____
Signed _____ Date _____

5

How to Overcome Stage Fright, Handle Hecklers, and Leave Your Audience Cheering for More

Three of the greatest challenges in being a professional speaker are: (1) overcoming stage fright; (2) facing hecklers effectively; and (3) knowing how to give your audiences just enough, so they will want you to come back and tell them more. In this chapter, we give you a variety of tips and insights gleaned from our own experiences, as well as the experiences of many top-name professional speakers.

HOW TO GET PAST THE BUTTERFLIES AND ONTO THE STAGE

If you love speaking to audiences but have a bad case of stage fright, you are certainly not alone. *The Book of Lists* ranks speaking in public as the number one fear in the world.

Not surprisingly, the question we are asked most often in our seminars for speakers is, "Do you ever stop being afraid?" The answer, of course, is yes . . . and no. If your knees knock, your heart pounds, and your mouth is dry, you are in good company.

Helen Hayes, the great dramatic actress who has a lifetime of performing experience, says she is always scared before she goes on stage. Butterflies in your stomach are normal. "The trick is to get those butterflies flying in formation," says Cavett Robert, Chairman Emeritus of the National Speakers Association.

Steve Allen, one of the world's best-known performers, finds it odd that the speakers' and performers' fear is called "stage fright." That implies, says Allen, that it doesn't really happen until we are *on* the stage. In reality, he adds, we begin getting scared months before, when we first accept the assignment.

You may not be able to get rid of your stage fright completely, but you *can* learn how to control it. Being brave is feeling your fear but doing a great job anyway. Charles Lindbergh talked of fear after he flew alone across the Atlantic in his tiny plane in 1927. He said, "What kind of person would live where there is no daring? I don't believe in taking foolish chances, but nothing can be accomplished without taking any chance at all." Professional speaking is a daring business, so stage fright or no stage fright, you must be willing to stand up and speak from your heart to your audience.

The Three Best Ways to Conquer Fear

When we hear a speaker who seems a genius, we are dazzled by his or her self-control. We think we have seen a natural talent who has not a twinge of fear. What we actually have witnessed, however, is preparation, perseverance, and enthusiasm in disguise. The professional speaker (1) plans; (2) prepares; and (3) rehearses. These are the three conquerors of fear. Utilize them to the fullest, and you can conquer your own stage fright. As that master of speech William Shakespeare once advised, "Screw your courage to the sticking place." If you plan, prepare, and rehearse, you can conquer the butterflies, get them all flying in formation, and do a magnificent job that is worth ten times your fee.

DOTTIE WALTERS' TECHNIQUES FOR CONTROLLING STAGE FRIGHT

Fear vanishes with your love of the people in your audience, your desire to help them, and your passion for your subject. Let these fill you up before you approach the stage. The Bible tells us, "Perfect love casteth out fear." Make up your mind to do the best job of your life for each audience. Approach each speaking engagement as if you might never get another chance to perform.

We have worked with thousands of professional speakers over a period of more than 25 years. During this time, we have come to the conclusion that the main reason speakers are afraid is because their thinking is concentrated on themselves. The fearful mind asks, "If I am not perfect, if every hair is not in place, if every fingernail is not the precise length, will I be ridiculed?"

What follows are Dottie Walters' own ideas, plus those of other well-known speakers, which can help you replace personal fear with positive thoughts and techniques.

How Dottie Walters Overcomes Stage Fright

The first time I spoke before an audience of 5,000, I was terrified. My lips stuck permanently to my teeth. My heart pounded so loudly I was sure it could be heard in the last balcony. Tiers of seats rose ahead of me like monster waves in the California surf. Then, I stumbled upon a tremendous professional speaking technique. Every actor uses it.

When an actor in a play turns in fear because he hears someone offstage, the audience gasps. Actually, there is no one offstage but the sound effects person. The frightening scene is in the actor's mind. But his shocked surprise is projected to the mind screens of the audience.

As I stood terrified on the stage that night, I began to visualize my home. I saw myself tucking my children into their beds with a soft pink blanket our family called our "comforter." We used it for anyone who was sick or extra tired. In a flash, I filled the whole auditorium with the "comforter" in my mind. Then I smiled and began. I received four standing ovations and five additional bookings that day.

Afterward, a woman came backstage and said, "How did you arrange to get that pink light into the auditorium? It was so pretty!" There was no pink light. She saw the loving comforter I had visualized. There is power in thought. As Anatole France, a Nobel Prize-winning writer declared, "To imagine is everything."

Professional speakers develop many different techniques to get themselves calmed down and ready just before they go on. Some do deep breathing. Others perform exercises. As I wait off stage with my mental motor roaring, straining against the minutes before I can let my energy flow, I use mental visualization. Here is exactly how I do it:

1. I ask my Heavenly Father for help, using the words of Saint Francis of Assisi, "Lord, let me be a channel of Your love."

2. I visualize the people sitting in my audience as I have seen them in my mental rehearsals. We are friends. I see them coming from a long distance. They are hungry, tired, discouraged. My modules of material are platters of delicious food which I have prepared. With all my heart, I want to give these good people my nourishing meal. I am filled with the spirit of my ideas.

3. When I hear my introduction I mentally "jump up" in my mind as I walk on stage. It is like pushing up from the bottom of a swimming pool and breaking the surface of the water. I walk in the sunshine of anticipation, excitement, and happiness. Albert Einstein called the feeling the "leap of the mind." Dr. Yoshiro NakaMats, an international speaker we represent who is known as "the Edison of Japan," refers to the sensation as "the big flash."

4. I look out into my audience, searching for the faces of all my friends who are hungry. My heart calls to them, "I am the one you have been waiting for! Eat! Enjoy!"

Though I have seen it happen many times, I am still amazed at how well the power of mental visualization works. People come up to me constantly after my presentations to say, "I came a long way. I needed help badly. You spoke just for me." *Just for me* is a phrase I hear repeatedly, no matter if the size of my audience was 100, 5,000, or even 14,000.

If you always speak heart to heart to your audiences, no matter how small or how big, and if you use the powers of mental visualization, you will be booked over and over again.

THE IMPORTANCE OF ADVANCED PLANNING

One excellent way to ease your nervousness and boost the confidence level of your performance is to engage in advanced planning well before your speaking engagement. Perhaps the best way to do this is to create an "advance needs" form that you can send to your clients. An advance needs form is simply a short document that specifies exactly what you will need to put on your program most effectively.

An example of an advance needs form is presented on the facing page. It is used by Pat Fripp, first woman president of the National Speakers Association. You can adapt the concept and format to your own presentation requirements.

THE POWER OF GOOD PREPARATION

To be paid for your performances and to keep getting more bookings, you must be very good on stage. This is the bottom line in professional speaking. You can ensure that you will be your best and in better control of your fears if you use the power of good preparation. Rehearse not only physically, but in the auditorium of your mind. Hear the roar of the crowd, the laughter, and the applause. Smile and turn to those friendly faces in your imaginary audience as you mentally deliver each punch line. Grin back at them. When it is time to perform your program before your real audience, you will exude confidence.

Rehearsal was very important to Dr. Victor Frankl, a concentration camp survivor who later became a powerful speaker. He said the only reason he survived the ordeal, while others gave up and died, was that he continually rehearsed, in the theater of his mind, the dramatic speech he would give after the war. Once he regained his freedom and became a speaker, Dr. Frankl told his audiences, "I've never given this speech before, never been here before, never seen you before, except in my mind. It is there I have performed this program a thousand times."

The message Victor Frankl brought to his audiences was that in the concentration camps, he shared the tiny amount of food he

Sample Advance Needs Form (PAT FRIPP)

Important Information When Patricia Fripp
Presents a Seminar for You

For a seminar, Patricia needs to be able to get into the meeting room two hours before she is scheduled to speak. Please clear this with the hotel.

She will need a paper flipchart, an overhead projector, and a screen. The overhead projector should be on a table, not a stand, set up to the right of her as she faces the audience, with the screen behind it. SEE BELOW:

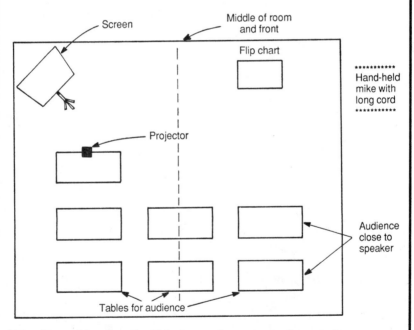

We will provide a handout(s) at no extra expense to you. At no extra expense to us, please have the handout(s) reproduced in sufficient quantity for the seminar.

If you have any questions, or have any problems complying with the above, please call us to discuss it further.

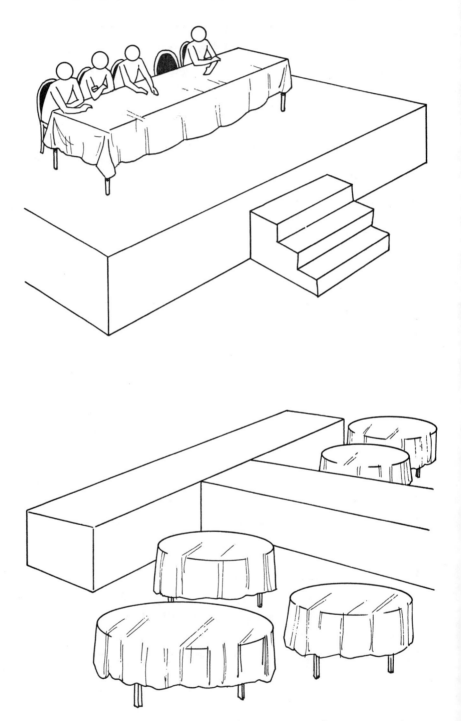

was given with those who were lowest in spirit. While he might be humiliated in every other way, he recalled, his captors could not take away his ability to care for others. The healing balm of loving and giving strengthened him as well as those he helped.

WHEN THINGS GO WRONG, USE THE OPPORTUNITY TO IMPROVISE

As you rehearse and as you speak, fill your mind with the spirit of benefits to your audience. We believe it is not possible to hold more than one all-encompassing emotion in your mind at the same time. Your clothes, hair, props, and materials are all part of your business. Make them as good as you possibly can. But having done that, let go of worrying about those things. If you focus on some possible fault in your appearance, that thought will fill your mind. When you step on stage, you will then be full of self-conscious fear.

Remember, it is okay if something goes wrong. You will then have the opportunity to use your skills and your brains to improvise. The new way you improvise to get the job done might be a serendipity, but it may also work out better than what you had originally planned.

FOUR GOOD WAYS TO HANDLE HECKLERS

Hecklers nearly always appear at evening performances, often after an "attitude adjustment" cocktail hour. Remember, the audience will be on your side—unless you respond with anger. Friends are everywhere; you have to make enemies. If you verbally attack one member of the audience with hostile and negative remarks, the rest of the audience may close ranks and side with the heckler.

Comedian Joey Bishop says, "You may come up with twenty-six witty heckler lines, but the drunk in the front row can always manage to come back twenty-seven times with 'Oh yeah?'" The following are some tips on how to handle hecklers.

1. If the heckler is talking to someone else, walk into the audience. Lightly put your hand on his or her shoulder.

Keep talking, stand close until they stop talking. Then walk away, still speaking as you go.

2. Have a few gentle jokes at the ready, such as "Excuse me, I work alone." Or, "Let's play a game! Only the person with the mike gets to speak." Say these with humor.

3. Tell the client's representatives (such as meeting planners) in advance how they can assist you if the need arises. (This is a last resort.) Explain that two of them can quietly come forward and ask the heckler to step outside for a phone call. Then the planners can talk to him or her out of the room or auditorium where you are speaking.

4. Try this idea that was used by Dr. Kenneth McFarland, the "dean of public speakers" who represented General Motors. Before delivering a speech, Ken always asked for the name of the most successful sales person in the company and placed it on a card that he kept at the lectern. If a heckler began to give him problems, he picked up the card and said, "Wait a minute! This must be (name of top sales person). Anyone who is so knowledgeable must be number one in this company!" Of course, the heckler was *never* the top producer. Dr. McFarland said this system never failed to quiet the heckler down.

THE POWER OF PERSEVERANCE

Sometimes, things simply will go wrong. A heckler will not quiet down, or there may be problems with the lighting or sound. Or you may draw a much smaller audience than you and your client expected. When these things happen, never respond with anger or vulgarity. Be the best you can be, no matter what happens. Your responsibility is to give a great performance, despite these obstacles and disappointments. Here is the "Golden Rule of Professional Speaking," from Bill Gove, the first president of the National Speakers Association:

> You are not responsible for your audience.
> You are responsible to them.

If you respond by doing the best job you can do, no matter what occurs, you can collect your fee. And people will remark,

"That speaker was magnificent, even under difficult circumstances."

If, however, you lose your temper or walk off the stage, you will lose the sympathy of the audience and your client. If you refuse to finish or otherwise are not professional, the client may refuse to pay you. You may also earn an unfortunate reputation. Before each speaking engagement, make up your mind to overcome problems by being constantly professional. Audiences will applaud you, and your clients will appreciate you, recommend you, and bring you back for more speaking engagements.

HOW TO END YOUR PRESENTATIONS ON A HIGH NOTE WITH Q & A . . . AND A TOP STORY

Question-and-answer sessions are a lively way to wrap up almost any professional speaking program. But there is a built-in danger when using this technique, unless you learn how to use a "top story" to bring your performance to a strong conclusion.

Many speakers finish the main part of their speech with their best, dramatic closing story, then call for questions. When that happens, the excitement level goes down, down, down. Once there are no more questions (a definite low point), the speaker has nothing left to say except "Well, um, thank you, and good night!" A much better idea is to save a good, emotional story to tell right <u>after</u> the Q & A session. Keep the questions and answers flowing smoothly and quickly.

Six Tips for Better Q & A Sessions

A question-and-answer session can be an effective part of your performance and your impact as a speaker if you practice six simple techniques. Many successful speakers use these techniques to stimulate audience participation and control the length of the session.

1. Begin the Q & A session by stepping downstage and raising your hand over your head. Smile at your audience, lean forward and ask, "Who has our first question?"

If the audience members are shy and no one responds, ask yourself a stimulating question, "Audiences often ask . . ."

2. It is a good idea to have at least one "helper" in the audience ready with a question, in case it is needed to get the audience started.

3. Speaker Rosita Perez prepares a series of numbered question cards, which she passes out in advance to her participants. She begins her question-and-answer sessions with a query of her own, "Who has question number 1?" That person stands and reads the card. Rosita answers and then asks for question number 2, and so on. This excellent technique gets the questions rolling and makes sure you are asked the right things. It is also her unique way of not forgetting important points she wants to make.

4. Always start your answers with, "Thank you for asking that!" or "Good question!" Some speakers thank each questioner by giving them a cassette tape. Audience members love receiving a gift. Of course, you will need a helper to run the gifts to your questioner. Questions will come fast when people see there is a reward.

5. If someone asks a question to which you don't know the answer, try this reply, "That's a grand question! Let's get some input. How would you wise people answer that one?" Someone in your audience may have an answer, and the response may stimulate you to come up with an even better reply.

6. If you are absolutely stumped by a question, try this response: "That's a good question. I will do some research on that and give you an answer later. Please give me your card after the program. And thank you for contributing that fascinating thought to our discussion. Next question."

If an attendee asks a question which is on a different topic, you can turn it into another booking by saying, "Thank you for that interesting question. We must stick to (your topic) today, but I do have another program on that very thing. I hope you will invite me back, and we can go over it in depth. Will all of you who are interested in that topic, please make a note on your rating sheets." You will then have an excellent opportunity to arrange a re-booking as you review the rating sheets with your meeting planner client after your presentation.

How to Get Back to the Top Story

Because you have one more good story to tell, don't let the question-and-answer period go on too long. Leave the audience wanting more. After a few questions, if you get a big laugh from one answer, that is a good place to make the transition from Q & A to your top story by saying, "Thank you! And now, before I say good night, and until you ask me back to speak for you again, I want to share this special story." Then deliver your story and leave your audience on a high emotional note. Great speakers begin with a laugh, end with a tear.

THE SCHEHERAZADE TECHNIQUE, OR HOW TO LEAVE YOUR AUDIENCES CHEERING FOR MORE

Many effective professional speakers practice what we call "the Scheherazade technique." This is the art of giving audiences just a little less than they want to know. (In *The Arabian Nights,* Scheherazade keeps herself alive night after night by telling the king spellbinding stories, but telling him just enough so that he is always left wanting to hear more.)

Here is how to take advantage of the Scheherazade technique. When your audience leans foreword, especially enjoying your material, and you see that your time is about up, pause and look at your watch. Then say, "I have much more on this subject, but let me summarize it quickly. I would love to be invited back for a longer program or seminar to give you this material in greater depth. I want you to have it." Often, at this point, the audience will burst into applause as their way of saying, "Yes, we want you back!" Remember, you are playing to two audiences. The main one, and the meeting planner who signed your booking contract. Applause for the idea of another engagement is a wonderful re-booking tool. There are two kinds of speaking clients. New ones and old ones. To obtain new ones takes much time, effort, and expense. To re-book over and over again with old ones is always the easiest and most lucrative way to work.

There is a big difference, of course, between leaving your audiences wanting more and leaving them feeling cheated. In each speech, give all the value you can in the time available. Rudyard Kipling once counseled, "Fill each unforgiving minute with sixty seconds' worth of distance run." Cram your speech with value, but like Scheherazade, don't take off all the veils or tell all of your stories at once. Leave your crowds hungry and cheering for more.

6

How to Set Up
Your Headquarters

One of the enduring images of success in business is to have your own office and staff of employees. Some popular speakers do, in fact, have large office facilities and a number of workers on their payrolls. But modern computers and communications equipment now make it possible to run a very successful speaker's business from a room, suite, or spare corner of your own home with your spouse, or one or two assistants.

We estimate that at least 85 percent of the professional speakers we book run their businesses from their homes. The home office's increasing popularity is indicated by the latest architectural home plans which often include two extra rooms: a home gym and an office. The National Work-At-Home Survey reports nearly five million Americans are now full-time home workers—an increase of more than 120 percent in the past two years.

If you plan to stay at your present job until your speaking business gets off the ground, setting up an office at home is a great way to start. Such an office has many advantages. Working at home eliminates commuting, parking fees, office rent, and other overhead costs. Speakers can work very effectively over the telephone, through the mail box, and over facsimile machines. Rather than have clients come to their office, speakers often meet clients while on the road, at the clients' offices, or at a hotel facility.

YOUR FIRST OFFICE

Robert Henry, a motivational entertainer-humorist, has two rooms in his home set up as his office. One is a storeroom for his press kit material, books and demo tapes. The other, with an outside door, has desks, telephones, and the usual business machinery. Other speakers, such as Sheila and Bill Bethel, have converted a guest house into an office. Maxine McIntyre, the "Silent Signal" speaker who specializes in seminars for police departments, uses a room of her home as an attractive and convenient home office. Earl Nightingale and his wife, Diana, have a writing studio, plus a complete recording studio and business office in their home. These speakers are typical of thousands who find home the best of all business locales.

FOUR TIPS FOR LOCATING AND EQUIPPING A HOME OFFICE

1. Do not set up your home office in a hall where there is traffic, near the kitchen with its loud noises, or in the living room, where you will disturb your family—and they will disturb you.

2. Choose a quiet, brightly lit place to work. If you do not have a spare bedroom or den to convert into an office, try starting with a corner of a bedroom where you can shut the door, a partitioned-off section of your garage, or a portion of your basement. Then work toward a separate room as an office as soon as possible. Quiet is all-important.

3. If possible, choose a room with an outside door and a separate bathroom, so your staff can come and go without disturbing the family. If need be, consider converting an appropriate section of your home to accommodate this type of office.

4. You can save money by purchasing used office furniture and equipment at first. Many advertisements in the classified advertising sections of newspapers feature used office equipment. Files and desks, sometimes beautifully refinished, can be purchased at a Goodwill or Salvation

Army store. Often, companies will sell you some of their smaller-sized equipment when they upgrade. Once you start moving up in the speaking business, you can replace your used office furniture with new items that reflect your success.

HOW TO ORGANIZE YOUR OFFICE

As your speaking business develops, you may soon have to keep track of hundreds, even thousands of inquiries and potential buyers. From the beginning, you need to develop three things: (1) an efficient method of storing promotional materials and correspondence to and from clients; (2) a system to trigger your call-back and follow-up efforts; and (3) a method for keeping billings straight. Many manual and computerized bookkeeping systems are available; the choice is up to you.

The Value of Color Coordination

You should also decide on a color scheme for your business correspondence right from the beginning. Start with your stationery. Then, as you add other items, such as custom mailing labels, they can be color-coordinated. Good printers will give you the name and number of paper and ink they use. Keep a record of this information so you can be sure to obtain a match on the next printing run. Another good idea is to ask the printer if there will be any waste paper on the job and if you can use it. For example, if you are printing post cards, the printer might be able to run your business cards in the same color ink on the end of card stock which otherwise would be thrown away.

FOUR ALTERNATIVES TO THE TRADITIONAL OFFICE STAFF

Once your career gets underway, you will discover quickly that you cannot do everything yourself. The efficiency and success of your business, therefore, will depend on having access to dependable, affordable assistants. There are at least four alternatives if you decide that you do not want, or cannot yet afford, a full-time office staff.

1. The majority of professional speakers must have at least one part- or full-time office person running things while they are on the road. In the early days of your speaking career, family members are the easiest and most economical assistants to employ in this capacity. Many speakers start on a shoestring in their homes and "hire" family members to be their staff. As these speakers become more successful, they often move to an office in a fancy building. But after a few years of being on the road, and driving back and forth to the office, they buy a larger home, streamline the business to its most productive areas, and move their office back home again. Often, they again call on family members to run the office and thus gain income formerly paid to outsiders.

   Many well-known speakers employ family members. Fran Tarkenton, the former Minnesota Vikings quarterback who is now a successful speaker, teams up with his daughter to run his office. Tony Alessandra, a prominent sales speaker, has his brother handle his direct mail marketing. IBM speaker Buck Rogers' career manager is his daughter. Sales speaker Jim Cathcart's wife works as his office manager. Pat Paulsen, the political comedian, has two offices, both run by family members in their homes. Norm Rebin, the stellar Canadian speaker, employs his wife and daughter to run his office from their home. All of these people are extremely successful professional speakers whose fees are $4,000 to $15,000 per presentation.

   Your family is very interested in your career, so they make the best partners you can find. We have always included our children in our businesses, talked shop with them, asked for their opinions, and worked with them as a team. The result is that all three are now very successful business people. They tell us that their practical experience in our family business was an invaluable help in developing their own careers.

2. If you are currently employed and plan to do paid speaking on a part-time basis, here is an idea. Ask a secretary in your present business to consider working for you in the evenings and weekends at his or her home. This person should know your wants, habits, and dislikes and be well-suited to assist you by doing such tasks as picking up your messages from your answering service, going to the post office to pick up and drop off mail, processing mail and orders for you, and making routine phone calls.

3. As your career develops, your office support needs will be sporadic. If you can set up a system to pay your assistants by the job, instead of by the hour, you will do better than having a helper sitting in your office full-time with work that is only part-time. Try using professional outside services for secretarial, copying, mailing, answering service, facsimile (FAX) delivery, collating, and bookkeeping needs.

4. Some secretarial services will send out a speaker's press kit and other promotional materials. They will keep your letterhead stationery on hand so that you can dictate letters to them over the phone, by FAX, or by audio cassette. In this way, you can keep your business moving ahead while you are on the road.

   By using outside services, you will do more than eliminate the hassle of having to keep many employee payroll records. Withholding taxes, vacations, sick leave and unemployment benefits will also be eliminated, thus saving money and keeping bookkeeping work down to a more manageable level.

AN OFFICE AT HOME VS. A "REAL" OFFICE

The size of your office depends on the scope of what you plan to handle in-house rather than "jobbing it out." Don and Jeff Dewar, speakers on participative management and quality systems, began their business in Don's garage, then moved into an industrial complex. Although the bulk of their business is training, they also develop custom training manuals, a space-consuming operation.

They bought two printing presses to print the manuals themselves. Their operation kept growing until it became the largest in-house printing facility in Northern California. However, the Dewars soon found that being printers, too, diverted time and energy from training and speaking, their main mission. They now job out the printing and have streamlined their business to fit in a smaller space.

If it is not convenient for you to set up a home office, you can consider as an alternative, teaming up with other speakers to rent office space. New office complexes frequently offer answering services, copy and facsimile machines, and the use of conference rooms to their tenants.

SIXTEEN WAYS TO SOLVE THE HOME-BUSINESS PHONE CRISIS

Home offices offer many advantages, but an office at home also can create problems if you do not include your family as part of your team and teach them how to represent you on the telephone. The following sixteen suggestions can help even small offices attain Fortune 500 professionalism and productivity through good telephone management.

1. Create the concept of a career team. Encourage family members and staff to project enthusiasm when they answer your telephone. When spouses, family, and staff are included in goals, plans, and rewards, they will be fervent in their support rather than resentful toward your business. Sally Rand, the famous fan dancer and magnificent businesswoman, once told us that her motto was, "It never happens by itself." Success in any business is no accident, so form your own quality circle of staff and family. When they help set goals, and are rewarded, they will become team players.

2. Teach family and staff to answer your phone with the right words and a warm, smiling, positive tone. For example, "Thank you for calling the Walters' office. May I help you?"

You and your company are judged by how well your phone is answered. A grumpy teenager with a mouth full of sandwich who mumbles, "No, dunno where she is. Call back." (Slam!) does not project a good business image and likely will lose the prospect. Potential clients may think: *If you can't teach your family or staff any better than that, how can you teach my employees anything?*

3. Install a separate phone for your business to avoid family problems. That way, when your spouse or son or daughter need to use the phone, you will not miss any calls. You may want to put in a two-line system, where the first line automatically rotates to the second line when the first line is in use. This will help you avoid missing calls. Another alternative is to continue using your home line for outgoing calls during business hours and leave your business line open for incoming calls only.

4. A separate telephone line and number for your business are important steps toward creating an air of professionalism. Too often, speakers just starting out try to skimp on costs. They install call waiting on their home telephone. Call waiting is a service offered by most local telephone companies. It simulates a two-line rotary system. When the phone line is in use and another call comes in, you hear a beep tone to alert you that another call is waiting. You are able to put the current caller on hold and answer the second call. However, you are limited to talking only to one caller at a time. Having call waiting installed on your home phone usually will not solve family conflicts over who gets to make or receive calls. The call-waiting feature can be quite annoying to both you and potential clients if you are trying to have a business conversation and your busy family keeps receiving calls. On the other hand, having a separate business number to advertise lends credibility to your professionalism.

5. Hold a family and/or staff training conference and discuss methods of answering the phone and taking messages. Whoever answers your phone should enhance

your image as a successful, highly-paid professional speaker.

6. Have message pads, client inquiry sheets, and pens ready by every telephone.

7. Practice what you teach. What your children see and learn in your home office will benefit them all of their lives. When Dottie's son, Mike, applied for his first job as a law clerk, he saw that the interviewer was swamped by several phones on his desk ringing at the same time. With a look, Mike offered to answer a line on one of the extensions. The interviewer listened with his mouth open as Mike charmed a caller using the business telephone techniques he had been taught to use at home. The interviewer dismissed all other applicants and hired Mike.

8. Remember that any company is the shadow of its owner. Show your staff and family members how to make a wonderful first impression. As the head of the business, you are the leader and the teacher. One of our favorite speakers, Ralph Waldo Emerson, said, "There is no teaching until the pupil is brought into the same state or principle in which you are. A transfusion takes place. He is you, and you are he. Then there is a teaching, and by no unfriendly chance or bad company, can he ever quite lose the benefit."

9. Try to answer your phone on the first ring to let callers know you are ready and able to help them. Be ready.

10. Do not let anyone answer your phone with "Hello, please hold." No one likes to be ignored or put on hold. It is most important that the person answering your phone projects a caring, friendly attitude. Teach staff to close with, "Thank you for calling us." Clients interpret a bored and uninterested voice as saying, "We don't care about you."

11. Convey the sound of success on the phone by moderating your voice tones. Show your family (and your secretary or inside booking person as well) the musical tones on an instrument, such as a piano or guitar. Then, train them to say, "Thank you for calling us!" by matching the

sound of each note as they go up the musical scale from middle C to G. Let them hear the difference between the tones of "hellos" that go up the scale (positive) or down (negative). Bringing the voice up at the end of a sentence works well, too, because it makes the listener lean forward, eager to hear more.

12. Hang a mirror by your phone. A mirror shows you how you sound to your clients. Your voice actually changes when you smile, so you will sound much better when you have a pleasant expression. A mirror with the word "smile" written on it will remind you that the telephone is the front door of your business.

13. Use a headset. The new headsets are lightweight and leave your hands free to take notes, type data into the computer, or look through files. A headset enables you to keep your head upright in a normal position so that you will project a more vibrant, outgoing, "professional speaker" image. Your hands can work a computer at full speed while you listen with a headset. George Walther, the telephone sales speaker, suggests a headset with dual earphones. This way, you can hear in both ears—a more natural way to listen.

14. Use a long telephone cord. It enables you to stand up, walk around your desk, step over to your file cabinet, pick up a file, etc. We like standing up when calling, and do this as a habit. The long cord enables us to move around, grab material, and keep our circulation moving. You can even open the door for a delivery person while you talk, or you can do a couple of wall push-ups. A long cord enables you to sound full of life, excitement, and dynamism because you feel physically better if you haven't been sitting all day while you talk on the phone. A long cord is an investment well worth its low price.

15. Set up your office for quick response. Be reachable. It is vital to respond quickly to telephone messages. When a bureau or meeting planner inquires about your availability for a program, an immediate answer is often needed. If you cannot be reached, you have lost the opportunity for that business. We once tried to reach a

speaker for three days, leaving messages on his machine. No response. Our client was waiting. This speaker lost a $5,000 engagement simply because we could not reach him. His lack of professional response forced us to find another speaker for our client. So we called Alan Cimberg and reached his answering machine at his office in New York. In less than two hours he had returned our call, even though he was on a tour in London! That is professionalism. Responding to every telephone message promptly, which means within three hours, is the way to jump ahead of your competition.

16. Avoid the game of telephone tag by leaving a complete message on your answering machine, or with your answering service, or secretary, saying when you will pick up messages. If your telephone machine message says only, "Leave your name and number," you must call back after every call. Sometimes that leads to repeated callbacks trying to get the message through. A better way is to invest in an answering machine that records long messages from callers and have your outgoing message say: "Please leave your entire message. You have all the time you need." Often, the caller then can leave all of the necessary data, so that no call back is required. This idea eliminates the annoyance of missing calls and saves some of the time and money involved in long-distance calls. Other advantages of using an answering machine are discussed later in this chapter.

USING ANSWERING SERVICES TO ENHANCE YOUR BUSINESS

It is difficult, but not impossible, to find an outstanding answering service. One that really cares about you is worth its weight in gold. A good service should sound like it is your own staff, in your office, taking care of your business.

When Tom Winninger, a very successful speaker whose topic is marketing, first began his business, he employed a handicapped woman to answer calls for him in her home. When Tom wasn't at his office, his calls were automatically forwarded to her home phone. She answered her line as if it were Tom's business line. Tom says this approach had a tremendous advantage over a traditional answering service. The woman worked only for Tom, and she cared how she did her job. In the past, we used the services of a person with arthritis. We transferred our business calls to her phone. The professionalism she demonstrated when answering our calls created a wonderful relationship for us and our clients.

The most efficient answering services offer toll-free lines on a 24-hour, 7-day-a-week basis in all fifty states. They will take both messages and orders for you, including credit card information. Good answering services will let you call in with information about where you are performing, so callers can be directed to you. These efficient answering services act as a part of your business team. We work closely with our own answering service, calling them at set times each day. We send them all of our promotional material, along with thank you notes for their fine work, and gifts to let them know how much we appreciate them. You should strive to build a warm relationship with your answering service, and make them part of your winning team.

THE ADVANTAGES AND DISADVANTAGES OF ANSWERING MACHINES

Some people refuse to talk to an answering machine, but this hostile attitude toward mechanical devices is becoming almost extinct as more and more business people find new ways to use the machines. When you purchase an answering machine, look for one that is voice-activated and offers unlimited message space. It should continue recording as long as the caller is speaking and not cut off in mid-sentence.

Be sure your machine will allow you to call in and pick up messages while you are on the road. Keep in mind that if you record a new, short, informative message reply each week, your answering machine will serve as another medium for advertising. Do not use music, phony voices, or poems in your message. These can be very irritating to clients or speakers bureaus who want to reach you. (Especially, if they are calling long distance.)

What follows is an example of an answering machine message

that has worked very well for us. You can adapt it to your own business.

> "Hello, this is (your name). I am sorry I am not in my office at the moment. I am on the road, but I call in often. I will get right back to you. Please leave your entire message with all the details I will need to return your call with the information you need. Give me your name and a telephone number where and when I can reach you. Take all the time you need. Thank you for calling me."

Once you begin to use a message similar to this above, be sure that you *do* pick up messages often and return calls immediately. Remember: The time to follow up on a lead is always RIGHT NOW. The longer a message goes unanswered, the less chance you have of closing the booking.

If you have just begun your speaking career and are still running your operation with little or no staff, consider having two phone lines installed that use the rotary system described earlier in this chapter. You may want to put your answering machine on the second line, especially when you are in the office alone and are holding important business conferences by phone on line-one. Have the answering-machine message on the second line say something like this, "I'm on the other line with a client conference call right now. I should be able to call you back within twenty minutes. Please leave a detailed message about the information you need from me, so I can be prepared and ready to help you when I return your call. Thank you for calling."

EFFECTIVE WAYS TO ORGANIZE YOUR SUPPLIES AND SPEAKING MATERIALS

Once you set up your office, you will find that it will quickly fill up with supplies, promotional materials, press kits, research files, and machinery such as answering machines, computers, and printers. If you keep your supplies and materials organized, you will be able to handle more business efficiently and effectively.

Speakers with the real drive to succeed write books, articles, and press releases which enhance their expert image and increase their bookings and fees. All of these projects will take up considerable office space, because you must keep many copies of these materials to send in your press kits to meeting planners and speakers bureaus. Each prospective client will need to receive copies of the materials that show you as an expert on the topic under consideration. If you write as much as you should, it will soon become almost impossible to keep all your materials straight without office pre-planning. Here is a great example of pre-planning that can help you stay organized.

Somers White, a former Arizona state senator and now a world-class professional speaker, has one of the best-organized speaker offices in the industry. He had a carpenter build narrow shelves in vertical rows. At the top of each shelf is a small sign bearing the name of a type of business Somers addresses: "Banking," "Insurance," "Sales," and so forth. On the shelves beneath these headings are stacks of articles he has written, copies of testimonial letters, and complete handout materials for his programs on each particular subject. The shelf system makes it very easy for him to find and pull a specialized press kit for each inquiry. At the bottom of the stack on each shelf, Somers keeps the original document in a protective envelope. When he runs low on copies of a particular item, the document is easy to find for duplication.

Tom Winninger, a top sales speaker, uses this same shelf scheme in his office, and we have adapted it in ours, as well. However, Tom uses cardboard racks which are designed for shoe storage. They can be found in most variety stores. They come with nine little storage holes in each container. The cardboard racks cost under $15 each and perfectly fit a standard 8 1/2 in. x 11 in. or even 14 in. sheet of paper. The cardboard storage units are much less expensive than hiring a carpenter, and they can be found in attractive shades that match your office. Since they are lightweight, as well, they are easy to add to or move around as your business grows.

TWELVE TIPS FOR BETTER SCHEDULING

One very important function of a well-organized office is to help you keep track of the dates, times, and locations of your speaking engagements, meetings with potential clients, and other important matters. The following tips can help you develop better scheduling habits and a highly efficient scheduling system:

1. Remember, speakers sell dates. The speaking dates on your office calendar are your inventory, your stock in trade, just as your products are.

2. Get a large, three-or-more-year calendar. Successful speakers often are booked a year or more in advance. Even as a beginning professional speaker, you must be able to track your future whereabouts for several months ahead of time. Your calendar should hang on the wall directly in front of the phone, next to your menu of topics, your fee schedule, a mirror, and your goals. If your office is computerized, this information should be easily accessible from your computer, in a program whose files can be opened and the data available to you in less than ten seconds.

3. For a variety of reasons, many successful speakers limit the number of speeches they will accept in a year. These reasons include a desire to avoid fatigue in order to offer top performance, a desire to be at home with family, or even a desire to maintain a certain income level. Jim Cathcart, recent president of the National Speakers Association, has steadily grown in his speaking career, raising his rates each year. When we interviewed him for an issue of *Sharing Ideas,* he told us that he had just raised his keynote fee to $7,000 per program and planned to take only sixty programs per year—a gross of $420,000 for speaking only. Remember, most professional speakers double their fees by charging for consultations and product sales. Therefore, $840,000 might be a reasonable estimate of this speaker's annual earnings. Since speakers are booked a year or more in advance, a good scheduling calendar must be at the center of their business.

4. You have the option of utilizing calendar programs that run on your computer or a variety of manual calendars. If you work with a manual calendar, use self-adhesive tags or markers of different colors to indicate pending dates, definite contracted dates, and personal days such as dental appointments or special family events. Buy plastic markers or tags that are easy to write on and to change.

5. Keep a United States map and world map with time zones close to your phone, along with a book that lists zip codes and telephone area codes. Remember, speaking can be an international business.

6. Always consider the travel time from one speech to another. When a client or speakers bureau calls to inquire about your availability, don't just look at the blank spot on the calendar and say "Yes, it's clear." Look at the dates on either side of the proposed event. Note your location the day before, and the travel time from venue to venue, to be sure you have time to move from one day's engagement to the next, allowing for canceled flights and delays.

7. Check the "real time" it takes to arrive at the venue in question. Example: On a map of the United States, Wyoming looks close to Denver. Denver is easy to get to from most other major cities. Therefore, you may figure that you should be able to make a Wyoming date on time with no problem. But this may not be so. Check with your travel agent. How many local flights actually go to that area of Wyoming from Denver? How far is the venue from the airport? One hour . . . six hours? What is the ground transportation situation?

8. Figure the estimated travel time involved so that you will arrive in a refreshed and alert manner. Allow for late plane arrivals, to be sure you will have time to get some rest. It is always best to arrive the night before an event.

9. Go over these points with the client meeting planner. For example, your client may plan to send a limousine or small plane to transport you to an isolated resort. Find out exactly how you are to get to the program and how long the trip will take. (Check to be sure local transportation runs on weekends and/or at night.)

10. Consider the time of year the meeting is being held. Are there likely to be any weather problems? What are alternate means of transportation in case of blizzard or storm?

11. When booking flights through your travel agent, never take the last possible plane that will get you to the speech exactly on time. If that flight is canceled, you have no other options left to get you there. Speakers are paid not just for the time they are present on the platform, but for taking the personal responsibility to be at the presentation site refreshed and on time, ready to give the best performance of their lives.

12. Carry with you the clothes and materials you *must* have to give the speech. Many speakers say, "There are only two kinds of luggage: carry on and lost." Find bags that you can carry on comfortably. Keep a set of the smallest size necessities (toothpaste, brush, etc.) packed and ready to go, and pare these necessities down to a minimum. Also pack a small travel steam iron. The dry cleaning facilities may be closed when you arrive. You can usually ask the hotel staff to supply an ironing board in your hotel room. Ship your speaking materials, props, and handouts ahead by Federal Express or United Parcel Service, so you will know they have arrived ahead of you. Call before you leave and confirm their arrival with the bell captain at the hotel or conference center to which they were sent.

THE COMPUTER DECISION

Many speakers are adding computers rather than typewriters to their offices because computers can do more tasks, faster. A computer and the right software can simplify bookkeeping, product inventory, booking records, writing (articles, books, speeches, letters), handout production, slide-making, mailing lists, and labels. You can keep your office in full production while you are on the road by using a portable computer and a modem to send work home electronically via the telephone line. We find that more and more communications are arriving on computer disks rather than on paper from meeting planners and from speakers who write for our newsmagazine, *Sharing Ideas.*

Top speakers are business leaders. As a leader you should learn how to use a computer. Many people may have avoided computers like the plague in the past, but by the year 2000, only eleven years from the first publication of this book, you will be considered illiterate if you do not know how to use a computer. The following is an example of how fast the world is going to computers.

When we bought our first computer, our little grandson came over and watched Lilly practicing.

"Can I play too, Lilly?" he asked.

"No, sweetie, this machine is very expensive, not a toy. Lilly is doing hard stuff here today," she answered. Lilly was reading the manual and trying to figure out just how to turn the thing on. "Let's see, where does this go?" she said to herself.

"Auntie Lilly," the little boy said, "that's your *system* disk. It goes here, in the internal drive. Plug in your mouse over there." He had been taking a computer class all year at school.

Once you master using a computer, you will not want to go back to a slower, old-fashioned typewriter for any price. However, do not throw away your old manual machine. It can be a good tool to have handy if the power goes out for an extended time.

Introductory computer courses are available from many sources. Check with the nearest community college or private computer training company. It is no longer just a "good idea" to learn about computers. Today, such knowledge is mandatory. Computers now are as common in offices as copy machines or telephones.

CLIENT TRACKING METHODS

Computers and software supply the best systems for tracking data, but there are other methods to get you started if you are just beginning to be a professional speaker. For example, you can use 8½ in. × 11 in. file folders that are filed alphabetically according to the buyers' company names. Also, you can use a small file box to create a tickler file. Each client and/or potential client should have a matching 3 in. × 5 in. card with the date listed that you need to call that client again, and the cards should be filed by date. A tickler file created in this manner is easily portable, ready for follow-up in your office, or to be taken with you so you can make phone calls on the road.

In your office, as each date in your tickler file comes up, you can pull all the client records you need to take action. Speaker Tom Winninger uses a system of colored tags to help him establish priorities for which clients should be contacted first. Winninger ranks the clients in three categories:

1. People you *must* call back on that date.
2. People whom it is a very good idea to call back on that date.
3. People to whom it would be nice, but not urgent, to place a call on that date.

Before our speakers bureau became computerized, we used the following new client inquiry form to help us keep track of essential information. Change this form to suit your own business. Never fail to fill it out on every incoming booking inquiry. Use it for calls from bureaus, clients you solicit yourself, and those who call you direct.

Before sales speaker Steven Cates switched to a computer system, he used a form similar to ours. He took it a step farther, however, and had his forms printed up in triplicate. One copy went into the client folder; one went into the file by location of the meeting. The third copy was filed by call-back date.

PLANNING OUT-OF-OFFICE WORK

Smart speakers have developed a system for working away from home, because proper time management is essential to continued success. A speaker may be away from the office for one day, sometimes two, or even for a week or more before returning home. Speakers who are unable to work away from their office often have stretches of time on the road with nothing to do, while in contrast, back at the office, the pile of work and research to be done grows ever larger. The solitude of travel can be a wonderfully productive time, if you are prepared with the tools to use such time to advantage. You might use some of these speakers' ideas for time management.

Make a plan for out-of-office work. Plan your calendar months in advance, noting which speeches and articles you can

NEW CLIENT INQUIRY FORM

LEAD ORIGIN _____ TODAY'S DATE _____

CONTACT _____

COMPANY _____

CARE OF _____

ADDRESS _____

CITY _____ STATE _____ ZIP _____

HOME PHONE _____ WORK PHONE _____

BEST TIME OF DAY TO REACH YOU? _____

ASSIGNMENT INFORMATION:

TIME _____ HOURS TO SPEAK _____ WHEN _____ WHERE _____

OBJECTIVES _____

_____

THEME _____

TYPE COMPANY _____

IN AUDIENCE _____ AGES _____ Ratio of MALE/FEM _____

BUSINESS RESPONSIBILITIES _____

FROM WHICH PART OF THE WORLD _____

BUDGET _____

WHAT OTHER SERVICE MIGHT I HELP THEM WITH? _____

SPEAKERS USED BEFORE? _____

DECISION MAKING PROCESS _____

write while on the road. Be sure to pack a folder with the information you will need to accomplish these goals, along with whatever supplies you need to write your material. Follow these tips:

1. Use simple, yellow-lined legal pads, pencils, and 3 in. × 5 in. cards.
2. Rent a typewriter from the hotel.
3. Take along a laptop computer and several disks.
4. Use a small audio cassette recorder for dictation, and utilize the hotel's secretarial service to transcribe the tape.

When we interviewed Steve Allen for *Sharing Ideas,* he told us he keeps a number of small audio recording machines around him at all times. Each has a cassette in it labeled for a different project he is working on. It is then easy to travel with one machine or pick one up in the office to work on a project.

Be sure to take along a folder of office stationery and your address book, some attractive post cards printed with your picture, and some stamps. You may want to get an important letter or proposal into the mail while you are away from the office.

Make arrangements for your mail to catch up with you if you will be gone for a long period. Or, have someone at your office read your mail to you daily over the phone. Be prepared to give instructions for an appropriate reply.

A laptop computer is a wonderful new asset for all of us on the road. You can write letters, articles, proposals, and then give the disk to a service at the hotel to print them out on your stationery as well as mail them, or you can mail your disk to your office to edit and take appropriate action.

Some speakers now hook up a modem to their laptop computer and send materials from their hotel rooms to their offices. The work they send in can be edited and processed by their staff. Messages and other information also can be sent from the office to the speaker.

Another method of getting your work to your office for completion is to use a public facsimile machine. Most hotels have fax machines available. If you do not have one for your own office, you can make arrangements with a nearby office or secretarial service to send out and receive your facsimile messages.

A less effective, yet still workable, method for preparing a variety of material is to use an audio cassette recorder. You can dictate onto a cassette while on the road, then mail the cassette or carry it back to your office to be translated into business letters or speeches. Some of these recorders are now so small that they can be carried in a purse or a man's inside pocket. We see many business people dictating into their recorders on airplanes or in airports. Imagine getting all those thank you letters done in the air as soon as you finish your program, while they are fresh in your mind.

CONTROLLING PRODUCTION AND QUALITY

If you try, you can find many ways to get more productive time and action into each day. Plan better. Waste less. Swing on each task with authority. Make a list of each goal, then figure out how to reach it. You can do it. You know how better than anyone else.

Keep your eyes on your destination, not on any small failure. Production means going around the temporarily bad situations and planning how to create new markets.

Make sure everything you do is top of the line. Give your clients your best, then do even more.

SETTING SPEAKING AND BUSINESS GOALS

When prospective speakers call to ask for our advice, we often ask them, "What is it you want to do?"

When they answer, "I have no idea," there is not much anyone can do to help them. It is as if they are asking a traffic cop for directions, then saying that they have no destination. We love the words Cecil Rhodes, the man who built the railroads in South Africa, used to greet new arrivals in his country. Instead of saying "Hello," he asked them, "What is your dream?" He hired only those with dreams.

Set your speaking goals. Goals are dreams with a deadline. Put them up where everyone in your office can see them and make every bit of work you do propel you toward them. When you reach those goals, aim for new ones immediately. Put up the new goals like an athlete raising the height of the jump bar.

Dr. Yoshiro NakaMats, an international speaker we discussed in Chapter 5, sets goals for each new project with visualization. So far, he has registered twice the number of patents that Thomas Edison did. Among his 2,380 patents are the floppy disk and the digital watch. Dr. NakaMats says, "You must use your life. You must use your life fully. When it is time to die, if you were given a creative potential of eight and you have only used six, you will die unsatisfied. If you were given a potential of eight and have expanded it to a twelve, you will die satisfied."

Cavett Robert, Chairman Emeritus of the National Speakers Association gets a similar message across in a slightly different way, "Don't go to your grave with your song unsung."

Looking at your goals on a daily basis helps your mind focus on where you are going. Put up a picture of your own dream close to your telephone. For example, this dream might be a beginning goal of two paid speeches per week at $1,000 each, a total of 104 per year, plus doubling your fees in product sales. This would give you a total gross of $208,000 for your first speaking year. You might write it out like an algebraic formula:

$$2S \times \$1,000 \times 52 = \$104,000 + \text{Consultations \& products of } \$104,000$$
$$= \text{Yr. Gross of } \$208,000.$$

Next to these figures, put up a picture of a family goal—maybe a child's college graduation, a boat, a plane, or a summer home. Conrad Hilton always put a picture over his phone of each hotel he dreamed of buying. Then he made his dream come true. The trick is to make every stroke of work that you do hammer out a path from where you are to your goal—until the dream becomes reality.

The best way to make your speaking dreams come true is to help meeting planner clients achieve their objectives. Let your family know you are working toward making all clients happy, satisfied, and content. Therefore, every letter, phone call, and performance must be aimed at fulfilling your goals. Explain that you need their help pulling together on the oars of your business. Ask your staff and your family for ideas about how to reach these goals.

We have seen instances where the actions of a family or staff member almost sabotage a business. This is because they feel left out. A favorite old poem, "Outwitted" by Edwin Markham, explains how to overcome their negative attitudes by making them part of your winning team:

> He drew a circle that left me out.
> Heretic, rebel, a thing to flout.
> Love and I had the wit to win.
> We drew a circle, and took him in.

Lavish praise and rewards on your staff. The day you achieve your goal, reward them. Then set up a new and higher goal.

TEN TECHNIQUES FOR HIRING AND TRAINING AN INSIDE MARKETING PERSON

One of the first people you may want to add to your growing staff is an inside marketing person who is good at selling a speaker's services and products. Once you decide to look for an inside market specialist, you may want to use some of the following techniques:

1. Be sure to put the words "telephone" and "sales" in your ad copy. There is no use hiring someone who dislikes either one.
2. Put your phone number in the ad. Have them call you. Listen to their voice projection and their telephone personality.
3. Look for someone who loves to serve customers on the phone. Our daughter Lilly left several jobs because she was told she "talked on the phone too much." We brought her into our company to talk on the phone all day with outstanding results.
4. Watch for workers with successful sales experience.
5. Observe how prospects move when you meet them in person. One way is to arrange so that they must walk a distance toward you. Watch the walk. People reveal their life force in their walk. Another way to judge by movement is to have interview candidates come in one at a time. Get up

and move the interview chair away a few feet away after each applicant leaves. Then ask the new applicant to "Pull up a chair." You will be astounded by the results. You will hear responses ranging from "No, I like it where it is" or "Move it where?" to "I would be glad to." The reply will give you an instant view of the cooperativeness, pleasantness, and attention concentration of the applicant.

6. Ask candidates when they want to start. If they say "right now," hire them. Someone who gives excuses for not beginning will continue to give you excuses for not producing or showing up. (Unless they must give notice at another job, of course.)

7. Have the new worker sit by you while you make the calls for the first day. Next, sit by him or her and listen for at least two days more. Praise every good thing that is done.

8. Show the new marketing person how to keep records of calls made and bookings closed.

9. Pay a good salary, not a high one. Pay high commissions with bonuses and/or perks.

10. Ask the marketing person about personal weekly goals. Put those goals on the wall, then reward the achievement of those goals. Help other employees set their sights up each time they achieve their mark. Increase the commission percentage as the goal goes higher.

Remember the advice given by Knute Rockne when he was asked for his formula to bring out the best in his team members. He responded, "Some players need a pat on the back. Some need a kick a bit further down. I give each team player what they need to get them going."

Give your office staff what they need to get going and keep going. In turn, they will do their very best to help you speak and grow rich.

7

How to Speak and Grow Rich
with High-Profit Seminars

Seminars are one of the most profitable enterprises in the speaking industry. For that reason, many speakers now produce their own seminars and market them to corporations and specialized public audiences, such as investors in real estate or precious metals, people who want to start their own businesses, and thousands of other business and personal audiences.

Seminars are so popular, in fact, that they have even spread to resorts and gone to sea on cruise ships. Today, many speakers and their audiences enjoy mixing learning with pleasure.

If your seminar has the right ingredients and back-of-room products to sell, it can be a great revenue producer. For example, many technical seminars, such as those for consultants, doctors, dentists, and other professionals, charge attendees up to $1,000 and more for a one-day session. Those who register are willing to pay such fees because a good seminar can help them enhance their careers by increasing their knowledge and income-earning potential.

Twenty-five participants at $1,000 each translate into a gross of $25,000 just for registrations. Additional income can be gained from back-of-room (BOR) product sales (see Chapter 10). A real estate seminar leader reports typically that his BOR product sales usually equal the amount his seminar grosses from registration fees.

Therefore, he brings in about $50,000 for each seminar that draws twenty-five attendees.

SEVEN WAYS TO PROFIT FROM THE SEMINAR MARKET

You can profit in at least seven ways from the popular and expanding market for seminars:

1. You can produce and sell your own seminar to the public.
2. You can offer in-house seminars to corporations.
3. You can work for seminar companies that hire speakers on a per-day basis or for a flat fee.
4. You can speak on a share-the-gate basis for impresarios who sponsor seminars.
5. You can pay a seminar promotion company to produce and market a program for you.
6. You can cash in on the growing popularity of fund-raising seminars.
7. Organizations such as colleges, churches, and other groups stage seminars and book speakers on a share-the-gate-basis.

Each of these methods has its own requirements, and we will discuss them in turn. We will also show you the ingredients that go into a successful seminar and explain how you can adapt your materials for seminars at sea or foreign resorts, as well.

PRODUCING AND MARKETING YOUR OWN PUBLIC SEMINAR

Producing your own seminar and marketing it to the public can be tough and risky business but also very rewarding. When you are the impresario of a public seminar, you reap all the profits. But you also take all of the financial risks.

To offer a seminar to the public, you must make all of the arrangements yourself, including locating lists of prospects, writing advertising copy, printing flyers and posters, sending out direct mail pieces, reserving a seminar site, and taking care of refreshments. In short, you must act as your own sales agent, publicist, meeting planner, site arranger, promoter, playwright, and star of the show. You wear all of these hats, and more, when you offer your own seminar.

Then there is the matter of what each attendee will get. Your seminar may or may not include a workbook and some cassette tapes in the registration fee. You may even opt for a low registration fee, try to draw a large crowd, and count on some additional income from the educational items sold at the back-of-room display.

Many seminar speakers offer attendees their own products on the seminar's subject, and display related books ("recommended reading"), albums, and videos by other authorities in the field, as well. These products often are discussed in the seminar, and attendees appreciate having easy access to a wide range of recommended learning materials. The back-of-room display saves them time, since they do not have to search through stores and catalogs to find the products they desire.

Many seminar leaders think of their BOR table as a miniature information store that stocks the best materials available on their topic. Starting the "store" and keeping it stocked does require an investment. But most publishers are glad to offer you their materials at from 40% to 50% off retail. You can then sell them at the retail price and bank the profits.

A good seminar leader constantly reads new books and reviews the latest audio and video materials on the seminar's subject and adds the best ones to his or her display.

Barney Zick, who is well-known and successful in real estate, developed a major mailing list of people interested in investing in income property. Now he markets his seminar to his mailing list. Zick charges an average fee for the seminar, then offers his special materials on income property as back-of-room products. He reports that his average product sales alone are $20,000 per performance.

Here is another example. An expert on state tax preparation offers a public seminar for the 54,000 income tax preparers in California. He spends one month a year in the state capital, revising and updating his material. He publishes a large annual book which is the top reference manual in his field. For publicity, he publishes a simple newsletter on his subject and lists the locations of his seminars. It is mailed twelve times a year to the 54,000 tax preparers, at a low subscription price. Thus, he is well known in his target market.

The tax expert offers three-hour seminars, with question-and-answer sessions, every Saturday during eleven months of each year. He uses no outside help or assistance and offers no refreshments. He takes advantage of low-cost locations in each city, such as community centers and schools, and works a circuit covering locations all over the state. His seminars are ticketed at only $50, but his essential book, describing all of the new changes in state tax law, is sold back-of-room at a high fee. His average gross is $5,000 per seminar. Four seminars per month for eleven months give him an annual gross income of approximately $220,000.

HOW TO SELL IN-HOUSE SEMINARS TO CORPORATIONS

Corporations often find they do not need a full-time seminar leader or trainer on their payroll. As a result, they contract with outside speakers who are experts in different fields as they need them.

Corporations are businesses. There are directories of corporate meeting planners, such as The Salesman's Guide, Inc., 1140 Broadway, New York, NY 10001 which lists 15,400 corporate meeting planners. This company also has a directory of Association Meeting Planners.

Your material is focused on certain business or professional markets. When you call or write to corporations and offer them a "hot" topic which is needed in their field, they will be interested in using you. For example, two New York actors offer a seminar on "Stage Tricks for the Courtroom" to large law corporations.

To sell corporations, track down the companies who need your subject. Call them and ask for the person in charge of training. Some speakers work exclusively for corporations. They often work under contract for only one large corporation such as IBM.

THE ADVANTAGES AND DISADVANTAGES OF WORKING WITH SEMINAR PRODUCERS

A number of seminar-producing companies now contract with speakers to deliver a given topic several times a week on a specified circuit. One circuit might be the Far West, while another covers the Northwest and Alaska, and yet another covers the Southwestern United States or overseas.

Speakers are hired to present a seminar owned by the seminar company, and the seminar's subject may or may not be one that the speaker has gained experience with previously. If the seminar company buys your seminar for a fee, you and other speakers alike may present the program on the circuit arranged by the seminar company.

At a seminar company, the subject matter is the star, not the speaker. These companies often have a number of speakers on the road at one time, each giving the same seminar. Each circuit is set up so that the speaker can complete one program, get on a plane or bus, and go on to the next program for the following day. A typical schedule is two daily seminars, a day off, then two more.

Seminar companies pay a smaller fee per engagement than the amount speakers can earn as keynoters or seminar leaders for conventions. They also pay far less than you can earn by presenting your own seminars. But the series of programs is assured. For example, a contract might be signed for 12 seminars at $700 per day plus all expenses. The speaker then would net $8,400 for three weeks' work. All expenses are paid by the seminar company.

What Seminar Producers Can Do for You

Seminar producers are companies that market and produce a speaker's seminar. They usually do not take a cut of the profits. Instead, they charge a flat fee, which is usually $10,000 or more. Some seminar promoters, however, find a hot topic, do all of the marketing and promotion, and hire a known speaker on that topic to present the seminar. The promoter pays all the bills, including the speaker fee, and keeps the difference in gross sales as the profit.

Rosalie Wysocki, a successful Canadian speaker, often works for a travel agency which books her to speak to their overseas tour groups. The trip is income tax deductible for the attendees because there is an educational one-hour lecture offered each day of the trip. The speaker is paid for the programs, plus all of the expenses, and enjoys a marvelous vacation as well.

THE BIG-RISK TAKERS: IMPRESARIOS

Impresarios work on a much larger scale than seminar producers. Impresarios hire a hall such as a sports arena or theater, then contract with several famous speakers whose names will pull in the crowd. They arrange for advertising and promotion, sell tickets, handle back-of-room sales, manage the program, pay all of the bills, and (they hope) make a profit. The large facilities they use may seat an audience of 5,000 to 7,000. Recently, Zig Ziglar and John Molloy appeared for impresario John Hammond at Madison Square Garden in New York. Hammond, 1988 President of the National Speakers Association, is one of the finest impresarios in the United States. Dottie Walters has appeared at many of these large programs and shared the platform with Zig Ziglar, Dr. Norman Vincent Peale, Dr. Robert Schuller, and other famous speakers. Speakers may work for impresarios for a share of the gate, for a flat fee, or sometimes just for the opportunity to sell their products at the back of the room. We know of one case where product sales are so high that the speakers pay the impresario for the *privilege* of speaking, then selling thousands of dollars worth of their books, audio albums, and videos BOR.

HOW TO CASH IN ON FUND-RAISING SEMINARS

A variety of organizations sponsor seminars as fund raisers for their treasuries. They work with speakers and seminar leaders on a "share-the-gate" basis. Share-the-gate seminars are done with hospitals, churches, colleges, universities, "free colleges," associations, Chambers of Commerce, and other groups. Any group interested in fund raising likely will listen to your proposition for a seminar project, especially if it is closely suited to their members.

The trick is to find the groups that will tie in best with your subject. In a share-the-gate, the speaker supplies the program. The sponsor provides the hall, refreshment breaks, travel expenses, advertising, their list of prospects, postage, and printing. Often, the speaker's products are offered back-of-room. The usual arrangement is a fifty-fifty split of the gate, although different organizations work at various percentage levels. A one-day seminar co-op can easily net $5,000 each to the speaker and the sponsor as their share. When you establish a successful co-op with one organization, ask them for the list of other groups affiliated with them, such as other churches of the same denomination. Ask for a letter of recommendation. Use this letter to offer the same co-op seminar to the related organizations.

For example, Alan Cimberg, a superb sales speaker, works often with the Sales and Marketing Association. This association has chapters in every major city, and Cimberg has presented seminars at many of the chapters. When you have good success with a local group, ask if their association has chapters nationwide or worldwide. It is possible to stage fund-raising seminars in many cities and countries, offered by the local chapters of the association. Be sure to send an article about the successful seminars to their national trade journals.

OTHER MARKETS FOR SEMINARS

Many organizations present seminars on a regular basis as an on-going part of their educational programs. Thus, they are always looking for new subjects. And they have the resources to back up their programs. They have lists of former seminar attendees, as well as their own printing facilities, newsletter, a publicity department, and sometimes even their own radio or television show.

Numerous colleges produce catalogs of their business extension courses, both in the United States and worldwide. These classes are taught by professional business speakers and are arranged on a co-op, per-head, or fee-per-day basis. Call and discuss the possibilities and requirements with nearby colleges. Then expand to their county, state, national, and international counterparts.

HOW TO FIND COMPANY SPONSORS
FOR SEMINARS

Companies often look for speakers who can act as spokespersons for their products, services, or public image. The speaker may travel to many areas, present speeches and seminars, and often participate in media interviews to promote the sponsoring organization's products, services, or image. If you are an expert in a special field, consider contacting all of the large corporations or organizations in your area that relate to your topic.

Dr. Kenneth McFarland, often referred to as the "dean of public speaking," began exactly this way with General Motors. Bill Gove, the first president of the National Speakers Association, represented Minnesota Mining and Manufacturing (3M). Ira Hays began the same way with National Cash Register. Judith Briles is the spokesperson for Clairol products. The Canon Home Copier company hired Paul and Sarah Edwards, speakers and experts in the area of home businesses, to speak on television across the nation to promote Canon's products. This proved to be a perfect tie-in. While the Edwards' promoted the Canon copier, they inevitably promoted themselves and their seminars, as well. This sort of sponsorship creates winning situations for everyone concerned.

A sponsor company may be interested in using a speaker on a fee, per-head, or per-seminar basis. Jim McJunkin, a top sales trainer for a major typewriter manufacturing company, staged retail sales seminar programs on salary for the company's retail distributors. When he went into his own sales seminar business, he signed his former employer as his first client. Then he branched out laterally to companies in related fields. His income has shot up to $5,000 per day. His background and success with his last employer became the basis for his good reputation and success in the seminar world.

FIVE INGREDIENTS FOR
SUCCESSFUL SEMINARS

If you decide to create and market your own seminar to the public or to corporations, the following ingredients are essential for success:

1. Your seminar must appeal to a specialized market. In other words, it must have a niche, such as meeting the information needs of state income tax preparers.

2. You must develop a list of good prospects in your market. If you cannot identify a large potential audience or many companies that might want your seminar, you will not have enough buyers for your speeches and products. You might consider a high-priced seminar for a small market, or a lower priced one for a large competitive one.

3. The subject of your seminar must be something that the individuals and corporations in your target audience will need and want.

4. You *must* be recognized as an authority in the seminar's subject matter before you take the program to the marketplace. People want to learn from successful experts, not unknown orators.

5. You must develop good marketing skills and make astute use of direct mail, advertising, and promotion.

HOW TO REACH THE RIGHT SEMINAR PROSPECTS

We received a call for advice recently from a man who had lost more than $5,000 promoting a seminar that brought in only two registrants. His topic was "Making Money Fast," and the registration fee was just $25. He had bought expensive ads on the financial page of his local daily newspaper. He had guaranteed a large attendance and paid a high price for a seminar room in a very expensive hotel.

We believe he went wrong in his focus. First, his program and price did not appeal to the financial page readers, who probably thought both the title and fee were a con. If the fee had been $500, if his name had been known in financial circles, *and* if his title had been "Careful Investment Strategies," he might have obtained ten attendees and a profit. His title and price, however, were aimed at people with lower incomes, most of whom were not readers of the financial page.

He could have reached the right audience if he had used the

local talk shows for publicity interviews, advertised in the shoppers, and held the meeting at a lower-priced location. Also, if he had raised his seminar fee to at least $100, his title might have worked, and given him a profit, instead of a dead loss.

ADAPTING YOUR SEMINAR FOR CRUISES, RESORTS, AND OTHER SETTINGS

Cruise ships, exotic resorts, and other facilities dedicated to comfort and pleasure are an increasingly important marketplace for professional seminars and speakers.

Many new cruise ships with meeting facilities have been launched, so that conventions are booked on board cruise ships featuring four to five "enhancing" speakers per trip for regular vacationers. Many seminar subjects are offered to passengers: gourmet cooking, self-improvement, how to invest, and hundreds of other topics. There seems to be no limit to the subjects that cruise ship travelers enjoy in a seminar or speech.

One type of speaker who is popular aboard cruise ships is the "destination" presenter. This speaker's program topic ties in with the history of the destination or with the flavor of the cruise. For example, Eskimo culture is explored and explained during Alaskan voyages, while Britain's Crown Jewels are a popular subject on the cross-Atlantic run to London on the QE2.

Cruise ships usually pay money only to the evening entertainers, such as magicians, singers, and dancers. Speakers and seminar leaders typically work on a trade basis. They are given passage for themselves and sometimes a guest in exchange for presenting one or several sessions during the cruise.

Business and personal topics alike are popular with cruise-ship audiences. For example, Tom Leech, author and speaker on "How to Put on Meetings," has presented his subject while cruising across the Atlantic on the QE2. For presenting his seminar on a cruise, he traded for a $9,000 trip. Numerous speakers present their programs while sailing on the South Seas, traveling up the Amazon, or even stern-wheeling it up the Mississippi River.

You may obtain a list of cruise ships from a travel agent, or work with speakers bureaus who specialize in cruise bookings. To catch a cruise company's attention, tailor your area of expertise to the needs and interests of a cruise ship audience. Space futurist Paul Hanover's usual seminar topic is "Living in Space." When he aimed his program at a shipboard audience by changing his topic just slightly—to "Will Your Next Cruise Be in Space?"—he was snapped up by the QE2 for a voyage to London.

A one-man show, "Mark Twain" speaker performed during some of the Halley's Comet cruises to the South Pacific. The real Mark Twain, it was pointed out, had been born on one swing of the comet and died on its return.

Finding that special niche can make all the difference. Believe it or not, a speaker who presents a three-dimensional show on the sinking of the Titanic is constantly employed aboard cruise ships.

To put on your own seminar in a resort area, you proceed just as you would in arranging for one anywhere else. The resort lends itself very well to a high-priced, executive or family retreat program. Often these seminars are sold to individuals, or they can be sold to a corporation which wants to send a team of managers or engineers, etc., on an educational retreat.

The advantage to the attendee is a tax deductible mini-vacation, in addition to the valuable material he or she will learn in the seminar. Famous seminar leaders, such as Ed Foreman, offer seminars for executives in this manner. Often fifty to sixty attendees come to spend the weekend, be inspired, learn stress-reducing and health skills, and come away refreshed and inspired. Fees per attendee can be from $1,000 on up. Some executive seminar leaders include the hotel and food, others have the attendees pay for their own. These are usually scheduled for Friday evening through Sunday afternoon.

TAX TIPS FOR SEMINARS HELD ABOARD SHIP OR AT RESORTS

You may offer executive retreat seminars that can qualify as a double win: knowledge and tax deductions. However, the rules can get trickier when cruise ships or resorts out of the United States are involved. Before planning to sell such a seminar, you should check with the Internal Revenue Service and find out exactly what you must do so that your seminar registrants can qualify for a full or partial income tax deduction. Tax rules change each year, so be sure to update your material frequently.

TAKING ADVANTAGE OF A THREE-WAY PROFIT POSSIBILITY

You may be able to sell tickets to the cruise or rooms at the resort and make a markup on those, at the same time that you sell registrations to your seminar. You also can sell your products during the program, giving you a three-way profit possibility. The ingredients for success in this type of seminar are: (1) an enticing title and topic; and (2) a group of wealthy people who want a special program that will help them enhance their businesses or practices, and who might like to take their families along on the trip. Naomi and Jim Rhodes put on very successful dental seminars which are an example of this kind of program. The Rhodes' seminars are held in resorts, on cruises, and in beautiful hotels around the world. All of their materials, including their newsletter and catalog, are aimed at the dental world. Their seminar topics include business practices, patient relationships, selecting top employees, and training. For the dentists' spouse and children, they offer positive-thinking seminars. The Rhodes include their own children as seminar leaders for the young people. Their name has become a household word in their specialized field.

SEMINAR PUBLICITY TIPS

Once you have located a market for your topic, you then can begin working to make yourself familiar to your potential audience. For example, consider starting a newsletter aimed at your market. We publish *Sharing Ideas,* a large magazine. By means of our publication, we reach our target market on an ongoing basis. We carry features, interviews, news, and testimonials, all specifically for speakers, meeting planners, and speakers bureaus. The National Speakers Association took a survey recently of the top independent publications professional speakers read most. Number one was *Success Magazine. Sharing Ideas* was second. Because we are finely-tuned to our market, speakers put us ahead of *Inc.,*

Psychology Today, the *Wall Street Journal, Business Week,* and *Working Woman.*

We also publish an updated calendar of upcoming seminars in each issue, including locations. We find that listing the whole year's seminar dates is very beneficial. If you only advertise one date at a time, many people will not be able to attend. Giving them a choice increases the chance that they will register. In case of sickness or other unexpected event, a registrant unable to come on the date for which he or she originally signed up can have the opportunity to come to any of the cities where you offer your program on any of your other dates. Listing a series of dates also lets prospects know you are successful at what you offer. Our experience with direct mail shows that what works best is a series of three large postcards mailed to potential attendees in the geographical area where our seminar will be held. We give new information and an up-date on each card. We mail them three weeks apart to subscribers of *Sharing Ideas* and to our entire mailing list in each area.

Two companies who will list your public seminar topic and dates on a nationwide computer network are the Seminar Information Service, 17752 Skypark Circle, Suite 210, Irvine, CA 92714, and Skiebo, 44 Forster Ave., Mount Vernon, NY 10552. Many daily newspapers have a seminar section where you can advertise the seminars you sell to the public.

You may also want to consider trading mailing lists with others who offer seminars on topics related to yours. People are creatures of habit. If they will attend one paid seminar, they may be very interested in another on a similar subject. We find that people who attend sessions on how to present workshops or seminars are very interested in our seminar on "How to Enter the World of Paid Speaking." Trading mailing lists with other seminar leaders helps everyone.

TURNING PROFITS FROM KEY MAILING LISTS

The secret to profitable public seminars is good marketing. You can pull in responses and registrations by using direct mail to specific markets, newspaper advertising, and specialized magazine advertising in trade publications aimed at a particular market. Develop a mailing list of your own from every attendee and inquiry. We use our rating sheet at every seminar. At least 50 percent of our attendees give us referrals. We mention that person's name on our first mailing to the referral. We find that 75 percent of our seminar attendees come through recommendations from past attendees. Consequently, we use testimonials in every mailing and advertisement.

INVESTING IN SEMINARS FOR YOURSELF

Watching a professional seminar leader put on a full-day seminar is an excellent way to learn the topic they offer, and also to study their seminar techniques. Experienced national seminar leaders, such as consulting expert Howard Shenson, offer sessions on "How to Put on Seminars." He gives novice seminar leaders the benefit of his long and successful experience, while focusing on topics such as where to advertise, how to find the right mailing lists, and what locations and prices are best. Instead of relying on trial and error, you can shorten your learning curve by using the advice of people who know the business. Learning from the experts is called "P.F.O.P.E."—Profiting from Other Peoples' Experience. From them, you can learn how to pick out a location that will double your attendance and how to avoid pitfalls such as local holidays, parades, building remodeling, heavy rock concerts, and lawn mowing right outside your seminar window. Once you have selected a site, study the room setup and see how well it works with your particular kind of topic. Check out the refreshment and smoking policies, and how long and how often to allow for bathroom breaks. These details can be learned by attending seminars on how to put on seminars and also by attending any successful seminar. Take notes on ideas that make the seminar run smoothly and profitably. Then think of ways to apply the good ideas to your own seminar business.

8

Selling Your Programs to Meeting Planners

To succeed as a paid speaker, you must understand what professional meeting planners do and how they work. You also must make yourself known to as many meeting planners as possible. They are the buyers.

A QUICK LOOK AT THE MEETING PLANNING BUSINESS

A meeting planner is the person in charge of organizing a meeting, a conference, or an entire convention on behalf of an association or corporation. The association or corporation hires the meeting planner to plan and arrange the event. To get the job done, the meeting planner then becomes a buyer of services, including the services of professional speakers.

Today, more than 9,000 meeting planners are members of professional associations such as Meeting Planners International, the Professional Convention Management Association, and the Society of Company Meeting Planners. Easily double that number work in smaller companies or belong to other associations. Meeting planners book directly as well as through speakers bureaus and agents.

How Meeting Planners Book Speakers

Meeting planners choose from hundreds of speakers in one field, just as real estate buyers often have many choices of houses in one particular area. Just as a home buyer looks for exactly the right dwelling, a meeting planner searches for the perfect speaker for an event, meeting, or convention. To get a booking, you must convince a meeting planner that you are the speaker he or she is seeking.

How do meeting planners book speakers? The most popular ways were determined in a recent survey co-sponsored by the National Speakers Association (NSA) and the American Society of Association Executives (ASAE). Meeting planners were asked, "Where do you currently locate the speakers you book?" Respondents to the survey were allowed to check more than one means of locating speakers. Their responses were as follows:

Word-of-mouth and references	80.2%
Seeing speakers at other conventions	56.1%
Through speakers bureaus and agents	45.6%
Speakers brochures and marketing material	29.1%
Universities	24.1%
Current celebrity personalities	23.6%
Speakers directories and advertising	14.3%
Convention bureaus	6.3%

A meeting planner may decide to book you by using just one of the means listed above. But more often, a booking usually takes many seeds planted over a period of time to bear fruit. Getting a booking from a meeting planner is a cumulative process. Meeting planners may see your direct mail piece, then later read about you in a speaker's directory. They may notice an article you have written for their trade publication, then talk to other meeting planners who have booked you. Finally, a speakers bureau may call a meeting planner and ask for the special requirements of their group for a scheduled convention. The meeting planner describes what kind of speaker is needed, the speakers bureau suggests and recommends you, and "click," the meeting planner says, "That speaker sounds good. I have heard about that person."

The smart speaker uses every effective avenue to reach buyers. Thus, if you seriously plan to become a successful professional speaker, you must first become an expert on sales and marketing. Everything you do—how you prepare your business materials, how you handle your incoming and outgoing telephone calls, how well you keep in contact with your clients before, during, and after your performances—are all part of booking yourself. Meeting planners are your target market.

FOUR WAYS TO CAPITALIZE ON THE NEEDS OF MEETING PLANNERS

You should not neglect any of the pathways to bookings revealed by the survey. But here are four tips and ideas to help you capitalize on the top three methods used by meeting planners.

1. Take advantage of the meeting planners' reliance on "word of mouth and references" by using your rating sheets diligently. Ask your respondents if you may quote them right from the rating sheet. Letters of recommendation also can be very valuable. Send these endorsements in your press kit to meeting planners in fields appropriate for your program.

2. Since meeting planners say that they like to "see speakers perform at other conventions," you should invite meeting planners, speakers bureau representatives, and publicity sources to attend every program you offer. Make every performance a showcase.

   Be willing to do a program at no fee if it places you in front of the right buyers. At all conventions and meetings where you appear, leave a trail of handouts that buyers can follow back to you. (If the speaking date was booked by a speakers bureau, be sure everything you hand out shows the name and address of the *bureau,* rather than your own.)

3. Increase your opportunities by being aware of the meeting planners' reliance upon the advice and professional recommendations of agents and bureaus. Before every performance, be sure to invite bureau representatives to come and

"catch" you. (Ask permission of your meeting planner first and offer to pay for your guest's meal.) Work with as many non-exclusive bureaus as you can.

4. Print the following questions in bold letters on a sign and place the sign on the wall over your desk, "Why should they pay for my talk? What are the benefits they will receive? Which groups will benefit most from my program?" These are some basic questions of quality control and marketing that meeting planners will want answered.

Why Meeting Planners Choose Particular Speakers

The NSA/ASAE survey also illustrated why meeting planners choose certain speakers over other speakers. The meeting planners were asked to "rate the importance of the following attributes in making your choice of the keynote/principle speaker at your convention or major meeting." The attributes that they checked as "extremely important" or "very important" are as follows:

	Extremely Important	Very Important
Industry authority	51.2%	27.5%
Nationally recognized	32.4%	31.0%
Published	6.3%	9.3%
Has audio tapes	7.3%	5.3%
Is on video	6.4%	5.4%
Author of books	1.9%	5.3%

The Six Best Places to Locate Meeting Planners

Your success as a professional speaker can depend, to a great degree, on your willingness to woo meeting planners. The first step in the process, of course, is *finding* meeting planners. Below, we have listed what we consider the six best places to look for them.

1. *At the library.* Ask the reference librarian to assist you. There are local, state, and national directories for virtually

every kind of business and association. Write down the information you need. Or, better yet, copy the name and address of the company that publishes the directory, then write them and order a copy for yourself.

2. *In your audience.* One or more meeting planners may be watching and listening at your next speech. Ask for referrals to meeting planners on your rating sheets.

3. *Among friends and acquaintances of the meeting planner who is your current buyer.* Remember that referrals and word-of-mouth recommendations are the main avenue that meeting planners use to select speakers. Market yourself by asking for referrals from your meeting planner to other meeting planners.

4. *Among groups related to your current buyers.* Build your connections laterally. For example, if you have begun with banking, approach meeting planners for banks in the same company first, then meeting planners at other banks. Work citywide, then statewide, then nationally.

5. *Among businesses in related fields.* Keep stretching out laterally. After banks, to continue the example, the next step would be to try the meeting planners for financial planners, stock brokers, and other groups or organizations in the financial world.

6. *Right next to you.* Use the power of networking. You likely belong to associations, groups, or a church. Talk to the people you meet there and tell them what you do. They may be the door to the best series of engagements you have ever had. Always carry your business cards with you and exchange yours with theirs.

THE PROFESSIONAL APPROACH TO WORKING WITH MEETING PLANNERS

Many speakers tell us, "Don't ask me to sell myself to get bookings." But we know from long experience that you must be a good sales professional to have a thriving career as a speaker. The most successful professional speakers work hard at marketing, publicity, negotiating contracts, and closing bookings, as well as at speaking. The key area for sales involves meeting planners.

Meeting planners may be attracted to you by your performance abilities or by high-quality promotional literature. Or, they may have received some glowing recommendations from a speakers bureau. But most will insist on meeting you in person, and hearing and seeing you perform, before they book you. When you are to be interviewed by a meeting planner, go to the session dressed as a professional speaker. No one gets a second chance at a first impression. Your material and presentation must be tops, but you must look the part of a professional, as well. Follow these tips for best results:

1. You are not dressing for a cocktail party—no dangling earrings or loud ties.

2. Project a sharp, competent, business-like image. When you do not have to worry about your hair and your clothes, you can concentrate on the needs of the meeting planner.

3. If you have suggested that you and the meeting planner get together over lunch or dinner, you should pick up the tab. The meeting planner is your prospect. Never drink alcohol during the business meal. It lessens your chances of being sharp and may offend some meeting planners. Keep careful records of your expenditures. Much of the expense of the meal is deductible on your income tax.

4. Bring a big, yellow legal pad to the interview and take copious notes. Some speakers carry a small tape recorder and ask if they may tape the interview, because they want to prepare the program exactly the way the meeting planner wants it.

5. Ask gentle questions. Then, after you have listened to your client's needs, feed the information they have given you back to them, in different words. They might say, "We want serious content, nothing frivolous." You could reply in person and in your proposal, "I pride myself on the heavy content of my material, delivered with light humor."

6. Get the buyers to describe what types of programs have been especially successful in the past. This will help give you an idea of what they want. Ask what their goals are for this presentation. Then combine what they have given you with your own expertise and submit that as a proposal.

7. Make sure you have with you a few copies of your brochure, plus your press kit filled with all information, and your contract and proposal for the possible booking. Also have any other pertinent information with you at the site of the interview. You do not want to have to say, "Oh, I forgot to bring that." Such an oversight does not help you project an image of being professional and ready to work.

8. When you are face to face with meeting planners for the first time, do not brag about how good you are or how many speeches you have done. Ask about *their* accomplishments and needs. Focus on *them* and how you can help them. Many excellent books, albums, and talks are available that focus on different methods of selling and related skills such as how to read and use body language. You can study them all and improve your personal skills. However, we believe that one attribute is more important than all others in closing sales. It is the mind-lock of sincere interest in the buyer by the seller.

9. Use tact rather than too much frankness, especially at the first meeting. For example, if a meeting planner mentions that she loves dogs, do not respond with a true confession, "I hate those dirty beasts—they give me hay fever." Instead, keep the negative thought to yourself and try to say something positive that is also true, such as, "My mother has a darling dog, too." Then move on to something else. The trick is to get in the "me, too" attitude so that you and the meeting planner share some common ground.

10. Maintain eye contact. Be friendly and helpful. Smile. While it is great to be interesting, it is much more powerful to be *interested*. The most precious gift you can give a meeting planner, and the least expensive one, as well, is your full attention. In return, you receive the contract

you have been wanting: a booking that will help boost you into a long and prosperous speaking career.

Seven More Helpful Techniques for Making a Lasting Impression with Meeting Planners

Use the following techniques to sell prospective clients:

1. Repeat the meeting planner's name whenever possible during the interview. Everyone loves the sound of their own name.
2. Ask for their business card, make a note on it to yourself about what they want. Add a personal word or two about them that will trigger your memory and help you restart a personal conversation or send a follow-up inquiry later.
3. Ask them for a second business card. Even more important than giving them your business card, is getting theirs. We suggest you explain that you know someone who will be of assistance to them, or who needs them, and with their permission, you would like to pass the second card on. (Then do it.)
4. Use "power" words in your conversations with potential buyers. Some of the most "powerful" words are: You, Can, Guarantee, Proven, Easy, Quality, Urgent, Today, Save, Money, New, Opportunity, Win.
5. We have a sign in our office that says, "Four things hard to hide: Arrogance, Drunkenness, Selfishness, Insincerity." Each of these conditions show with glaring clarity. It will not matter if you are dressed for success or have the latest haircut if your attitude is false and self-centered. Current surveys show the era of "What is in it for me?" is over. Today's successful business people project the attitude of "How can I best help you?" Caring and sincerity are in.
6. You never know who you may meet or how important that person might be to your career. So we advise being interested in, kind to, and appreciative of, everyone you meet. The positive words opposite those four negative ones on our office wall are: "Sincere," "Aware," "Caring," and

"Thoughtful." Put them up on your wall. They are as full of golden business nuggets as the Rand mountains in South Africa.

7. Utilize the "professional" handshake when meeting prospective buyers. For best results, practice these techniques:

   a. Use a gentle, but firm touch that says, "I like you." Be careful of squeezing too hard—you could leave black and blue marks. Look down and see if the woman or man is wearing a ring. Don't cut their hand.

   b. Bring your other hand over and place it on top of theirs for a moment. It tells them you are concerned and listening.

   c. Let go quickly. Holding on too long makes people feel uncomfortable.

   d. Step forward and smile. That projects warmth.

   e. Look into the person's eyes and give the gift of full attention.

   f. Concentrate on answering the question, "How can I help and serve this person?" Project sincerity and caring.

CLOSING THE DEAL

One of the most important factors in closing any sale is to get the contract to the buyer. When a meeting planner expresses interest in booking you, mail the contract or send it by facsimile ("fax it") that day. Do not delay. Enclose a letter reviewing all of the terms and desires of the group. This one technique will close 50 percent more bookings than any other one we know.

Another useful technique for closing a sale is to show the client that you truly care about their interests. Stanley Marcus of Dallas' Neiman-Marcus store personified this attitude when he helped his customers to "invest" in elegant fur coats. "I want you to have it, you deserve it," he told them lovingly. He said he never met a customer who did not agree that they deserved and needed the best.

If the word "sell" bothers you, perhaps these six pointers will help:

1. The word "sell" comes from a Scandinavian root, "selzig," which means "serve."
2. To serve, you must think in terms of your prospects' needs and wants.
3. To learn what their needs and wants are, all you have to do is to ask them gentle questions.
4. Use Dottie Walters' four magic sales words: "Tell me about it."
5. Listen and take careful notes on what your prospects want.
6. Give them what they ask for—joyfully, gladly. You must *want* them to have the very best.

USING QUESTIONNAIRES TO DEFINE YOUR AUDIENCE

Once you close a booking with a meeting planner, you should begin right away to prepare for your program. A vital step will be to tailor your material to your expected audience. First, of course, you must find out *who* your audience will be and what are the expectations of the meeting planner who is buying your service.

To achieve these goals, many successful speakers send a questionnaire to the meeting planner well ahead of their scheduled appearance. An example of our questionnaire is included later in this chapter. Questionnaires take time to fill out and require several days to travel through the mail. But they are a valuable research tool that can help speakers and meeting planners achieve the best results. Consider using FAX transmissions instead of the mails.

Over the years, speakers' questionnaires have been growing in size. Today, several speakers boast that they request as much as eight pages of information from a meeting planner. Not surprisingly, many meeting planners who fill out speakers' questionnaires often complain that they already have given the speakers most of the same information over the phone. "Wasn't the speaker listening? What are we paying $5,000 for?" the meeting planners ask.

The questionnaire you design for your speaking engagements should not be so long that it becomes a burden to meeting planners. Before you send it, fill in as many blanks as you can, using the information the meeting planner has already given you. Then, if you need more details you can call the meeting planners and ask a specific question or send them a copy of the partially completed form and ask them to fill in the blank portions. If you use a computer to maintain your questionnaires, filling in the additional information you need can be simple. If you do not use a computer, it still should not take long to fill out the questionnaire by hand with the information you gather.

A SAMPLE SPEAKER'S QUESTIONNAIRE

To help you design your own pre-program questionnaire, here is a sample of the one that has proven very effective for Dottie Walters.

Pre-Program Questionnaire

This pre-program questionnaire is for Dottie Walters' presentation to

your group on _____.

We need your help! Dottie would like to specifically meet your needs with her presentation. Please take a few moments and give us the answers we need.

We have filled out the answers to the questions below to the best of our knowledge. Please doublecheck our answers and make additions and corrections. Fill in the questions we left blank. We were uncertain of this information and thought it best for you to provide it for us.

PLEASE: Send us any printed information on your group that may help us. Corporate report? News publications? Etc.

Return this questionnaire to:
Dottie Walters
PO Box 1120,
Glendora, CA 91740
no later than: _____

If you have any questions, call 818-335-8069

Presentation Title _____ Date _____

Time Frame? Start Time _____ End Time _____ Any breaks? _____

What is on the program just before Dottie speaks? _____

What happens on the program right after she speaks? _____

_____

_____

Appropriate dress code for presentation? _____

Conference theme? _____

Specific purpose of this meeting (awards banquet, annual meeting,

etc.) _____

Specific objectives for Dottie's presentation? _____

_____

_____

Sensitive issues that should be avoided? _____

_____

_____

Introducer's name? _____ phone #_____

Is there any publicity work Dottie can do for you while she is at your
event? Radio or television? Please let us know ahead of time, so we
can arrange travel. _____

_____

Who are the other speakers on the program?

Speaker _____ topic _____

Speaker _____ topic _____

Speaker _____ topic _____

What speakers have you used in the past that covered topics related
to the material Dottie will be presenting for you?

_____

_____

What did you like and/or dislike? Without their names if you would
like, but do comment on the material they used!

_____

_____

Name three main movers and shakers of your group that will be in Dottie's audience. With your permission we would like to contact them for more research information on your group.

_____ phone _____

_____ phone _____

_____ phone _____

What would make Dottie's presentation really "special" for your group?

_____

THE AUDIENCE

Number attending? _____ % of male to female _____

Spouses coming? _____   Average Age _____

Annual Average Income _____   Income range _____

Educational Background _____

Major job responsibilities of audience _____

DETAILS ABOUT YOUR AUDIENCE

Problems? _____

Challenges? _____

Breakthroughs? _____

What separates your high-performance people from others?

_____

TELL US ABOUT YOUR INDUSTRY

Problems? _____

Challenges? _____

Breakthroughs? _____

TELL US ABOUT YOUR ORGANIZATION

Problems? _____

Challenges? _____

Breakthroughs? _____

Significant Events? Mergers, relocations _____

_____

Will Dottie's presentation be taped? _____

If you wish, Dottie will make her educational materials available to your audience, so that they may continue the learning process at home. There are two ways this can be arranged. Please check the one that is the most appropriate for your group.

A. ___ Group purchase in advance for each attendee, at wholesale.

B. ___ Materials made available at the back of the room after the presentation.

IF YOU CHECKED "B," please make sure that:

1. Nothing will be on the program directly after her presentation and that there will be a break for at least 20 minutes.

2. A table will be made available for her to place her materials by the exit door.

3. Someone from your group will assist with sales.

TRAVEL INFORMATION

Location of presentation and venue name _____

_____

Address _____ Phone _____

Location at the site, room-rate, etc.? _____

Airport to arrive at _____

How will Dottie be transported from the airport to your site?

Taxi? _____ Rental Car? _____ Pick-up person? _____

Pick-up person's name _____ Phone _____

If an emergency occurs on the way to the site, who would be an alternate contact if you are unavailable?

Name _____

Business Phone _____ Home Phone _____

Other _____

SEVEN WAYS TO HANDLE "NO"

When a potential buyer tells you "no," you naturally will feel dejected for a while. It can help to remember the words of Bill Marriott, "Failure? I never encountered it. All I ever met were temporary setbacks." Nevertheless, a "no" does hurt. Take heart, there is a cure for rejection. Positive action. An old football coaching slogan goes, "Show me a good loser, and I'll show you a steady loser." We suggest that you not be a good loser. Instead, be a great retriever of "lost" situations. Here are seven tips to get you started:

1. The meeting planner may have wanted you, but was vetoed by someone else in the company. Assume this is the case and stay on their side. A speaker we know sends a little gift to every meeting planner who rejects him. "Hope you will keep me on your mind for next time," the card reads. Meeting planners often move from one company or association to another during their careers. They will remember how helpful and charming you were and will call you for another booking.

2. If you are rejected this time, call the meeting planner and say you hope the meeting will be successful and that he or she will think of you for another occasion. Mention that if anything should happen to the speaker they have chosen, you would be delighted to stand by. Many a stand-in has had a start when the star "broke a leg."

3. Call the planner when the meeting is over and ask how it went, or drop a card saying you hope all went well. Keep in touch. Make the meeting planner's success a great concern of yours. Remember, people who hire speakers do so again and again.

4. Ask the meeting planner who rejected you for a reference for a group he or she knows would be suitable for your material. Meeting planners know each other. Write thank you notes for leads.

5. Be like the friendly character in the poem by Robert Louis Stevenson, "Leary the Lamplighter." Leary went "posting up the street," lighting the oil street lamps each night. "You can always tell where Leary has been, by the warm

light he leaves behind him," wrote Stevenson. The story, illustrating leaving the lights lighted in peoples' hearts was one of the favorites of Dr. Kenneth McFarland, the famous General Motors speaker. Leave the lights of caring lit.

6. Speak well of other speakers. Never criticize. Talk only about the future. This is the way to leave a warm light on and the door wide open. Stay visible. Stay friends. Try again.

7. Generally, you must approach at least five prospects to sell one booking. On the four with whom you don't connect, leave the door open. Remember that a "no" now can turn into a "yes" later, particularly if you succeed in making a lasting impression. We often receive calls from buyers that we did not close with in the past. They remember our sincerity, hard work, and honest interest in their needs, even though they did not buy the services of a speaker from us the first time. A speaker who truly wants to build a successful, well-paying career will, as we do, always strive to keep the lights of goodwill burning.

The time will come when you will hear "yes" instead of "no." The same buyer who has just turned you down may welcome you in the future. People to whom we made unsuccessful proposals long ago now call to do business with us. Recently, a man from Australia called our bureau and asked us to take over the booking of all the speakers he uses there on a regular basis. He had been on our mailing list for more than five years. What happened? His situation has changed. He has new investors, and now he is ready to use us. It is a happy day when a "late bloomer" calls and tells you, "Now!" Stay expectant. Seasons change. Those seeds you planted will eventually sprout, and when they do, how delightful you will find the fruit.

HOW TO CHANGE REJECTIONS INTO BOOKINGS

When you are just starting out in the speaking field, you will hear the word "no" more often than you will hear the magic word "yes." How you respond to rejections can have considerable bearing on your success. If you get angry or feel defeated, you may overlook many opportunities to change a turndown into a booking or to sow some seeds for future appearances. The following is an example of how one professional speaker turned a rejection into a triumphant tour with return engagements.

Mike Podolinsky, whose seminar topic is "Customer Relations," planned a honeymoon trip to New Zealand and began marketing himself to groups there. At first, the hotel association turned him down. In their letter of rejection, they explained, "Our members own small facilities. They have a hard time coping with the big hotel chains."

Rather than being discouraged, Mike immediately sent back a proposition for training sessions on "How to Compete with Big Hotel Chains," a seminar on competitive customer relation strategies. He recognized the call for help in their refusal. By giving them exactly what they needed, he got the contract.

While in New Zealand, Mike also arranged to speak free to several business groups. He wrote ahead and invited the local bureaus and agents to attend. Because of his free speaking, he was able to arrange for thousands of dollars in "perks," as well. Not only was the magnificent honeymoon paid for, he also laid the groundwork for highly paid return engagements. He was on tour number two of New Zealand and Australia as we were writing this book.

The moral is: always adjust your proposal so that it fits the client's particular audience need. Be willing to change your material and terminology to suit the group you are addressing. Get the meeting planner to help you achieve the right focus. For example, dentists have "patients"; attorneys have "clients"; salespeople have "customers." Be aware of each group's problems and needs—and talk about them. Don't constantly refer to sales*men* if a group also has saleswomen. Use the term "salespeople."

However, you should not fall into the trap of thinking you can change your material and pretend to be an expert on something you are not. Know when to say, "Let me have my bureau call you to find an expert in that field." Then add, "When you need my topic and area of expertise, I will be pleased to serve you." You will be remembered and respected by meeting planners.

HOW TO KEEP YOUR EXPENSES WITHIN MEETING PLANNERS' BUDGETS

Meeting planners expect to pay for speakers' travel expenses, hotel accommodations, airport to venue transportation, meals, and all other reasonable "out of pocket" expenses in addition to the speaking fee. Therefore, be sure to include the phrase "plus expenses" on your fee schedule, your quotes to buyers, and your contracts.

Ask your client to describe their policy on first class or business airfares. Many Fortune 500 companies do not allow their own executives to fly first class. Do not insist that you must have better accommodations than their CEO. State on your fee menu schedule and your contract what your standard policy is. Remember, the more restrictions you put in front of a client or bureau, the harder you make it for them to book you. We have speakers who want us to obtain all sorts of special privileges and concessions. If we have another speaker who is equally as good and who does not create problems over the issue of expenses, our bureau will call that less-demanding speaker. Make it easy and simple for people to work with you—and they *will* work with you.

Some old-time speakers say, "I spend so much of my life in the air, I can't survive if I fly coach!" The presidents of major corporations likely are not going to fly coach either, but they charge coach expenses to the company and pay the differences themselves.

If you insist on flying first class, pay the difference between coach and first class, or use your frequent flyer points to upgrade. Ask for a clarification of the client's policy first, then make your arrangements. Always offer to adjust the airfare if you go on to another speaking date, or are coming back from one. Share the savings with both clients. You will be remembered and thanked for your consideration, and that can translate into future business.

Many new meeting planners see advertisements for supersaver fares, "Only two-hundred dollars round trip, California to New York." When you tell them you will pro-rate expenses, they may think they will be charged a third of the $200 super-saver they may be expected to share with two other clients.

Unfortunately, super-saver fares are rarely usable for professional speakers. Super-savers are non-refundable. They cannot be changed. And speakers often must make changes in their schedules. Such tickets usually are only good for round-trip flights. If you fly from one date to another, then on to two more, there is no way to use round-trip tickets. Even standard coach expenses often are based on a round-trip basis.

In reality, the meeting planner will get your bill for the buyer's share of the regular one-way flight. If the series of one-way tickets, even though pro-rated between many clients, is more expensive than if the client had purchased a full round-trip ticket with no other clients to split the expense, you have a problem.

One way to handle this is to not make the offer to pro-rate until your other speaking stops are set. If pro-rating will save your client money, call and tell them what you have arranged. Otherwise, accept the amount of one round-trip ticket from your location to the venue, then apply it to your total travel bill.

How to Achieve a Good Understanding on Expenses

Meeting planners tell many terrible war stories about ridiculous amounts of expenses submitted by speakers. Our personal philosophy is to go low on expenses, never high. As one way to reduce costs, as well as tension, we recommend that speakers carry packets of coffee and tea, and oatmeal bars, or other nourishing snacks in their bags.

When your plane is late, and you have half an hour to shower, dress and review your notes, you will be glad you do not have to wait for room service for a cup of coffee or tea and a strengthening bite or two.

Never charge your own business or personal phone calls to the client. Put those calls on your own credit card. It is permissible, however, to charge for clothes pressing services. But remember, no bureau wants to hear from an angry meeting planner who is upset because the speaker has overcharged on expenses.

To illustrate this point, here are some complaints we have heard from meeting planners regarding expenses charged to their corporation or association by speakers:

Dinner for one, $195, including an expensive bottle of wine.

Car rental, when the speaker lived only 45 minutes from the meeting site.

A $5-per-attendee "handout fee," when the handout was only a one-page flyer.

A $1,000 personal phone bill charged to a client on the tab for a speaker's hotel room.

Such extravagant expense billings make meeting planners and speakers bureaus disgusted and angry with the speaker. It kills any future business with that speaker no matter how good they are on the platform. We have heard meeting planners say that it is not so much the amount of the expenses but *the idea* of overcharging that rankles them the most. Meeting planners and the bureaus who serve them naturally will opt for other, more scrupulous and talented speakers on their rosters. When a speaker pulls overcharging tricks on expenses, he or she is dropped by the client and the bureau—and the word gets around. You should use the golden rule when listing expenses.

Three Tips for Achieving an Understanding on Expenses

1. Make sure the meeting planner knows well in advance what you will charge as fees and normal expenses.

2. When unexpected expenses arise, discuss them with the meeting planner and speakers bureau. Avoid last-second surprises. Meeting planners generally do not mind paying expenses, but they do mind unfair surprises. Speakers bureaus must be involved in disputes over expenses, because meeting planners hold bureaus responsible for the conduct of the speakers they recommend. Expenses are part of the contract the bureau negotiates with the client.

3. Keep careful records of your expenses. Some will be deductible from your income taxes. Those that the buyer will pay should be carefully listed on an invoice. A sample invoice for travel expenses is presented on facing page.

Travel Expense Invoice

For speech performed on _____ Event _____

Airfare Total _____ Prorated _____

Mileage:

From home _____ Taxi/limo airport to hotel _____

Hotel _____

Phone expenses at hotel _____
(only those calls related to this job)

Meal, date _____   _____

Meal, date _____   _____

Meal, date _____   _____

Meal, date _____   _____

Shipping of materials   _____

Other   _____

                         _____

    TOTAL   _____

George Walther, the famous telemarketing speaker, sends an excellent expense form to meeting planners. The first section tells his clients exactly how he arrives at their prorated airfare. The second section shows how much each client pays toward the total ticket price. Walther then highlights the savings in terms of both percentage and dollars, a touch that meeting planners especially appreciate. Here is his form: (next page)

I am committed to keeping your travel expenses as low as possible while still traveling first-class. I do this by utilizing discounted airfares in combination with low-cost upgrade stickers and certificates wherever possible and also prorate airfares when I schedule more than one engagement on a single trip. The following rather complex computation is a bit tricky to follow, but rest assured I have done my best to be very fair with your airfare allocation.

If you wish to decipher these computations, here's how they work: First, I check the current OAG (Official Airline Guide) to find out the regular, first-class airfare between Seattle and your city. Then, I do the same for all clients on a single trip. After totalling the first class airfares as if I had taken each trip separately, I determine what percentage of the total is fairly allocated to each client.

As you know, airfares often make little sense, but this is the fairest approach I have been able to devise.

Finally, I total the cost for the actual ticket I purchased, usually an unrestricted coach airfare, and add the cost of all upgrade certificates and stickers, to determine my total actual cost. Then, that cost is divided among the clients on a given trip according to their percentage of the total as shown below.

What this all boils down to, is that the billing I have included for you represents a substantial savings when compared with regular first-class airfare.

The complete computation follows:

Prorated Airfare Computation If Flown Separately

Client	Routing Basis	First-Class Round Trip*	Percent of Total
A	SEA-BOS-SEA	$1,402	25.4
B	SEA-DTW-SEA	1,386	25.2
C	SEA-FAR-SEA	1,154	21.0
D	SEA-ORD-SEA	1,566	28.4
	TOTAL	$5,508	100.0

As Actually Flown

SEA-BOS-DTW-FAR-ORD-SEA	$1,610.50
Upgrade stickers, coupons, and certificates	310.00
Total Actual Airfare	$1,920.50

Client Allocation

Client	% of Total	Airfare Billed	Airfare Saved	% Saved
A	25.4	$ 487.81	$ 914.19	65.2
B	25.2	483.97	902.03	65.1
C	21.0	403.31	750.69	65.1
D	28.4	545.42	$1,020.58	65.2
TOTAL	100.0	$1,920.51		

Source: March 1, 1988, Official Airline Guide

WHY YOU SHOULD BE THE "MEETING PLANNER'S ASSISTANT"

A good and caring attitude toward the work that meeting planners do will help you land future bookings. Once you are at the lectern speaking, you are the star. But in the minutes and hours before your appearance, as well as afterward, you should think of yourself as "the meeting planner's assistant."

While you are at an engagement, keep in mind that you are a contractor, paid to do exactly what the meeting planner has specified. The meeting planner's concern is to make the event smooth-running, pleasant, and beneficial for all who attend. His or her job depends on that outcome. Do everything you can to assist the meeting planner. Ask how you can help. If the meeting planner has to move some furniture, pitch in and help. If you need props or last-minute items for your speech, run your own errands. Be flexible if your time or room has to be changed. Never sulk or scold. **Assume things will go wrong, and cheerfully be ready to help make them go right again.**

Some speakers, unfortunately, do not adopt a caring attitude toward the needs of meeting planners. The problems they generate are reflected in the recent NSA/ASAE survey. When meeting planners were asked, "How often do you run into problems and concerns with the professional speakers you book for your meetings?" they responded as follows:

Problem	Always	Frequently
No opportunity to personally preview the speaker	5.9%	46.8%
Speakers not tailoring presentations to my specific group	6.4%	41.2%
Speaker doesn't respond to requests for pre-meeting information	6.4%	40.7%
Speaker too difficult to contact prior to meeting	3.4%	32.8%
Speaker concentrates too much on selling him/herself or a given product endorsement	2.0%	23.2%
Speaker won't give hand-outs	1.0%	21.9%
Speaker not accessible to members after session	2.5%	15.3%
Poor delivery by speaker	0.5%	14.1%

No matter how small the issue or item, strive to be known among meeting planners as a problem solver and a promise keeper. Never cause them to worry or wonder if they have made the right choice. Show them that they have chosen wisely, and they will reward you again and again with bookings.

9

The Advantages of Working with Speakers Bureaus and Agents

Once you are receiving solid fees for your bookings and spin-offs to speak elsewhere, it is time to consider the advantages of working with agents and speakers bureaus.

Agents and speakers bureaus offer professional speakers a variety of valuable services. They can handle many of the tasks that are difficult or impossible for an individual performer to accomplish without sacrificing some of his or her development as a speaker.

THE AGENT'S ROLE

An agent signs an exclusive contract with a speaker to handle all of the speaker's business. In most cases, agents are paid a salary by the speaker or a percentage of the speaker's income. Obviously, not every speaker can have an agent. The words "agent" and "celebrity" go together like ham and eggs. Agents usually do not work for noncelebrities. However, if you become a household name and are able to command speaking fees of $10,000 to $50,000 and above, you will have agents wooing *you.*

The agent represents the speaker in negotiations for speaking engagements. Often, the agent also handles the publicity for a speaker and arranges promotional articles, book publishing contracts, and radio and television appearances. Some celebrity speakers have agents who handle all of their business affairs, as well.

Agents occasionally call themselves "personal management companies." They help design speakers' brochures and demo tapes, and handle all other matters related to the speaker's bookings and other business. Some personal management companies work for a small stable of speakers, charging each of them two or three thousand dollars a month as a basic fee, plus all expenses of telemarketing and mailings, and a percentage of all bookings. Naturally, these companies promote and sell only the speakers who are paying members of their group.

Since you are not likely to attract an agent in the early phases of your speaking career, we will focus most of this chapter on the advantages of working with speakers bureaus. We will also show you the proper ways to develop a mutually beneficial relationship with as many bureaus as possible.

THE TWO TYPES OF SPEAKERS BUREAUS

As soon as your fee for a keynote presentation tops $1,000, you should begin to identify which commercial speakers bureaus match your topic and fee level. There are two types: (1) the community service or public service bureau; and (2) the commercial speakers bureau.

A community or public service bureau sends speakers into the nearby community to present programs at no fee, usually for public relations purposes. Community service or public service bureaus may be operated by large organizations such as hospitals, which send doctors or hospital executives out as speakers. The bureaus may also be operated by large companies, utilities, or political parties, which will offer their executives or leaders as free speakers to publicize their organizations.

The second type of bureau is the commercial speakers bureau. Commercial bureaus are much like travel agents. They are paid a commission only on the engagements they obtain for the speaker. Thus, they do not book free or low-fee speakers.

Unlike agents, commercial speakers bureaus are not responsible for the balance of a speaker's engagements, media interviews, mailing, advertising, training or coaching, or additional promotions. However, some speakers bureaus offer these services separately, and charge for them.

Commercial bureaus focus on selling speakers' services to their own client meeting planners. Commercial bureaus are similar to the employment "headhunters" who go on "search and find" missions for clients that are seeking skilled managers or executives.

Thus, when professional speakers talk about working with "bureaus," they usually are referring to the commercial bureaus, which book paid speakers on a non-exclusive basis. At present, there are approximately 350 non-exclusive commercial speakers bureaus in the world. Since they are non-exclusive, you can be listed with many bureaus. Each bureau develops its own niche of clients. A good way to build your speaking career and increase your opportunities is to constantly work on building relationships with bureaus who will book you. At the same time, you should keep your friendship and team spirit bright with the bureaus who already work with you, because they will continue to work with you.

THE HISTORY OF SPEAKERS BUREAUS

At the turn of this century, speakers bureaus sprang up in the United States to handle the booking business of star speakers. The Redpath Bureau of Boston was one of the earliest. Redpath brought Charles Dickens to America to give dramatic readings from his books, which he also autographed and sold at the back of the auditorium. Dickens sailed on one of the first Cunard vessels, a sidewheeler. The weather was so stormy, he wrote a story about his cabin being awash with a foot of water, and sold it to a magazine upon arrival. Thus, Charles Dickens spoke and wrote for money. He autographed his books to help boost their sales. Nearly one-hundred years later, this is the same procedure professional performers follow as they speak and grow rich.

The Redpath Bureau also booked Mark Twain, Winston Churchill, and many other celebrity speakers, including a woman who was billed as the "Joan of Arc" of the Civil War. The poet

Ralph Waldo Emerson drove down from Concord to Boston in his buggy to perform for Redpath. Emerson demanded a full $5 fee per performance, plus a special contract clause: "oats for horse." Today, professional speakers always receive transportation, travel and hotel expenses, paid by the groups who book them.

With the building of railroads in the United States, a new concept was born, the Chautauqua circuit. It began in 1874 as a series of adult education tent meetings on Lake Chautauqua in New York state and soon spread from coast to coast. Separate bureaus ran their own "circuits" of Chautauqua speakers under contract. The speakers and other performers appeared in tent shows along the railroad lines, moving on to a new town each day.

The Chautauqua speakers, lecturers, and entertainers were of a high moral caliber, which was important to audiences, because multiple season tickets could be sold in advance to entire families. Farmers saved all year to buy the precious Chautauqua tickets. P.T. Barnum, the American showman famous for his outrageous publicity stunts, spoke for the Chautauqua. His subject was the "Philosophy of Humbug." Barnum was a good speaker, as well as an expert on his topic. He also autographed copies of his books at the table at the back of the tent.

Chautauqua speakers earned fees ranging from $100 to $1,500 per program. The modern speaking term "circuit" started with the Chautauqua and still refers to a series of programs contracted with one speaker. After movies and radio appeared, the Chautauqua gradually died in the late 1920s, but not before its circuits had become a gigantic network covering all of the United States, Canada, Australia, and New Zealand.

The people who owned the Chautauqua circuits went into other forms of the business. Many of their children and grandchildren are in the speaking and speakers' bureau business today. The speaking business gets into the blood and stays there.

THE BUSINESS OF SPEAKERS BUREAUS

As you saw in Chapter 8, speakers bureaus are a very valuable resource to a meeting planner. Instead of having to call and screen speakers one at a time, the meeting planner can have the speakers bureau's expert counsel, and the availability and fees of hundreds, even thousands of speakers.

When you have become a professional speaker and are ready to work with several non-exclusive bureaus, you should always be willing to look at the speaking business through their eyes. A speakers bureau's greatest worry is the possibility of losing a client who books speakers through them on a regular basis. A bureau could lose this important source of sales just by booking one speaker who is not what the client wanted or who does not give a program that lives up to promises. If the speaker bombs, the meeting will be a disaster. The meeting planner who accepted the speakers bureau's recommendation will not be a hero to the association or corporation who pays their salary. In fact, their job might be in question.

Thus, the reputations of both the speakers bureau and the meeting planner are on the line with every speaker. The meeting planner wants a great program, plus a pleasant, cooperative speaker. The speakers bureau wants satisfied clients. This is why bureaus not only search for the most talented speakers they can find, but they also watch closely for speakers who possess two other qualities: the ability to be client pleasers and team players.

Therefore, you should not be surprised when a bureau says it wants to get to know you and learn more about your character and reputation before it adds you to its list of speakers. Representatives of the bureau also will want to review your program in person before they agree to represent you and will carefully check your credentials and your client and other bureau recommendations.

With this in mind, you can use a simple technique to make yourself and your expertise known to speakers bureaus. When you have a booking in a particular city, be sure to invite local bureau representatives to come and hear you. Remember, the bureau representatives will be doing more than just watching your performance and the audience reaction. They also will want to know what kind of a business person you are. They must be sure you are a person of integrity and dependability, as well as talent.

HOW BUREAUS LIST SPEAKERS

Speakers bureaus list you by your expert topic and by the amount of your fee. Since bureaus list hundreds, or in many cases, thousands of speakers, topic is virtually the only way to keep track of who does what.

Beginners often call a bureau and say, "I'm a terrific speaker. I can talk on ANY subject." However, the clients of speakers bureaus do not want random oratory. They want expertise! It is crucial to your career that you develop a specialty.

IMPROVING YOUR PACKAGING SO BUREAUS CAN BOOK YOU

Speakers who come to our bureau for professional advice usually have many skills, but often, they do not have the "packaging" they need to make them look like the experts they really are. To succeed as a professional speaker, you must have a solid, attractive business package that includes a professional-quality press kit, good demo tapes, and a fee schedule. Your business package also will make all the difference to bureaus in their efforts to close bookings for you. For example, Floyd Wickman, whose topic is real estate sales training, increased his speaking business income by over $200,000 the first year after speaker packaging expert Nat Starr (Nat Starr Speaker Packager, 2396 Atlas Dr., Troy, Michigan 48083) designed his business materials. They included press kits, demo tapes, letterhead, contracts, envelopes, labels, business cards, and the cover design for his audio cassette album. The colors, designs and type all synchronize, creating a professional package to match his professional presentation.

You cannot book yourself for high fees, nor expect bureaus to consider booking you, if your materials are shoddy. We are always flabbergasted by speakers seeking bureau representation who write to us in pencil on yellow-lined pads. Their competition has full-color press kits with beautiful foil accents. Bureaus need good tools from you before they can get good bookings.

As you saw in Chapter 3, it is the speaker's responsibility to create these tools, and provide them to the bureaus and clients you book directly. Without them, you put the bureau in the position of being asked to dig a ditch without a shovel. Bureaus are like manufacturers' sales representatives. They must have attractive catalogs and samples to do a good job of selling your programs.

If you are serious about wanting to speak and grow rich, you must work to create materials that project the image of a million-dollar speaker. It does not matter how good you are or how good the bureaus think you are. They absolutely cannot work for you unless you give them the tools they need.

HOW BUREAUS BROKER WITH AGENTS

When a client asks a commercial bureau for a celebrity speaker who is signed with an exclusive agent, the bureau contacts that agent. The bureau arranges to "broker" with the agent. Brokering means that the bureau and agent share the commission. The International Group of Agents and Bureaus holds a "Brokering Fair" at its conferences. Each agent or bureau tells about its exclusive speakers and gives out "one-sheets" with the speakers' pictures, descriptions, fees, and demo tapes. Other bureaus are invited to book the speakers on a brokering basis. This system is similar to the multiple listing service used by real estate agents.

Occasionally, an otherwise non-exclusive bureau will sign an exclusive contract with a speaker. Sometimes, bureaus carry "partially exclusive contracts" with speakers. These contracts cover specialized geographic areas or markets. A speaker may have ten, fifty, or one hundred non-exclusive bureaus working on bookings with different clients at the same time. However, the first bureau that calls the speaker for a date is given the privilege of closing the sale.

SERVICES OFFERED BY BUREAUS

Speakers bureaus offer many types of services to professional speakers. Some perform management services. Some are meeting planners themselves. They produce an entire convention or conference for their client associations and corporations. In this case, the speakers bureau books all of the speakers, entertainers, and music for an event. For example, our bureau frequently books as many as ten speakers for one convention.

We, and many other speakers bureaus, also offer training and consultation work for both speakers and meeting planners. Some bureaus provide advertising, public relations, packaging, and other services for a fee.

For example, a number of bureaus produce matching "one-sheets" for each of the speakers they represent. They will print one for the speakers they choose to represent and mail it to their clients. The charge to the speaker for this service and material typically is about $800.

Some bureaus and agents will produce a videotape of your presentation for approximately $5,000 or an audio cassette tape for approximately $1,000.

Many bureaus also provide the speaker an opportunity to participate in a showcase presentation. The speaker often pays a fee to appear on the program. All bookings generated by the event go through the bureau which stages the showcase.

Four Key Questions to Ask a Bureau

When contacting a bureau for the first time, you should ask four key questions. These questions will help you determine if there is indeed a match between what you can offer and what the bureau needs. The questions are as follows:

1. Do you specialize in certain kinds of speakers? Some bureaus deal exclusively with special types of speakers, such as sports figures, entertainers, politicians, religious figures, and even race car drivers and pilots.

2. What are the average fee levels of the speakers you book? Some bureaus specialize in lower-priced speakers, while others focus their business on speakers who command high fees. If your fee is $2,000 for a keynote, and their average speaker is booked at $10,000 per performance, you are approaching the wrong bureau.

3. What are your requirements? All bureaus will want to examine your professional demo tape, press kit, audio albums, books, publicity, fee schedule, and other items. However, many bureaus have additional requirements, as well. Some typical requirements are listed below.

   - A registration fee ($350 is not uncommon) is required by some bureaus.
   - A number of bureaus charge speakers a yearly or monthly fee, which may cover services such as publicity and packaging.

- Annual speakers' directories are produced by some bureaus. If you are accepted by such a bureau, you will be asked to advertise in this publication. Each speaker pays for his or her advertisement (usually $200 to $300). The advertisement works for you all year and costs less than printing, postage, labor, and the mailing lists you would pay for if you sent out your own materials. The fact that the bureau has accepted you for its directory is also viewed as an endorsement.

- Bureau representatives will want to see you perform in person so they can judge your professional ability. One way to get the attention of bureaus who match your fee and topic is to invite local ones to review you each time you perform.

- Some bureaus offer review services or "directors notes" for a fee. These are a splendid way to obtain coaching and expert advice. A bureau may review your performance and tell you that you need to work on certain areas before you are good enough to rate a substantial fee. If this happens, study the findings, work hard to improve, then invite the bureau back to hear you again. Remember: bureaus work constantly with meeting planners and know the market.

4. What is your method of doing business? Bureaus and agents charge different percentages. Also, they each have their own manner of paying speakers. Ask in advance so that there will be no misunderstanding about how they do business. If the bureau uses a contract with speakers as well as with meeting planners, ask for a copy of this contract. Study the terms and be sure all are agreeable in advance. Do not wait until you are booked by a bureau to ask them how they will handle the payment.

SPEAKERS BUREAUS AND COMMISSIONS

Whoever books a speaker receives a commission, just as a sales representative for a manufacturer is paid for the orders he or she obtains. In the past, speakers often told their agent or bureau, "I want to net a certain price for this job. It's none of my business how much you add on top for yourself."

Today, many non-exclusive bureaus will not book speakers who ask them to "add on" to their fee in this manner. Over the years, the practice of adding on has caused problems and created many "war stories" in the speaking industry. Here is an example of how adding on works. A bureau asks a client, "What is your budget?" After the client answers "$10,000," the bureau then calls the speaker and says, "How much do you want to do this job?" The speaker says, "I want to net $5,000." The bureau then calls the client and says, "Okay, you've got your speaker for $10,000." That is "adding-on." The speaker gets $5,000, and the bureau keeps the rest. With add-on speakers, agents and bureaus charge the buyer whatever the traffic will bear.

Eventually, however, the meeting planner client will find out that he or she has paid $5,000 more for that speaker than their meeting planner friends have paid. Naturally, the meeting planner then becomes angry at the bureau and spreads the word that a bureau did them wrong. This hurts the business of all bureaus.

Adding on often is mentioned as the main reason that only 25 percent of all speeches in the past were booked through agents or bureaus. With the new policy where agents and bureaus refuse to work with add-on speakers, that low percentage is rapidly improving.

HOW TO BE A GOOD INVESTMENT FOR SPEAKERS BUREAUS

Since the client is the most valuable part of a bureau's business, speakers ask bureaus to take a risk each time they book them. The bureau has advertised, sent out mailings, made thousands of phone calls, and worked hard in many other ways to obtain the trust of its clients. In short, they have made a big investment in each client. They always want to please their clients so they will continue to use the bureau's services on a regular basis.

To protect their investment, speakers bureaus need speakers who understand the importance and fragility of this relationship. The bureaus need speakers who understand that they, too, represent an important investment.

If you are pleasant to work with when dealing with the bureau, the bureau will tend to trust you to treat their clients in the same way. This is an important advantage toward getting bookings. There are many speakers who speak on your subject. It is a competitive market, and clients are hard to find. As many as twenty speakers a day call every bureau office. If you can make a match with a bureau, you have secured a wonderful business partnership. If you can work on a team of twenty non-exclusive bureaus who book you for the first year at $1,000 for just one program per month, you will gross $20,000 monthly. That makes a gross annual income of $240,000.

Novice speakers often feel bad when they call bureaus and are turned away. Many new speakers have no idea that they are asking the bureau to make a large-dollar investment in someone with no experience or track record. One inexperienced speaker who had never performed for a fee called a bureau, demanded a number of services, then also asked for a $2,000 cash allowance to live on until the bookings began!

No bureau will put up thousands of dollars for a novice speaker's career. You must develop your own professional business tools and skills. When you are good, have developed fine tools of the trade, and are earning a fee of at least $1,000 per program, you are ready to begin to woo the bureaus.

SUPPORTING THE BUREAU AND PLEASING THE CLIENT

Too often, when working with a speakers bureau, a speaker is focused on just one thing: the immediate date under discussion. He or she wants that booking at all costs. A speakers bureau, however, looks at a much bigger picture. They want to book all the slots at that convention, and all slots for the next twenty years at all their client's meetings. Then they want this client to refer their bureau to their meeting planning friends.

A speaker who is booked by our bureau, then neglects to help us secure the goals we have just listed, is not a good investment. Speakers we work with most often promote our bureau as we promote them. We think of this kind of speaker as one who pays us dividends on the time and effort we invest in them. They are team players. We reach for their telephone numbers first when working on a date.

For example, speaker Gene Harrison has attractive tent cards printed at his own expense, which he places at each attendee's place when he conducts a seminar or a keynote we have booked for him. The cards read: "Thank you for inviting me to be your speaker. If I may serve you again, in this organization, or in any other in which you hold membership, I will be grateful. If you need any other kind of speaker, please call my bureau, Walters International Speakers Bureau." He lists our address and phone number, not his own. Since Gene works with several bureaus, he no doubt has similar cards printed with their names and addresses, too. He takes along the ones printed for the bureau who obtained the booking for him. He is a great investment for any bureau who books him.

Other speakers print our name and phone number on all of their handouts, promotional materials, and giveaways. Any speaker who takes the time and trouble to work with a bureau in this way makes sure that he or she is a gilt-edged investment.

When our speakers are great on the platform, professional, pleasant, cooperative, and promotion minded, we can count on receiving at least five additional bookings from that date. The original meeting planner will re-book, as will several others who are in the audience. We record the number of additional bookings the speaker brings us from each performance.

It is essential that all three parties involved in a potential booking—the speaker, the bureau, and the client—work as a united team. As a professional speaker, whenever you talk to a client about a bureau, you should do your best to help promote and instill confidence. Promote the idea that by using your bureau they will get the best service possible. And remember that both you and your bureau work for the meeting planner client. Whatever the client wants and needs is the first consideration. The client is king.

Unfortunately, correct procedures and ethics are not always clear between speakers and bureaus, sometimes through a misunderstanding of how the system works. Here are some problems and workable solutions:

Problem #1: Loyalty to Bureau

The question of loyalty to our bureau by a speaker has come up twice in our experience with new clients—with opposite results. In the first case, we had worked a long time to get to the point of booking a specific date with a new client. A bureau often invests at least $1,000 in time, postage, advertising, long-distance calls, attending meetings, and other means, while searching for a new client. We suggested Speaker #1 who had just signed with us, for this new client. His topic was ideal for our new client's needs. We looked forward to a long association of booking many more dates for this speaker to the client and other clients.

Then the client asked to talk to our speaker directly, before the contract had been signed. We gladly gave him the speaker's number, believing the speaker would be delighted to help us close this first booking. The new client said to the speaker, "Do we have to use a bureau? Can't you cut your price if you and I work together?" The speaker replied, "Once a bureau or agent gets involved, I don't have any choice. I am stuck. We have to work through the bureau. If I don't, all of the other agents and bureaus will get mad at me. They know each other."

This speaker had the opportunity of selling our new client on the advantages of having bureau back-up, selection, negotiation, and speaker knowledge free through using professional services. He also had the opportunity of receiving not only this first booking, but many, many more through our efforts. Instead, he implied that it was better to go around us, his own "sales rep," and that he preferred it that way.

That speaker did not receive the booking from us. We booked the date for another speaker. Who told us the story? The client, when he called to ask us for someone else. He found Speaker #1 was disagreeable and dishonest in other ways. We immediately pulled Speaker #1 from our files. He had killed the golden goose of our bureau bookings.

On a different occasion, here is how Speaker #2 handled a very similar situation. When the client asked for a cheaper price if they could "bypass" the bureau, Speaker #2 answered, "My professional fees are always the same, if you call me or my bureau. So their tremendous service is free to you. I would not do you a favor if I went around my bureau. Using them is a great advantage to you. They have several thousand speakers available on every possible topic. They always look out for your interests. If something happened to me, they would have a back-up speaker there for you immediately. They chose me for you out of hundreds of possibilities because they are good at making the right match."

We know Speaker #2 told our client this, because the client was so impressed with the speaker's honesty and integrity, he called and told us. We book Speaker #2 several times a month—forty-eight bookings a year from us amounts to about $144,000 in gross bookings a year. We know he is popular with several other bureaus, too. He is a team player and a good investment for his bureaus. Speaker #2 takes good care of golden geese.

Problem #2: The Touchy Business of Spin-offs

A spin-off is a booking which a speaker receives from a company whose representative happens to be in the audience while the speaker presents a program for another client. Spin-offs are a touchy area with bureaus and speakers. Bureaus feel speakers owe them a commission on spin-offs, even if the buyer calls them directly. There is nothing that pleases a bureau more than to have a speaker call and give them a new client through a spin-off.

Most bureaus want spin-off clients directed through them. A few small bureaus want the speaker to handle the contract and send them a commission. In our case, we want all such business to be transacted by our bureau, because we try for several other speaker bookings at the same event. Ask each bureau you work with how they want spin-offs handled, and keep careful records of all such bookings.

Problem #3: Handling the Repeat Engagement

If the same client, or another branch of that client, invites you back for another engagement, it is referred to as a "second time," or "repeat engagement" booking. Some bureaus expect their full commission on repeat bookings, while others expect only a partial sum. All agree, however, that a commission is owed to the bureau that booked the speaker originally. To avoid misunderstandings, you should ask each bureau you work with how they want to handle repeat business. Most will want you to direct the buyer back through the bureau for negotiations and contracts.

When you are called directly by the buyer in any situation where a bureau is involved, you should make the client feel comfortable and negotiate in a way that is best for the client. But you should close the deal by saying, "Now that that's all settled, I will call my speaker's bureau to set up our contract."

This makes the client happy, because you gave them your attention, and your bureau happy because they can again sign a contract with their client. It also gives the bureau that important option of booking other speakers as well for the same meeting. Another aspect is that this transaction tells the bureau you are to be trusted, and that trust certainly makes them think of you when the next call comes in.

Problem #4: Keeping Track of Leads

When you work with many speakers bureaus, a system for accurate lead tracking is essential, if you wish to maintain and build golden relationships with those who obtain bookings for you. Lead tracking means that you must keep scrupulous records of incoming calls and be sure to ask, "How did you hear about me?" then carefully recording and processing the answer.

If the lead has occurred because of something done by a speakers bureau, you should collect the information, then turn the contract-writing over to the bureau that made the solicitation with this client.

If the lead did not occur because of a bureau, you still need to know how it originated. Then you can begin to get an idea of which method of advertising or promotion is bringing you the best results.

In our own lead-tracking efforts, we like to use a form which puts the origination question right at the top. We also are very careful to send a thank you card to friends and business associates who give us referrals. Those cards go out the same day that we get the referral.

Unfortunately, some speakers do not keep records on how their business originates. It is always tempting to just grab an inquiry, but that is a very short-sighted approach. One speaker who wanted our bureau to book him told us, "I can't be bothered asking people how they heard about me." Afterward, he couldn't understand why we were not interested in working with him. As long as you practice the right attitudes and take the honest approach to the speaking profession, many friends, meeting planners, and bureaus will continue to refer business to you.

Problem #5: Scheduling and the Bureau

When a bureau calls you to discuss a possible booking, they disclose the date under consideration. You are asked to put a "hold" on that date. Sometimes, however, the client must have board meetings on the matter, so nothing may result immediately from these efforts. The bureau may work on one booking for you for more than a year.

In the meantime, the meeting planner may be fired or promoted. A new meeting planner then comes on deck, and the client's needs may change. Finally, the client decides to book you, but calls you directly after looking at the materials and letters the bureau or you have mailed.

If you have kept good records, you will know what is happening and to which bureau you should turn to complete the booking. You should keep your records in duplicate and filed by the meeting planner's name, by the company name, and by the date of the program. This may seem like too much, but it is not. Meeting planners often move from place to place. Companies and associations sometimes change their names. But the date record will remain intact and give you another chance at retrieving the correct information. You will then be able to give the inquiry back to the bureau that has worked so hard to sell you.

Our bureau pays commission checks to speakers who refer clients to us. We have a database that keeps track of exactly how every client first heard of us. We always ask "How did you hear about us?" because we believe in rewarding and thanking people. When the reply is, "Oh, somebody told me about you"; we say, "We want to send them a thank you. May I hold while you get me their name or number?" It takes just a few seconds of gentle probing to find out, but the information can mean a great deal to your reputation and success in obtaining additional business.

Problem #6: When Two Bureaus Work on the Same Booking

If several bureaus work for you, record keeping is even more important. Some meeting planners call several bureaus at once. They ask each bureau to make ten suggestions to them. If you do not keep records of who suggested you for which job, the bureaus can cross paths over you. You could even have two, three, or four bureaus suggest you for the same job. Then the bureaus will fight over who got to the client first.

When this happens, the only fair thing is to hold the date for the bureau who called you first. Your records should show whose inquiry was first. Then, when other bureaus call you questioning your availability on this date for the same buyer, you should tell them that you have already made a commitment.

Some bureaus do not want to let you know the name of their buyer until the deal is a sure thing. So if another bureau calls you for the same date, but you don't know the name of the buyer involved, let the new bureau calling know what the problem is, then try to get a clear date from the first bureau. If it is not the same buyer, but the first bureau's buyer is just being slow about making a decision, you can tell the first bureau that you can only hold that date for another week. After that, you can give the date to the second bureau. This gives the first bureau a chance to close the sale.

Problem #7: What to Do When a Bureau "Comes In Behind You"

Often, when a new client calls our bureau, they say, "Find out about Speaker X for me." We call Speaker X and learn that he himself has been trying to sell to that same client. Or, he has already been hired by that client in the past, but there apparently has been a change of meeting planners. Does Speaker X owe our bureau a commission when we close this booking?

The first time this situation happened, the speaker was Nido Qubein. We told Nido not to worry, that we would back out of the deal. But he insisted that we work on it for him. He insisted that he pay us the standard commission. He felt our recommending him and closing the sale was commissionable. This same situation since has happened to our bureau repeatedly, with hundreds of other famous, successful speakers. At first, we thought this situation seemed unfair. The speakers were asking us to work on their own clients and prospects. Then we realized that they were hoping we might be the added touch that could close the deal. The "plus element" we provided was worth the price of our commission to them. It was also a strong step in cementing our speaker-bureau team into a solid, permanent relationship with a view toward many more golden eggs.

Problem #8: Why Closing Bureau Doors Is Not Profitable

We once called Speaker Y and told him about a booking we were working on for him. We always reveal the name of our client. He told us he had mailed a brochure to this client a year before. Then he said, "I'll just take this booking over. You back out."

We hung up. Then we called our client back and immediately booked another, equally qualified speaker for them. We pulled Speaker Y from our files. The golden goose was dead.

Remember: When a client is still talking to bureaus about other possible speakers, and the contract for you is not yet signed, nor the deposit paid, you do not have that booking. Speaker Y told us with his actions that he did not want to be on our team. It is better to invest part of your fee on a commission to a bureau than to lose all of the fee to another speaker or another bureau and their speaker, and lose the goodwill and future bookings from the bureau, as well.

In addition, the goodwill created by speakers who behave as Nido Qubein and many others do, is bound to land them many more bookings. Beginning performers do not realize that bureaus have many choices of speakers. When all other things are equal, such as ability and content, the speaker who cooperates most effectively with the bureau is the natural choice. Good relationships with solid, ethical bureaus can do a lot for your speaking career. When you find bureaus you can trust, look for good reasons to give them commissions. They, in turn, will reward you with bookings.

A SAMPLE AGREEMENT BETWEEN SPEAKER AND SPEAKERS BUREAU

Once a speakers bureau or agent is willing to represent you, you will be asked to sign an agreement or contract. Below is an example of the agreement we sign with speakers. The signing occurs only after we have seen them perform in person, after they have provided us with all of the tools of the trade, after we have checked their references, and after we feel they are suitable for our clients. Each bureau and agent has its own contract. (See facing page.)

SPEAKER'S AGREEMENT
Walters International Speakers Bureau

Billing, Fees and Terms

1.   Walters International Speakers Bureau (referred to as WI) will receive a 25% commission, paid from your standard fee, on all engagements booked for you. The gross fees you give us to quote must be
the same as the ones you quote when other clients call you direct.
We will not add our commission to the top of your standard fee.

2.   You will honor fees we have quoted for you if you have agreed
verbally by phone. You agree not to raise your fee for that particular
client, for that date.

3.   WI will issue the contract and handle negotiations with all
clients.

4.   WI sends the booking contract to the client. The client pays 25%
down to WI to secure your hold on the date. This is referred to as the
"holding deposit." The 25% is also our commission. The 75% balance
is paid to you directly on the day of the presentation by the client.
You agree to send a bill to the client for expenses, ahead of the date
if possible, and no later than a week after the performance.

5.   We will send a reminder of your speaking date and the terms of
the contract to the client 10 days before the program. We will send
a copy to you.

6.   You agree to provide us with your current fee menu for each type
of presentation you offer. If you offer a discount for additional programs at the same event, or a discount if a minimum purchase of
products is included in the contract, you agree to indicate how these
discounts apply so that we may negotiate on your behalf. You agree
to notify us at once of any changes, and to honor all commitments to
clients made before the changes are received at our office.

Expenses

7.   You agree to make your own travel arrangements, unless the
client wishes to do so themselves. (We will notify you of the client's
wishes.)
You agree to submit vouchers and bills for reimbursement.

8.   You agree to inform us of your travel requirements before we suggest you to a client, so that we may include them in the contract. (Many clients will not allow first class air.)

9.   You agree that all travel expenses shall be pro-rated with other clients on the same speaking trip, whenever the pro-rating will offer an advantage to both meeting planners involved.

10.   You agree to travel and food expenses for one person only, unless approved by WI and the client before the contract is issued.

11.   You agree that you will not charge any personal or outside business long-distance phone calls or liquor to the client.

12.   If you charge our client for anything other than coach air, airport taxi, and two moderately priced meals (if needed), such as any other expenses or handout materials, you agree to advise WI before we send out our booking contracts. These items must be included in the contract. Our 25% commission is not charged for any transportation or meal expenses.

13.   You agree to let us know immediately if you do not receive your check from the client at the booked engagement. WI will follow up and assist with the collection process. If there is any problem on the collection of your fee because the client goes out of business, you will receive 75% of any amount (including the deposit) WI has received. This does not apply to a client who refuses to pay because of clause #32 in this contract.

14.   If the booking date is canceled, and WI has already collected a deposit, we will send you 50% of what we have collected for holding the date.

Promotional Materials, Correspondence, Follow Up

15.   You agree to furnish us with one set of the following items: Professional demo tape before a live audience, professionally produced; a full audio program of your work; your professional press kit, brochure, photos, testimonial letters, fee schedule, and reprints of appropriate articles you have written. You also agree to have many sets of these same materials ready to send to prospective clients as we request them for bookings.

16.   We will call you to clear a booking date and confirm the fee on each prospective client and/or engagement. You then discuss any negotiation of multiple fees, products, etc. You will give us approval to proceed with this client on your behalf. We send you written confirmation of our conversation, with the prospective client's name, address, and phone.

17.   We will often ask you to send your press-promotional package to the client, from your office. We will supply you with our labels and business cards to place on your brochures and promotional materials, covering any place your own address appears. You agree to place our labels on materials you mail to our clients.

18.   You agree to send your package of materials to our client the day we call you. If you are away on the road, you agree to make arrangements for someone else to send your package out promptly.

19.   You agree to send our client a personal letter in your package, stating you have been requested by WI to send your material. You will ask them to call Lilly Walters at Walters International Speakers Bureau, (818) 335-8069, if they have any questions.

20.   You agree to copy us on all correspondence with our client at all times.

21.   You specifically agree to not call our clients, or prospective clients without checking with us first. We call our clients frequently to follow up for you.

22.   Our policy is to have you speak to our client directly as soon as it is appropriate, but only upon our specific request. Sometimes we need your assistance to help us "close" the booking. However, often a client uses our bureau because they don't want to talk with multiple speakers "up front." We always do what makes the client most comfortable. We expect your full cooperation.

23.   Clients often want an immediate answer on availability and contract terms. You agree to maintain an answering service or other means of reaching you promptly. You agree to return our call on the day we place it.

24.   You agree to send out your materials to our client on the day we call you. Delay can mean we both lose the booking. (We are competing with other bureaus and their speakers.)

25.   If the client decides you are not the speaker they want for this engagement, we will notify you by mail immediately, so that you can take our temporary hold off the day.

26.   If our client decides that they want you, we will call you immediately with the confirmation of the booking. We will send a contract to the buyer and copy you when it is returned to us. We guarantee full disclosure to you.

27.   If the client decides to book you, you will send a photo and bio to them and a short description of the talk you are planning for them, or any other information the client requests.

General Etiquette

28.   You agree that you will not give out the name of our client or information about their future speaker needs with other speakers or bureaus.

29.   If you receive a letter of recommendation from one of our clients, you are not to use it in any promotional material to other bureaus or speakers.

30.   If a prospective client calls you direct, we ask that you always answer their questions regarding your relationship with us. You may discuss your fees with them. This is appropriate because we will never quote different fees than those you quote yourself.

31.   Once you or your office has given your commitment verbally to WI by phone to hold a date for a client, we will negotiate in your behalf. You will not release this date for other buyers, bureaus, agents, your own personal business or for any other reason without checking with us first.

32.   You will engage in no vulgar language, dirty jokes, off-color or inappropriate material, excessive drinking or other unprofessional behavior, either on or off the platform, as designated by the client. If you persist in such behavior or use material that the client specifically

asks you not to use, you understand that you will forfeit your fee and expenses for the engagement, if so requested by the buyer.

33.   You agree to keep in touch with WI, letting us know your whereabouts at all times, and will send us your updated literature and any fee changes.

34.   If more than one bureau calls you for the same client and date, you agree that the first bureau to call you on the date is the one you work with for that booking. You agree to tell the second bureau you are already pledged with another bureau for that same client.

35.   You agree to keep careful records of how your inquiries originate. You will call WI immediately when you receive an inquiry from any of our clients.

Repeat, Spin-Off, Future Business

36.   All business and inquiries at any future date from clients booked for you by WI will be referred to our Bureau. Refer all arrangements and negotiations to us. You agree not to engage in separate contracts with our clients.

37.   On every incoming call to your office, you agree to specifically ask, "Where did you hear about me?" If the client says, "The Walters Bureau recommended you," you will ask all the pertinent information about the booking, then turn that client and the information over to WI. There is no time limit.

38.   You agree to keep careful records of the source of your bookings. If WI is in any way connected to a booking, you agree to call WI and have us handle the contract. If the caller says, "I heard you at a speech you did in _____," you will research your records to find how that date was booked for you. If it was a booking made by WI, you agree to refer this new spin-off lead back to WI.

39.   You agree to inform WI of all spin-off business. Spin-offs are inquiries you receive as a result of an engagement WI set up for you from someone other than the booking client. Example: Someone in the audience from a different company or association requests

information about you. WI will handle the contracts on all spin-offs from any bookings we obtain for you.

Product Sales & Referrals

40. Any product sales at the performance must be cleared and arranged with the client first. If we arrange for a quantity purchase of your products as a part of the contract, we require a 10% commission on the gross of products sold.

41. Referrals: If you have a lead you cannot handle, or a date you are unable to make (with clients other than the ones we book you with), we appreciate your turning the lead over to us. We keep careful records of these leads and will send you 10% of the gross fee on the first booking.

Miscellaneous

42. We appreciate your being an on-going subscriber to *Speakers and Meeting Planners Sharing Ideas Newsmagazine.* We will feature you in our publication. *Sharing Ideas* is mailed to our bureau clients. It helps us to suggest you. We appreciate your enthusiastic support, in the same spirit that we give it to you.

43. Walters International, Royal Publishing and all of its employees are not responsible for any injury you incur while on an assignment or in anyway associated with an assignment you are performing for a client booking we obtain for you.

Most Important of All

44. You agree that we will work together as a Three-Way Team. We want our clients to feel that WI is an extension of your office and of theirs. We serve them and you. We need your help. Please back us up with everything you do. Let the client know they receive the very best for themselves by using both of us. Our job is to make your booking go smoothly and successfully, so that this client will use you again, and use our services again. Thank you for your support.

Failure to perform any of these requirements, points 1 thru 44, will mean that Walters International Speakers Bureau must eliminate you from our rolls.

Please tell our clients, "Thank you for booking me through Walters International Speakers Bureau."

WE COUNT ON OUR SPEAKERS TO HELP US PLEASE OUR CLIENTS:

Welcome to our Team.

Speaker agrees to above terms of this document.

Signature_____ Date_____

Company Name_____

Address_____

City_____ State_____ Zip_____

Work Phone_____ Home Phone_____

General Topic Areas_____ Best Known For_____

Main Background Specialty_____

Heavy Experience in Which Industry?_____

Please attach your commissionable fee schedule.

THE POWER OF AGENTS AND SPEAKERS BUREAUS

Once your professional speaking efforts are put into motion and settle into a solid, productive, upward path, speaker's agents and speakers bureaus can help you get your career into high gear. As your bookings increase, so will your income and visibility— and your success will generate even more speaking engagements. At this point, you will truly be speaking and growing rich. And, as the next chapter shows, audiences will demand more from you than just spoken words and good feelings. They will want products, too, that capture the essence of your spirit and expertise.

10

How to Boost Your Profits
with Speaker Products

Paid speaking is the front door of the mansion you have entered with the information in *Speak and Grow Rich*. Speakers are actually in the information business. As you develop your subject, study it, write articles about it, and come to new conclusions. You will find room after room of opportunity opening before you. You are not limited to the spoken word on the platform, but only by the idea, and the value of the idea or information.

The same information you use in your speech can·be sold in standard versions, and in customized programs which you will create especially for individual companies and associations. You can create videos, audio albums, workbooks, consulting sessions, training materials, reports, magazine articles, posters, accessories, and even software programs based on your original speech. These are the valuable ancillary rights of your speeches. They are at least half of a speaker's income.

This chapter focuses on how you and your audiences can profit from the products you create on your subject. Speaker products are sold in five primary ways.

The first is to sell large quantities of your items to the corporation or association who books you for a fee. The client gives these items to your audience as part of the educational material in their convention package.

The second is to offer your product as a "gift with a seminar registration" when you produce your own seminars for the public. The price of the seminar is increased. You pay wholesale for the gift product, and the registrant perceives the gift at the retail price. This is highly profitable.

The third is to sell your products to attendees at your autograph table at the back of the room after your programs, often in a power pack.

Fourth is to sell your products to the public through appropriate catalogs and direct mail. These sales are referred to by speakers as "passive income."

Fifth is to sell a large quantity of your product to a company such as a bank to use as a gift to their clients for opening a new account; or a magazine as a subscription gift promotion. This can lead to your becoming a paid spokesperson for their company. Speakers make television appearances, write articles, and speak on behalf of the sponsoring company for additional fees.

You will receive royalties if your book, cassettes, or videos are published by major companies and distributed by them. However, the most lucrative part of your product income will come from your own sales in the ways we have listed, because you receive all of the profits.

Sales of speaker products can do more than boost your level of income. Having the products available also can add credibility and prestige to your power position as an expert. Professional publicists find it much easier to promote you as a speaker and expert if you have created books, audio cassette tapes, or video tapes on your topic.

HOW AUDIENCES CAN PROFIT FROM YOUR PRODUCTS

Audiences who like you will want to buy products associated with your topic. Speaker Brian Tracy reports that his multiple cassette and video albums were created because his seminar attendees kept insisting that they wanted something that would allow them to re-listen to what he had said. Keep that fact in mind as you embark on your own speaking career. Surveys show that attendees can only absorb and remember 20 percent of any program. We learn best through repetition. If you have materials for your audience to purchase, they can continue learning from and enjoying your expertise—at work, at home, or driving in their cars.

Your Recordings and Books Can Change Lives

Another reason for creating speaker products is the personal satisfaction that you can gain through helping people. A prime example of how speakers help people is seen in Gil Eagles' story. He grew up in Africa, speaking Polish and Swahili. When he was sent to an English school, his mind went into shock. He was unable to learn to read or write. He developed a stutter and was considered unteachable. Then the Eagles family moved to America, and Gil worked as a busboy in their small restaurant in New York. One day, someone left a tiny promotional cassette in a booth. It was "Goal Setting" by former stutterer Paul J. Meyer of Success Motivation Institute (SMI), a producer of audio tapes in Waco, Texas.

Since Gil could not read, the talking cassette excited him. He took it home and played it on his younger sister's player. The material so inspired him that he went to a bookstore, bought first-grade reading books, and taught himself to read. Today, Gil is one of the most successful world-class speakers, famous in both the entertainment and business fields. Paul Meyer's recording woke his spirit. Keep this in mind as you write and record your own materials. Your material may be exactly what many hungry hearts are waiting for.

Here is an example of the impact of back-of-the-room products. New York attorney Adriane Berg is a speaker and financial radio show host. After we helped her increase her BOR sales from $300 to $2,200 per performance, she wrote us a special thank-you letter. While the additional money was great, she said, her special delight was in the increased donations she was now able to make to her favorite charity, Let Intervention Stop Abuse (LISA). She announced this contribution to her audience so that they benefited both by giving to a great cause and also by the content of her material.

SIX IDEAS FOR PRODUCTS AND MATERIALS YOU CAN SELL

Some of the products you can develop and sell are:

1. Standard and custom workbooks, which contain material directly related to the workshop you are holding. These can be sold either at the back of the room or included as a package for all attendees when asking a higher seminar fee.

2. Audio albums that contain your speeches or related subjects. Some speakers combine an audio album with a workbook to provide a package deal.

3. Instructional audio tapes. These usually include self-help exercises taken from your materials. Many speakers offer two to four albums, often in a "power pack," at a special price.

4. Video tapes. These can be used to augment any of your materials in very creative ways. Video tapes sell especially well if your subject is a visual one with demonstrations.

5. Topic-related items such as special calendars or charts. These products generally sell very well. For example, one speaker offers decks of playing cards imprinted with his body language material. Another speaker offers a mirror with the word "smile" printed on it. In her speech, she discusses the importance of smiling and looking into the mirror for telephone sales. Materials that are presented on computer disks are some of the newest specialty items offered by speakers.

6. Copies of articles and reports you have had published on specific areas of your information. These can be offered at an excellent fee via BOR sales or by mail order. Ten dollars for a package of five pages is not uncommon.

NOTE: Do not offer to furnish handouts, workbooks, and other products as part of your speaker's fee, unless you have already added the cost of designing and manufacturing these items to your fee. All extra materials you provide should be sold to the client for an additional fee. Some speakers sell rights to the client to reproduce and use their materials. Others supply the required quantity of the finished product, on a per item per attendee basis.

The best way to get your major products underway is to decide whether you want to write a book first, create a video cassette tape or audio album of your speeches, or sell the training materials you have developed. Once you decide, follow these steps we've developed.

FIFTEEN STEPS FOR CREATING YOUR FIRST BOOK

One way to leap ahead on the road to success and fame is to write a top non-fiction "how-to" book on your subject. Writing a book is hard work, but the long-term rewards and prestige of publication can be very important to your career. Here are fifteen steps that can help you get started:

1. If you have created a workbook for your seminars and speeches, you already have a viable book in the embryo stage. Rewrite at least three of the chapters in book form, rather than in workbook fashion. Then, create a table of contents and a chapter-by-chapter outline of the rest of your proposed book. These will be your sales tools when seeking a publisher.

2. Be sure to approach only those book publishers who publish the kind of material you present. Publishers are specialists, just as speakers and bureaus are. Some publishers look for recreational books on humor, science fiction, travel, or cooking, while others concentrate on business books.

3. If you don't know which publishers handle your type of book, go into a bookstore and examine a number of books on your topic, as well as related subjects. Buy the best examples of those books.

4. Study the books you have purchased. Then think of a new angle or "slant" for your material and send a query letter to suitable publishers. Enclose a copy of your outline,

three chapters, and table of contents with each query letter. The important thing is to make your book different from anything else available. Tell the publisher why people will buy your book.

5. When a book manuscript is purchased by a major publisher and printed, the author usually receives royalties of 5 percent to 15 percent for each copy sold, depending on the contract. You may even receive an advance against royalties, which is a lump-sum payment based on your estimated earnings from sales of the book. Since you will also be selling the book yourself, be sure your contract specifies a good price for your wholesale purchases.

6. Like speaking, the business of writing and selling books to publishers is very competitive. The odds against you are high, especially on a first book. Do not be hurt by rejection letters. If getting published was easy, everyone would do it. But being published can help your career tremendously, so do not give up. Dan Poynter, who offers seminars on publishing, says: "Each large publisher receives 15,000 to 20,000 unsolicited manuscripts per year." It is estimated that 350,000 books are actually written annually, but not submitted. Only 32,000 books go into print each year in the United States. The average nonfiction book has a run of only 5,000 copies before it goes out of print. But you often can sell this amount yourself in a short time because, as a speaker on your subject, you have a continuous, built-in, steady market for your book among the members of your audiences.

7. If the publisher lets your book go out of print, the publication rights can revert to you. If this happens, consider self-publishing as a way to keep your book available and making profits for you.

8. Sometimes a subject may be excellent for your speeches and seminars, but too narrow for a major publisher. If this is so, you can publish your books yourself. With the self-publishing alternative, you can make high profits from each copy sold. But the process requires an investment of money, and you may have to hire the services of

editors and book designers to ensure that you create a quality product. Many speakers self-publish their first books, then attract the attention of major publishers. One of the best examples is Zig Ziglar, who sold thousands of copies of his famous book, *See You At The Top,* before interesting a big publisher. Books are expensive to publish, but if yours sells well after self-publication, you will have proven that there is a market for your product. In this case, successful self-publishing can set you up as a good prospect for a book contract from a major publisher.

9. You can gain experience at self-publication by starting with the looseleaf workbook you use for seminar attendees. Have the workbook printed in book style and sell it to those who sign up. When you self-publish, you can expect to make up to 75 percent on your investment. But remember, you also must take all of the risks and do all of the work, or alternatively job it out.

10. You can sell the book separately or raise the price of your seminar and include its purchase in the fee. You also can merchandise the product in the other ways mentioned in this chapter.

11. Constantly gather new material and update the material you already have on your topic. Soon, you will have enough for another book, as well as an audio or video album. You can then work toward creating a power-pack of your own products.

12. Take part in a speaker anthology. Speaker anthologies are a sophisticated method of combining self-publishing and regular publishing. A number of speaker/authors are gathered together in one book. The word anthology comes from the Greek "antho," meaning flower, and "logia," collecting. This kind of a book or album is literally a "bouquet" of ideas on one topic.

13. The anthology should have a unified subject such as humor, communication, stress, or sales, etc. Each author writes one chapter on the pre-arranged topic. Royal Publishing, P.O. Box 1120, Glendora, CA, 91740, is an expert in speaker anthologies.

14. For some anthologies, four or six speakers get together and self-publish a book or audio album. With others, anthology companies do all of the work for the speakers. They find the other speaker/authors on the same subject, handle all of the publication details, then sell each author the books or albums at wholesale so that they can make a large profit when they sell them to their audiences. Some publishers offer individual dust jackets for each author, featuring the author's name and picture on the front and back.

15. In any kind of cooperative book, video, or audio album, each participant agrees to purchase a minimum number of products. The larger the purchase, the lower the wholesale price per item, and the higher the profits at retail will be.

TIPS FOR PRODUCING VIDEOTAPES AND AUDIO ALBUMS

Companies who publish speakers' videotapes and audio albums also look for excellent materials that fit their markets. Your topic and their marketing and distribution capabilities are the keys to success. You can approach these publishers in the same manner that you approach book publishers, but you should send them complete programs rather than snippets and outlines.

You also can self-produce and sell video cassettes and audio albums of your speeches. The anthology approach works very well for audio albums. It enables you to have high-class products to sell quickly at a profit to the audience. With anthology cassette albums, the speaker prepares only one cassette. The other five cassettes in a six-cassette album can be done by speakers on the same subject. Or it can contain the speeches of celebrity performers who are participating in the anthology. An anthology containing celebrity speakers gives you the opportunity to gain credibility and prestige because you will appear alongside the famous speakers as another expert on the topic.

The profits from anthology products are high, since the albums or books are sold by all of the participants to their own audiences. The participating authors effectively promote each other with every sale.

GOOD MONEY: PROFITING FROM SALES OF TRAINING MATERIALS

As a professional speaker, you will expend time, energy, and money developing training materials for your seminars. You can recoup your investment, and make an excellent profit by selling these training materials to seminar registrants and audiences. Training materials which continue the educational process are the easiest of all products to sell. They are sought after by seminar attendees, and are attractive to targeted buyers.

Training materials can also be packaged and sold with your book, video, or audio albums, to create a true power pack of products.

Another way to profit is to offer long-term, customized training materials for clients. For example, you could produce a series of twelve different training sessions on audio cassettes for a client's sales people. You could also prepare separate tapes for their sales managers with instructions, worksheets, and lesson plans for role-playing exercises.

Profits also can be gleaned from special handouts and educational materials prepared for your programs for corporations or associations. Negotiate the price for your customized material in addition to your speaking fee. Then ship your training materials to the client and bill for each person in attendance. Often, sales of these materials double, triple, or quadruple your gross income from the speaking engagement. An alternative arrangement is that you can send camera-ready flats to the client who will then print them. In the latter case, you will charge the client a one-time-use licensing fee. Because the material itself is customized, however, the client will still pay substantial prices, tied to the number of attendees.

Yet another possible source of income from training materials is to write a series of educational articles for a client's in-house magazine. If you write twelve articles, one a month, at $150 per article, a total of $1,800 can be added to your speaking contract with that client.

FOURTEEN WAYS TO PROFIT FROM YOUR PRODUCT SALES

Without products to sell back-of-the-room, you will miss out on many profit opportunities. But once you do have products, you will find new and unusual ways to make sales. The fourteen ways listed below can help you do a strong job of marketing your products for high profits.

1. Sell your products to major publishers who market them in bookstores and book clubs for in-advance deposits and continuing royalties. Purchase your products from them at wholesale for your own retail sales and earn the retail profit.

2. Publish your products yourself for sales directly to your specific audience. You will earn everything above your production and selling costs.

3. Join with other speakers in your field to produce anthologies and team products. Share the costs of production. Publicize each other through every sale and each other's product catalogs. You add distribution profits to sales profits.

4. Create generic and custom training materials for specific clients, for high consulting fees and continuing product income.

5. Give away a product as a gift with each seminar registration. One speaker increased the retail price of his seminar by $155. He gave away a $29.95 book, which cost him $5 wholesale. He has now registered 6,000 seminar attendees by this method, for a net profit of $900,000—more than he earned without the product as a registration gift at the lower seminar rate.

6. Negotiate quantity sales (at lower prices but still at a profit) to clients who will purchase products in advance to give to each registrant at a convention or seminar.

7. Use paid advertisements in appropriately targeted media to help sell your products. Or trade your articles to appropriate media for ad space for your products.

8. Make wholesale sales to appropriate catalog producers.

9. Advertise and sell your products via direct mail to companies and people interested in your topic.

10. Use drop-ship sales through magazines and catalogs that sell on this basis. (See item seventeen in "Twenty-Nine Tips for Boosting Your Back-of-Room Sales" later in this chapter.)

11. Set up a network of distributors who sell your products for profit.

12. Make your products available for back-of-room sales at the autograph table to those who have just heard you speak.

13. Advertise your product in displays at industry trade shows.

14. Promote your product as premiums. Various premiums often are given away by large companies to purchasers of their product. Products accepted as premiums may be sold in large quantities to the companies.

HOW TO CUSTOMIZE YOUR PRODUCTS FOR PROFIT

Many clients are very pleased when you agree to customize your materials for them, such as books, workbooks, training manuals, audio or video tapes. Many successful speakers establish a standard price for products sold as they come off the shelf, then set up higher fees based on two types of customized products:

1. Personalized (custom-cover with the name of the client only): Medium prices are charged, and volume rates are offered.

2. Customized (designed and written exclusively for the client): Products of this type command the highest prices, including consultation and writing fees. The client usually signs a contract to purchase future materials, and often additional training on a regular basis.

How to Charge for Custom Materials

Tom Winninger's techniques present an excellent example of how to profit from customized products. Tom follows the system discussed above when selling his custom sales training workbooks. He prints the workbooks, then furnishes them to his clients. They may buy a year's supply at one time, or purchase them on a monthly basis. The price rises according to the amount of customizing required.

1. He offers a standard product, which is generic training materials printed under his logo.
2. His next level of workbook is personalized. The front cover is designed to include the client company's name.
3. The third level of pricing is for customized workbooks. These materials are created exclusively for this client's needs. He starts from scratch, so he includes a fee for consulting as well as writing.

Many clients continue to buy Tom's workbooks on a regular basis. These sales are a continuing source of income and contact with clients. His clients bring him back again and again to speak, for consultation, to update the materials, and to train employees. Training manuals are a large part of Tom's gross sales.

Speaker Nido Qubein, whose topic is sales, utilizes an excellent audio album that can be customized for individual clients. He arranges for a special jacket with a picture of the company's president for the front of the album. Nido's picture and biographical information appear on the back. Nido does not produce the customized album himself. He sells his clients the rights to produce it for their sales teams, for a fee of $10,000. He has sold this same album on sales training to a number of non-competing companies.

RULES FOR TAPING: SALES AND ROYALTY RIGHTS

If you plan to produce and sell audio cassette tapes, keep the following important rules in mind. First, it is illegal to tape a speaker (or anyone) without prior written consent. If your client plans to sell tapes of your presentation at the event, those tapes will cut down drastically on your own product sales. If you plan to depend on tape sales for a part of your income, bear this in mind when you negotiate fees.

If a client wants to record your presentation and offer it for sale, ask for an additional fee for these ancillary rights. One way to do this is to charge an additional 50 percent of your normal speaking fee. For example, if you charge $1,000 as your initial base fee, you would instead charge $1,500 if tapes of your presentation are sold. If you agree to such an arrangement, be sure you do not sell your own reproduction rights when you sell the rights that allow the client to sell your tapes at an event. Specify in your contract that the client's tapes will be "for resale only at the 19___ convention, etc., and not to be sold in any other way, or at any other time." (This is called "First Rights Only.")

An alternative to the above plan is to charge the client a royalty fee of $1 per attendee at the convention. Note that this is not $1 each from those who buy the tape, it is $1 for each registered convention attendee. This amount is added to your contract in advance in the space you have provided. The same rule applies to the sale of video reproduction rights.

Always specify in your contract that you are to receive the master and several copies of the tape of your performance. Often, you can use these professionally produced materials by editing them for use as demo tapes, albums, and other products.

Welcome a client's desire to discuss the uses of your taped talk. Sometimes, the client will want to use the video to train field office people. Negotiate a deal for the additional use of your material. Discussion of this opportunity can lead to selling books, workbooks, audio albums, video albums, articles, and other materials—all to be used in the client's training program. You might negotiate a very large contract.

BOOKING THE SPEECH AND PRODUCTS TOGETHER

A speaker once called us for an emergency consultation. She had accepted a $1,000 speaking date plus the usual hotel and travel expenses. The fee was the top of the client's budget for her section of the program. While they had not asked her to furnish workbooks, she now realized her program needed them. She also wanted to include a cassette for each attendee to make her program most effective. When she checked into how much it would cost to produce these items, the total was $700, or 70 percent of her fee. She was in a panic. What should she do now? she asked us.

Fortunately, she had not discussed these handout items with the client at all. We suggested she ask if there was an additional budget for educational materials for this program. If so, we instructed her to say, "Would you like to make my section of the convention extra special by having an educational workbook and cassette provided for each attendee?" If the answer was yes, then she should continue, "Would you prefer to produce the materials from my original printing and audio masters, or should I do it all for you, and bill you?"

The client's answer was that yes, indeed, they had $1,000 earmarked for educational materials. The client gladly accepted her offer to produce the materials and ship them, because it was, for them, a very busy time. The speaker charged $1,000 for her materials. This gave her $300 over her own costs for her time in handling the production. The client was more than pleased, because their cost to produce the materials would have been far more than the $1,000. The speaker thus netted a $1,000 speaking fee, plus the $300 profit from the materials, and delivered a better program. It was a win-win situation for speaker *and* client.

THE ADVANTAGES OF SEMINAR AND CONVENTION REGISTRATION INCENTIVE GIFTS

Public seminars are often sold on the "two-step" system. The first seminar is free. It is used to attract attendees, arouse their interest, and sell them tickets to the paid, second seminar. A book or album usually is offered as a gift with registration to this second seminar. Often, an even larger package of materials is sold to attendees at the paid seminar.

A speaker, who presents seminars for insurance agents, offers a free book with each seminar registration. At the seminar, he offers a package of albums and marketing modules especially designed for his audience. The book gift with registration, he says, has increased his attendance by more than 100 percent.

Corporations and seminar companies buy products as registration premiums to increase attendance. Professional associations also use them to promote convention registrations, and can offer your materials for this purpose. Meeting planners often have a separate budget for educational materials. Your tapes and books can be the very things they need for some of the meetings they must arrange. Often, you can sell them 100 or even 1,000 items—enough for every attendee to receive a book, cassette, or other product. The glamour of your book and/or album in the convention pack will give attendees the feeling of receiving something of great value, because they will see the full retail price listed. But the client will have purchased them from you at a discount. In this case, everybody wins, including the speaker.

When Dottie Walters' first book, *Never Underestimate the Selling Power of a Woman,* was published, Prentice-Hall, Inc. arranged for the purchase of 4,000 copies by Tupperware so that its convention attendees could receive gift copies. A letter from the Tupperware president was included at the front of the special edition of the book. Tupperware later booked Dottie as their speaker for eight convention performances, where attendees received the books.

TECHNIQUES FOR BETTER BACK-OF-ROOM SALES

Unlike pre-sales, where the client buys enough products in advance for every participant, back-of-room sales occur because attendees want to invest in the products for themselves. BOR selling is sometimes called "selling products from the platform," a phrase which refers to the time a speaker uses during a program to talk about his or her products. Never devote more than a very few minutes to "selling from the platform." If you spend too much time describing your products during your program, your client will be resentful. It should not be necessary to dwell long on what is on the BOR table. When your program material is good, people will want more. The key is to perfect your presentation skills and speech content so that the audience likes you and will want to take you home with them. They will not be able to do that physically. But the BOR table will offer them the next best thing: your books, audio cassettes, videotapes, training materials, and other items.

Offering products at a display table at the back of the room usually is one of the most lucrative ways to sell speaker products. This is because the audience members or seminar participants are enthusiastic after hearing the speaker's program. Sales at one program can range from a gross of $4,000 on up to $22,000. This last BOR figure is the sales average of speaker Mike Ferry, who uses "power packs," "gift-with-order," and "discount-today-only" sales techniques.

TWENTY-NINE TIPS FOR BOOSTING YOUR BACK-OF-ROOM SALES

1. Refer to your BOR sales table as "the autograph table." This technique accomplishes several goals. It creates a celebrity image. It suggests that attendees can have something to do after the speech and encourages them to go to the autograph table and purchase products. It also encourages them to stay afterwards to speak to you.

2. Locate the autograph table between the exit door, refreshment area, and the bathroom. Accessibility to heavy-traffic areas is vital for best sales.

3. Have an enlargement made of your photograph, and engage a sign painter to mount it on a self-standing sign for your autograph table. It should say "(Your Name) In Person!"

4. Bring a large piece of colorful material to use as a table drape. Felt or knit is best, since these do not easily wrinkle. Stack up your products so they make an attractive display. Store extra supplies under the table out of sight.

5. Throughout your speech, make one or two subtle references to your products. (And be sure your references *are* subtle.) For example, do *not* say, "If you really want an answer to that, you must buy my book." This attitude makes the audience resentful. Instead, use this format.

"When I was writing my latest book on _____ (hold up your book), I discovered that _____ (set the book down again)." Or, "In my album (hold it up), I tell the story of _____. It illustrates the point of _____. Here is the story behind the story." Set the album down again.

6. Whenever you pick up your product on the platform, let your body language show that it is valuable. Charles "Tremendous" Jones, a famous motivational speaker, is a master at product sales. Charlie's unique style is flamboyant, but it works. He has one power-pack up in front with him. It is a boxed library containing several authors' sales and inspirational books. He treats each book as though it is a friend of whom he is very fond. He talks to the book, pets it, and hugs it as he shows it to the audience. He proclaims, "I _love_ Napoleon Hill. I want you to have him! You deserve him!" The power pack is a library of books he has personally chosen for the audience. They fill out the order forms found on their seats and hand them to him as they file out of the meeting room. Each person receives a hug. The next day he ships thousands of dollars' worth of power packs to his buyers. If your own power pack has $298 in products, and you sell 200 packs to an audience of 1,000, your gross will be $59,600. You do not need to sell them all.

7. Let the introducer be your sales assistant. Include simple, short material about your products in your written introduction. At the conclusion of your talk, have the introducer wind up with a conclusion that you have printed on the back of your introduction. For example, "Thank you so much! Our speaker will be available for questions at the back of the room at the autograph table. He has agreed to make some of his terrific books and albums available for us. The discounts offered are for today only, to this group. There is an order blank on the back of the rating sheets at your seat. Please don't forget to give us your comments on the flip side. Remember, part of every sale goes to our association's favorite charity. Please turn in your rating sheets with the order form on the back at the autograph table. Now, let's thank him again!" (While

this announcement is being made, take your bows and get to your product table before the crowd grabs you! Don't get stuck on the platform. Your presence at the autograph table can double your sales.)

8. You must have sales table assistants to make change and handle sales. They will leave you free to sign autographs and talk with people who enjoyed your presentation. Bring a relative or employee, hire temporary helpers, or find volunteers. Rehearse your helpers in simple sales techniques. Show them how to take credit card orders. If you plan to use volunteers, watch for attendees who come up to you before the event to chat and say they are excited to meet you. These are terrific people you should ask to help you. Offer volunteers an autographed book as a gift for assisting you. They will be honored and delighted. (Remember when you longed to be allowed to erase the blackboard for your teacher?) Be sure to send each volunteer a personal thank you note. When you give part of the BOR receipts to a client's charity, you often can ask for four or five helpers from the client group to help you with the sales.

9. Allow for break time. Make sure there is a 15-to-20-minute break immediately after your talk. If another speaker comes on before there is a break, you will lose most of your sales. Arrange this in advance with your meeting planner.

10. Remember, it is imperative that you get to the autograph table quickly when you finish your program. You court disaster if you do not do so. The following is an example of what can happen. A speaker at a large convention offered to speak free, because he thought he would have massive product sales afterward. He produced a new audio album for the event, in anticipation. But then he made a fatal mistake. The lunch break came right after his talk, so he closed his program by telling the audience that he was as hungry as they were, so he would see them after lunch at the autograph table. The crowd bolted for the door. He evidently thought food was more important than his materials, and so did they. They promptly forgot

him when the afternoon session started, and went on to hear other speakers. Not one came back to his sales table. His golden time was gone. He packed up his materials and left, angry at the crowd. But the fault was his, not theirs.

11. Some people come to your autograph table wanting to tell you long stories. But you can't let them monopolize you, because time is short. Take their hands and ask them to stay afterwards so that you can hear it all. This shows them you care. Do it kindly and with respect. Try this, "I would be so interested in speaking with you further, but I must autograph the rest of these books. Will you wait until I'm finished and we can have a really good talk?" If they say they can't wait, give them your business card and say, "Then please call me. I'd love to finish this talk later."

12. A prize drawing is a great way to increase the visibility of your products and to have the introducer talk about them. It is also an easy way to be sure you get your rating sheets returned. The introducer should explain that there will be a drawing for a free book, randomly selected from the rating sheets they will fill out, then hold up the prize book and mention the order form on the back of the rating sheet.

13. If you have arranged to give a donation to the group's favorite Little League team or other charity from your product profits, be sure the introducer mentions it. In your typed introduction, include a reminder that you and your materials will be available at the autograph table.

14. Everyone loves the idea of getting something extra when they buy. Barney Zick offers an anthology book as a free gift with the purchase of his power pack of three albums at his seminar's BOR table. Seminars traditionally have much smaller audiences than conventions, but he was averaging sales of 30 packs at $298 per pack, for a gross of $8,940. Then he added a "gift with order." He gave a book away with the purchase of the power pack. This practice has brought his sales up to an average of 68

packs per seminar—more than double his previous rate. His gross from BOR retail products alone now is more than $20,000 per seminar.

15. When you use an audience rating sheet, set up the reverse side as an order form. This saves time when attendees come to the table, and the technique helps you follow up after the event with those who are interested in more of your services or products. Offer your products in combinations or sets. Build a mailing list that includes the people who fill out your rating sheets. They are prime prospects for notification of new products, and other programs.

16. The ability to take credit cards as payment will dramatically increase your BOR sales. Go to the bank and obtain credit card merchant status. If you have difficulty obtaining this status, check the section on speaker resources at the back of this book.

17. Advertise your products. For speakers, the secret of successful product sales is the same as it is in any sort of marketing. Use targeted advertising media. If your material is on sales, then use the many publications on that subject. For example, you should not advertise a book or album on sales in a flower catalog, unless your material is customized for selling flowers and the catalog is aimed at florists. Your advertising copy should state the benefits the consumer will receive if he or she purchases your product. One of the finest copywriters and direct mail strategists in the United States, Bill Steinhardt, stresses the importance of putting benefits and more benefits into ad copy. He also recommends the gift-with-order technique. Always pack additional order forms in your outgoing packages, and retain the names of all buyers for future mailings. Consider releasing a new product each year, so that every buyer becomes an annual prospect for continued purchases.

18. The term "drop-ship" means that your products are advertised for sale in someone else's catalog, magazine, or direct mailing piece. The catalog "drops" the order in the mail to you, and you "ship" it. Here's how it works. The

producer of the catalog or magazine pays for the advertising. They sell your product at full retail, plus a shipping fee. They keep 50 percent (usually) of the retail price and send you (1) the balance, (2) the shipping fee, and (3) a label with the name and address of the buyer. You fill the order.

19. Drop-ship works well if you can buy your products in high enough quantities to get the wholesale cost down. For example: You buy a six-cassette album wholesale for $25. The retail price is $89.50. The drop ship catalog makes the sale and keeps $44.75. They send you $44.75 plus the $3 shipping fee. You pay your $25 cost of the album, making a $19.95 net profit. You also gain a prospect for future sales. You have no advertising or shipping costs. When you buy your albums in larger quantities, their individual cost goes down and you make even greater profits.

20. An important fringe benefit of drop-ship sales is that your name and products are publicized free. As your name becomes known in your field, you can raise your speaking fees. There are thousands of catalogs and magazines that do business on a drop-ship basis. Seek publications whose audiences have a keen interest in what you have to offer.

21. When you ship your products, include flyers about your availability as a speaker, and advertisements of your other products. These are called "bounce-back offers." The offer might read: "As one of our valued buyers, you will receive a 15 percent discount on any of the items in the enclosed catalog." Or, "With an order of $100 or more from the catalog, we will send you a valuable gift."

22. Try sales through distributors. Howard Shenson, Brian Tracy, Denis Waitley, and many other famous speakers set up distributors who sell their products and, in some cases, put on seminars for them. This is another way to multiply your gross income and your ability to reach the public. The best potential distributors for you can be found in your seminars. When attendees like the subject

and are enthusiastic about you personally, you can invite them to become distributors.

23. Create out-of-the-ordinary products. Many speakers offer their audiences items other than books or albums. For example, speakers on time management offer special calendars and appointment books. Others offer inspirational plaques and sets of special quotes on cards. Jeff Armstrong, who created "Saint Silicon," sells big posters of his famous "Keyboard Prayer" for computer users. Jo Brown, a telephone sales expert, offered telephone script cards. Elizabeth Kearney and Michale Joan Bandley sell tests which enable attendees to figure out what makes employees or customers tick. There are many other possibilities.

24. Equip your own "On the Road Product Store." Bring a cash box, order forms, pens, and gifts for volunteers to your program. Estimate how many products you hope to sell, then ship them ahead to the venue before the event. A second-day carrier will see that they are there before you are. Call and arrange with the convention center or hotel to receive your packages. If you run out of a product at your autograph table, do not sell the last remaining sample. You can take orders and ship the products if you keep at least one set of samples to show. When the engagement is over, the hotel concierge can ship any leftover products back to your office.

25. Learn about international business practice before attempting product sales. When you are booked to speak overseas, find out ahead of time about any restrictions that may affect you. Bringing products into a foreign country for resale can often be a challenge in the customs office. One solution is to bring only one set of product samples and a lot of printed order forms. Include the cost of shipping in your sales price. Ship the orders when you return home. You can autograph the items individually before they are sent. Be sure your order form specifies "U.S. dollars only." Another possibility for overseas product sales is to team up with a local distributor and have your products manufactured in the host country by

a local company. This practice saves taxes, tariff, and shipping costs.

26. When your client wants to tape your session and sell audio or video tapes to attendees at the convention for a lower price than your materials, you have a dilemma. Associations often sell such tapes for $5 or $10. Of course, it is not the same material, but as mentioned earlier in this chapter, it will certainly kill the sales of your higher-priced BOR package. Attendees will purchase the lower-priced convention tape, not yours. Here are some solutions to this problem:

   • You have the right to refuse to allow the client to tape, but you must do so well before the event. Be sure a prohibition line appears in all of your contracts.

   • You can offer a percentage of the sales of your products to your client if your package is offered instead of another made at the convention.

   • You can sell your client the royalty right to tape your talk and sell the tapes.

   For more information, see the previous section on "Rules for Taping: Sales and Royalty Rights."

27. Put together a power pack. A power pack is a package of items the speaker offers to the audience. It is often presented at a special price. A power pack typically consists of several albums, books, videos, and other items. Most frequently, the power pack is offered at a special discount "for today only," or with a gift with purchase. Our surveys show that audiences always buy the least-expensive product on the BOR table. If you display a $10 item and a $125 item, they will buy the $10 one. Therefore, never put a low-priced item out on the table with a power pack, unless it is the incentive "gift with order." The following figures show why careful display is important. Twenty percent of an audience will buy. In an audience of 100 people, 20 sales of a $10 item will give you a $200 gross. Products are usually marked up 100 percent over your cost, so your net profit is $100. However, if you offer a $200 power pack, the same 20 people will buy. But now your gross is $4,000 with a net of $2,000. Think "power pack" when you think of selling speaker products.

28. Constantly create new products. Increase the value of your products for your audiences by adding new items and topics to fit changing times. Fine-tune the impact of your marketing. Re-read your ads. Update them. Change a sentence here or a word there to further enhance their value. Stay on the cutting edge. Watch for successful ways of doing business by giving your attendees an easy way to buy more from you. One speaker has his attendees put their credit card number and expiration date on the back of their business cards to order his power pack. He asks those who want to discuss booking him as a speaker for their group to write the date of their program on their business cards. He has four different categories of items on which he asks for notes. Then as the people come up to him after the program, he puts their cards into his jacket in an internal "four-pocket filing system." Orders go in one pocket, requests for speeches in another, and so forth. We have used the same idea with great success.

29. Focus on your audience. Listen to their problems and their needs. If you create products to help them, you cannot help but succeed. Baseball's immortal Babe Ruth said when he was up at bat, he concentrated on the seam on the ball. Of course, he couldn't really see the seam as it charged at him at 90 miles per hour. He was talking about his mind's eye, his extreme concentration level. He, like Ralph Waldo Emerson, spoke of his enthusiasm engine. Babe had the greatest record for hits, but few realize he had a much greater one for swings. His concentration was so intense that when he swung and missed, he often spun around and fell on the ground. He swung harder than anybody else. Champions give it all they've got every time.

USING CHARITY TO WIN YOUR AUDIENCE AND BOOST YOUR SALES

Get audiences on your side by getting on theirs. Celebrities such as Sir Edmund Hillary, the conqueror of Mount Everest, often donate to charity a portion of the retail price of their books that are sold

BOR. In Hillary's case, the money goes to help build schools and hospitals for the Himalayan Sherpas. The charity donation is mentioned by the introducer and by the speaker. He often averages sales of several books per attendee by using this three-way benefit:

1. The audience wants to "take him home" in order to continue the positive experience.
2. They enjoy giving his autographed books as gifts.
3. They gain personal satisfaction by helping his worthy charity.

You can consider negotiating a slightly lower speaking fee for a charity engagement if the client will allow you to sell your products at the presentation, or if the client contracts for a large amount of your products in advance. We often negotiate $5,000 or more in advance product sales for a speaker, along with the speaking fees.

INCREASE YOUR PRODUCT VALUE WITH AUTOGRAPHS

An autographed book is worth more than one which is not. Ask any used book dealer. Ask yourself. If you had to give up most of the books in your own library (other than dictionaries and encyclopedias), which would you keep: the unsigned ones or those personally autographed by the author?

Literally thousands of people line up to buy Zig Ziglar's and John Molloy's books at their BOR autograph tables. People want to get close to them, meet them, and speak to them. Obtaining their autographs on their valuable products increases the value to the purchasers.

CURTAIN UP!

We suspect you may have thought professional paid speaking meant you stood in front of an audience and delivered a 45-minute speech before you read this book. We hope *Speak and Grow Rich* has opened the doors to the myriad of opportunities that paid speaking offers throughout the world.

You are standing in front of a gigantic building, ablaze with the lights of opportunity in every room. *Speak and Grow Rich* is a floor plan to the spiritual and monetary treasures within. We wish you the very best with your speaking career. Never stop learning and growing. If we may assist you as you speak and grow rich, be your mentors as we are to thousands of other speakers, just contact us at P.O. Box 1120, Glendora, California 91740.

Glossary

Agent: An agent is a person who represents speakers. Usually, a speaker has an exclusive agreement with one agent, which may include a guaranteed number of speaking engagements per year. The guarantee usually applies only to celebrity speakers. Speakers are clients of agents. Agents often are in charge of publicity and promotion for a speaker. Bureaus broker with agents for dates with their celebrity client-speaker who command fees in the range of $10,000 per presentation and above.

Autograph Table: Traditionally, this is the table where a speaker autographs books after a speaking engagement. Many speakers, however, use the term "autograph table" to also mean the table at the back of the room—the one from which they sell their products. See *back-of-room sales,* below.

Back-of-Room Sales: The act and process of selling books, tapes, and other products at the back of the room, usually immediately after a speech. Many speakers make a substantial portion of their income from back-of-room sales.

Billing: The order in which the names of speakers or entertainers are listed on a program, brochure, advertisement, or playbill. Billing also refers to the position in such a listing, such as top billing, second billing, and so forth.

Bio: A slang term for biography. See *biographical sheet,* below.

Biographical Sheet: A short document that lists a speaker's major credits and gives a brief history of his or her career. A biographical sheet is *not* a job resume or a vita. To remain true to its singular limit, a biographical sheet should be no longer than one double-spaced page.

Book: To reserve a date for a speaking engagement. (The term originally meant to reserve something by entering it into a book of record.)

Booking: The condition of being engaged to speak, as in "I have had 150 paid *bookings* this year."

Bounce-Back: An offer included with an order. For example, your materials are listed in someone else's catalog. They send you half of the retail price, plus a shipping fee. (This is called drop-ship.) You ship your materials to the buyer and include in the package a "bounce-back" order form of other items which the buyer can order directly from you.

Breakout: A type of session that occurs at a convention, when the main group of attendees are divided into several smaller, concurrent sessions that focus on different special-interest topics.

Brochure: A piece of promotional literature, usually professionally printed, which lists a speaker's major speech titles, notes from some of his or her most important recent speaking engagements, and includes testimonial quotes. For best results, the testimonial quotes included on a brochure should come from clients or famous people and focus on the quality, professionalism, and impact of the speaker.

Bureau: A booking or sales company. Bureaus are much like travel agencies, and they are nonexclusive. A speaker or meeting planner may work with several bureaus at the same time.

Buyer: The person or group representative who signs the contract and pays for the speaker. Usually, the buyer is a meeting planner employed by an association or corporation. A buyer is referred to as "the client" by speakers bureaus, and as "the buyer" by speakers' agents.

Byline: The acknowledgement of authorship for an article, short story, book, play, or poem, as in "By William Shakespeare."

Canned: A slang term for a standard speech or presentation. Often, the term "canned" is used in a negative context to refer to material that a speaker uses too often, without changes, in presentations.

Circuit: An old term from the Chautauqua days of the late 19th and early 20th centuries, when speakers were sent around the country on a speaking circuit as part of an educational movement.

Chestnuts: Stories that have been overused and are stale.

Client: Whoever is paying for a speaker's services. A company or association is the client when they buy a speaking engagement. A speaker may also be the client of an agent who is paid to "manage" them.

Community Service Bureaus: Sometimes called public service bureaus, these are speakers bureaus that send speakers into the community for little or no fee. The speakers educate the public on a particular topic or issue and promote the host company's interest.

Concluder: Remarks which conclude a program. Also known as a wind-up. Some speakers earn a second fee for concluders after doing a keynote speech or seminar at the same event.

Concurrent (sessions): Concurrent or breakout sessions (see breakout).

Consultant: A person who gives professional or technical advice for a flat fee or at hourly rates. Speakers often consult with clients to prepare custom material for programs or workbooks and earn an added fee for the consultation. An example of a consultant is an expert who observes how employees handle telephoned complaints, then prepares material for workshops to train employees in how to handle problem customers.

Contract: A formal legal instrument used to state the conditions of agreement between a speaker and a client, and/or a bureau. A contract spells out the exact terms of payment and performance.

Cooperatives: A group of speakers with varying areas of expertise, who team up to share leads and marketing expenses.

Curriculum Vita: Often referred to as a "vita." A vita is very similar to a resume. It highlights a speaker's education and key jobs held. A curriculum vita usually is used by a speaker in the academic community.

Date: The day set for a definite booking or engagement.

Date Clear: Formal permission to clear a date that is being tentatively held for a booking.

Demo: Audio or video demonstration tapes. Demos often are used to promote a speaker's services or speeches to meeting planners.

Dais: A raised platform. Also called a riser.

Direct: When a meeting planner calls the speaker direct, rather than going through an agent, bureau, or manager.

Elocutionist: Someone adept at elocution. An older term for a speaker that is not widely used any more.

Emcee: The master of ceremonies at a banquet or similar event. Sometimes spelled M.C.

Engagement: Used as a noun to describe a set booking or date when a buyer has secured the services of, or employed, a speaker.

Exclusive: When the speaker has signed an agreement with an agent to handle *all* of his speaking engagements. Bureaus then "broker" with the exclusive agent to obtain the speaker for their client. The bureau and the agent split the commission. An exclusive sometimes occurs on a regional or market basis. (See *partial exclusive.*)

Expenses: All normal out-of-pocket business costs incurred while the speaker travels to the client's event. These normally include airfare, taxifare, car rental costs, gratuities, special phone calls having to do with the event, meals, laundry, dry cleaning, pressing, and last-minute presentational materials. Expenses charged to the client should not include anything of personal nature.

Fee: The money paid by the meeting planner-buyer to the bureau or speaker per contract, exclusive of expenses.

Firm: A speaking engagement that is definitely confirmed as in, "I've got a *firm* for Baltimore on that date."

Flyer: A one-sheet piece of printed advertising, usually letter or legal size. These are often produced and distributed to help promote a speaker's products or services.

General Assembly: A meeting of all attendees at a meeting or convention. A general assembly occurs at a time other than a meal function.

Gig: A slang term meaning an engagement or booking.

Glossy: A photograph printed on glossy paper. Usually, the term "glossy" refers to a black-and-white promotional photograph of the speaker. Also called a "black and white" or a "B. & W."

Green Room: A room backstage where speakers wait to go on. Any room used for this purpose is called the "green room."

Gross: The total fee the buyer is charged for a booking, including agents' fees, but excluding speaker expenses (air and ground transportation, tips, hotels, and meals.) Bureau commissions are not paid on expenses. This is why they are excluded for this purpose.

Handout: Informative or educational material given to the audience at the speaker's presentation. Handouts often are in flyer form. The term, however, refers to any material that is handed out to the audience.

Hands-Free Mike: A microphone that attaches to the speaker's clothing and has no cord. It uses radio waves to work through the public-address system.

Head Table: The table at the front of a banquet meeting. This table is reserved for the key people at a meeting. Speakers are often expected to sit here during the meal.

Honorarium: An honorarium (professional speakers use the term "fee") is usually a small, token payment given to a public speaker. The term is used most often in the college market and by politicians.

(the) House: A slang expression used to signify the audience as in, "We have a full house."

In-House: An audience composed only of employees of the same company.

Impresario: A producer or director of a program or event open to the public, such as an opera, a concert, or a musical comedy. The programs staged by impresarios usually are held in large sports arenas or auditoriums. Speakers are hired on a fee basis or occasionally for a split of the gate.

Instant Demo: A recent experimental method in which a speaker's demo is played for prospective buyers who have called on a toll-free telephone line.

Intro: A slang term for an introduction. See *introduction,* below.

Introduction: A carefully written opener about the speaker, which is delivered by the introducer at the beginning of a speech. A good introduction gives some idea of the speaker's credits, achievements, and honors and also answers the question: "Why this speaker, on this date, for this audience?"

I.P.A. (International Platform Association): The oldest association of speakers, artists, poets, authors in the U.S. It meets once a year in Washington, D.C. Daniel Webster was one of its first members. It was run previously by Drew Pearson and now by Dan Tyler Moore.

Keynote: Originally, this term meant the fundamental point of a speech. Today, however, it refers to the main speech at a meeting or the speech in one of the featured spots at an event. The keynote sets the tone of a convention and carries out the theme. The keynote usually is connected with prime time, such as a meal function, or delivered to open or close an event, or given to the entire convention in the main room. Often, celebrity speakers give the keynote speech. It is usually the highest fee slot on the program.

Lavalier: A microphone that attaches to your lapel or part of your clothing, as opposed to a stationary or hand-held mike. This type of microphone often is connected via cord to the public address system. But some lavalier microphones are cordless and use radio waves. Originally, a "lavalier" was a flat, round, or oval ornament worn on a chain around the neck.

Lectern: A small desk or stand with a sloping top. Sometimes, a lectern has a light, a stationery or hand-held mike attached, or a shelf underneath. Often, a lectern is incorrectly called a podium. The term "lectern" comes from churches. Ministers developed lecterns to help them deliver their sermons.

Letterhead: Business stationery that contains a heading, usually giving the name of a business, its address, and telephone number. Professional speakers often use letterhead stationery to enhance their business and professional image.

M.C.: Master of ceremonies. The master of ceremonies at a meeting or banquet is often referred to as the M.C. or emcee. The person who acts as a moderator and connects the separate items at an event is often called an M.C., as well.

Manager: A person hired to manage a speaker's or entertainer's business and/or personal affairs. The job of manager may include marketing the speaker's services for more bookings or performing public relations work for the speaker.

Meeting Planner: A person who is in charge of all planning of a meeting. Meeting planners handle logistics, meals, hotel arrangements, room-sets, travel schedules, and often the hiring of speakers.

Menu: The fee schedule listing all programs and prices offered by a speaker.

Mike: A slang term for microphone. Many types of mikes are employed by speakers, including hand-held mikes with long cords, stationary mikes, clip-ons, and hands-free mikes.

N.S.A. (The National Speakers Association): An association for paid professional, business speakers. It is the largest association in the United States with 3,000 members. Headquartered in Phoenix, Arizona, the N.S.A. holds two annual winter workshops and one large convention.

Net: The amount of the fee the speaker will actually receive for a booking after agency or bureau fees and before expenses.

On-Site: An on-site location is a convention center or hotel where an event is held.

Orator: Someone who speaks eloquently in public.

Overhead Projector: A projector that produces screen-sized images from transparent, 8¹/2 by 11-inch pieces of film.

PA or P.A.: An abbreviation for public address system, the loudspeaker equipment that amplifies sound to the audience.

PR or P.R.: An abbreviation for public relations, which includes promotion, publicity, advertising, and all other tools used to keep a speaker in the public's eye. A public relations firm often books speakers for television and radio media. A PR firm may also arrange for articles about a speaker or written by a speaker to appear in magazines, newspapers, and other publications.

Panel: Speakers and others who are presented as a group to discuss a subject. At panel sessions, audiences often are encouraged to participate in a question-and-answer period with the members. Speakers may be paid to appear on a panel or offer this service free as an inducement to close a contract for a main event.

Partial Exclusive: When an agent or bureau has an exclusive contract with a speaker for a selected area, the contract is referred to as a partial exclusive. (For example, a partial exclusive covering only engagements in the college market, or only in Texas, etc.)

Perk: This British slang term is widely used in the United States. It comes from the word "perquisite," which means "anything received for work besides the regular pay." In the speaking industry, speakers and planners sometimes receive perks for using certain suppliers.

Planner: See *meeting planner.*

Platform: The raised area or dais on which speakers stand while they address an audience.

Plug: An advertisement, not in the form of a formal ad, but usually a mention—either written in a publication or given verbally from the platform to help promote a product, service, or individual.

Press Kit: A promotional package which includes the speaker's letters of recommendation, audio and visual tapes, bio, and articles written by and about the speaker.

Professional Speaker: A speaker who is *paid* a fee for performances, by a company, association, college, or impresario.

Promotional Package: See *press kit.*

Podium: Often, a set of risers covered with carpet, a small stage or a dais. The word "podium" comes from the same root as pedal and podiatrist.

Power Pack: A power pack is a set of speaker materials, such as three audio cassette albums plus a book, given as a gift with the purchase of the set. Of course, a power pack may be any combination of materials. But it is usually offered at a special "sale" price to the audience.

Product(s): Products are items which compliment the speaker's topic and are available for sale. A speaker's books, audio cassette albums, video-tapes, workbooks, posters, and other products may be sold by contract in large quantity to a client in advance for all attendees, or sold at the back of the room at an autograph table. The products can be sold singly or as a "gift with the purchase of" a power pack order, or used as a premium for seminar registration.

Projector: An apparatus for projecting a picture on a screen. Whether the device is an overhead, slide projector, or film projector, it is usually referred to as simply a projector. However, when requesting one for use at a seminar or speech, you should be very specific about the type of projector you will need.

Public Seminar: A seminar that is open to the public. Tickets are sold to individuals, often by a two-step method. First, a free seminar is offered as an introduction and inducement to draw a crowd. Then, tickets are sold to those who want to participate in the paid seminar that follows the free event.

Public Service Bureau: See *community service bureau.*

Public Speaker: Someone who speaks in public. Often, a public speaker is not paid for his or her appearances and delivers a political speech or a speech that promotes a particular cause, company, or organization.

Q & A: The question-and-answer session that follows a panel presenta-tion or speech.

Real Time: In the duplication process of audio and video tapes, a tape can be duplicated at a high rate of speed. Sometimes, especially on a tape that is being edited, the work must be done in "real time," meaning in the same time frame in which they were recorded, rather than at a faster or slower speed.

Referral: When someone, particularly a satisfied client, suggests or rec-ommends your speaking services to other buyers.

Repeat Engagement or Booking: When a speaker does a second or subsequent booking for the same client.

Risers: Short, portable platforms that are used to raise the height of the front of a room so that the panel, speaker, or guests at the head table can be seen by the audience.

Second-Time (booking): See *repeat engagement* or *booking.*

Seminar: A classroom-type lecture, which may last from one hour to sessions that span several days. A seminar usually is an educational session. At a convention, the break-out or concurrent sessions often are referred to as seminars. Handouts or workbooks frequently are distributed to the audience during seminars. (See also *public seminars*).

Seminar Leader: The teacher or expert who instructs a seminar's attendees.

Site: The location of a speaking engagement. Also called a *venue.*

Shill: A person planted in the audience to help the speaker. A shill may ask a pre-planned question to warm up the audience or be part of a pre-designed act. The term "shill" is sometimes used in a negative sense, referring to a person who poses as a bystander and who encourages audiences to buy, bet, or bid.

Special Events Company: A company that presents all kinds of special effects and theatrical acts. This type of company may contract to put on an entire convention or only parts of one. They sometimes hire speakers as part of their contract.

Sound: The audio amplification system for speakers.

Stage: The portion of an auditorium or room that has been structured into a formal area for productions or presentations.

Tailoring: When a speaker adjusts his or her material to the particular needs of an audience.

Technical Writer: Someone hired by a speaker to prepare scripts, workbooks, audios, videos, or articles on contract. Technical writing fees vary according to the complexity of the assignment and the time and effort required.

Testimonial: A letter of recommendation from a former buyer or organization that is familiar with a speaker's work.

Tentative: A tentative hold on a date for a buyer. This hold ensures the client that the speaker will not book another speech on this date, even though there is no firm commitment from the buyer that the engagement is definite.

Trade Out: An exchange or barter of services and/or products for all or part of a speaker's fee.

Trainer: Someone who conducts workshops. Participants are given assignments, break into small groups, then come back together to continue discussing a training subject. Often, this is called "hands-on" participation. A client may contract with a speaker to train employees in-house or at a conference or convention on a regular schedule.

Two-Step Seminar: A method often used in public seminars to sell a second seminar or a set of products. One seminar is given free, and attendees are encouraged to buy a second seminar or some of the products.

Venue: This term originally was used to mean the place where a court action or trial takes place. However, venue now often refers to the site of the meeting or event, which is usually a hotel, conference or convention center, college, or restaurant.

Vita: See *Curriculum Vita.*

Wings: The sides of a stage in an auditorium, out of the audience's sight, as in, "The speaker waited in the *wings* to go on."

Workshop: An educational, classroom-type session in which handouts and workbooks are often used. A workshop may last from one hour to many days. Workshop attendees participate in the discussion sessions and receive project assignments.

Resources for Speakers

The companies, associations, organizations, and individuals listed below offer a wide range of services, products, publications, and affiliations for speakers.

SERVICES FOR SPEAKERS

American Society of Association Executives
1575 Eye St., N.W.
Washington, DC 20005-1168
Publishes and sells advertising in a card pack that promotes speakers and is circulated to association members. Also publishes a speaker's directory.

Armed Forces Radio and Television Service
10888 LaTuna Canyon Rd.
Sun Valley, CA 91352-2098
Media service, often uses speakers.

Sue Avila, Publicist
1301 Teneighth Way
Sacramento, CA 95818
Publicity.

Bradley Communications
101 W. Baltimore
Lansdowne, PA 19050
Talk show publicity.

Edan Co.
158 N. Glendora Ave., #U
Glendora, CA 91740   (818) 335-2289
Credit card processing service for speakers with products.

Cassette Works
Box 158
Pasadena, CA 91102
Duplication of audio and video tapes.

Copley Photo Service
Box 190
San Diego, CA 92112
Offers a low-cost facility to duplicate black-and-white, glossy photographs. Professional speakers often require hundreds of copies of photos for their press kits and other promotional activities.

David Enslow
3119 Prospect Ave.
La Crescenta, CA 91214
Cartoonist who works with speakers.

Eric R. Voth
P.O. Box 9186
Akron, OH 44305-0186
Brochures, card packs, marketing of speakers' services and products.

Freedomike System
P.O. Box 1120
Glendora, CA 91740
Hands-free, wireless microphones.

Hour Power
P. O. Box 398
Crawfordville, FL 32327
Large, plastic scheduling calendars that hang on walls.

Kessler Management
10747 Wilshire Blvd., Suite 807
Los Angeles, CA 90024
Speaker management and public relations.

Kingdom Tapes
U.S. Route 6 East
Mansfield, PA 16933
Audio and video tape production.

L.R. Caughman & Caughman, Inc.
1256 Harvard Ave.
Claremont, CA 91711

Graphic designers and illustrators.

Military Library Mailing List
2460 Lexington Dr.
Owosso, MI 48867

Military mailing lists.

Master Cassette
2002 N. 25th Dr.
Phoenix, AZ 85009

Audio and video productions.

Nat Starr Associates
2396 Atlas Dr.
Troy, MI 48083

Packaging services for speakers. Also, brochure and material design.

Nightingale-Conant Corp.
7300 N. Lehigh Ave.
Chicago, IL 60648

Educational audio materials.

Publishers Photographic Services
266 Puesta Del Sol
Santa Barbara, CA 93105

Product photography.

Ron Fellows
2014 Siegle Dr.
Lemon Grove, CA 92046

Publicity card packs.

Russ Von Hoelscher
P.O. Box 546
El Cajon, CA 92022

Mail order and direct marketing consultant.

Speakers Source
P.O. Box 24147
Denver, CO 80224

Radio talk shows.

Steinhardt Direct
P.O. Box 7046
Shawnee Mission, KS 66207
Direct mail advertising consultant.

Suite 1000
4600 Park Rd.
Charlotte, NC 28209
Toll-free answering service.

Suzy Mallery Public Relations for Speakers
8033 Sunset, Suite 363
Los Angeles, CA 90046
Publicity.

TM Graphics
10708 Grovedale Dr.
Whittier, CA 90603
Overhead transparencies.

Vox Populi
15 Tech Circle
Natick, MA 01760
Telephone answering service and showcase.

Walters Speakers Services
P.O. Box 1120
Glendora, CA 91740
Speakers educational seminars and materials.

Irwin Zucker
6430 Sunset Blvd., Suite 503
Hollywood, CA 90028
Book publicity.

SERVICES FOR WRITERS

Book Publicists of Southern California
6430 Sunset Blvd., Suite 503
Hollywood, CA 90028
Publicity for books and authors.

Manuscripts International
408 E. Main St.
Dayton, WA 99328-1385
Editing for small presses.

Newsletter Clearinghouse
44 W. Market St.
P.O. Box 311
Rhinebeck, NY 15272

Help with newsletters.

Para Publishing
P.O. Box 4232-427
Santa Barbara, CA 93140-4232

Book publishing and publicity.

Phoenix Information Service
57 Main St.
Littlefork, MN 56653

Writing service.

ASSOCIATIONS FOR SPEAKERS

American Society for Training and Development (ASTD)
1630 Duke St., Box 1443
Alexandria, VA 22313

Trainers and in-house seminar leaders.

Australian National Speakers Association
Box 221
Paddington, Qld 4064
Australia

Professional speakers in Australia.

International Platform Association
2564 Berkshire Road
Cleveland Heights, OH 44106

Professional speakers.

National Speakers Association (NSA)
3877 North 7th St., Suite 350
Phoenix, AZ 85014

Professional speakers.

Professional Speakers Association
3540 Wilshire Blvd., Suite 310
Los Angeles, CA 90010

Minority professional speakers.

Toastmasters International
2200 N. Grand Ave.
Santa Ana, CA 92711
Communication skills enhancement.

ASSOCIATIONS FOR MEETING PLANNERS

American Society of Association Executives (ASAE)
1575 Eye St., N.W.
Washington, DC 20005-1168
For association executives and their suppliers.

Association of Conference and Events Directors, International
Colorado State University
Rockwell Hall
Fort Collins, CO 80523
For directors and suppliers of conferences and events. Specializes in the academic world.

Institute of Association Management Companies
335 Commerce St.
Alexandria, VA 22314
For association management companies and their suppliers.

International Special Events Society
3288 El Cajon Blvd., Suite 6
San Diego, CA 92104
For planners and producers of special events for meetings and their suppliers.

Meeting Planners International
1920 Stemmons Freeway
Dallas, TX 75207
For meeting planners of all types and their suppliers.

National Association of Exposition Managers
334 E. Garfield Rd.
P.O. Box 377
Aurora, CO 44202
For exposition planners and their suppliers.

Professional Convention Management Association
100 Vestavia Office Park, Suite 220
Birmingham, AL 35216
For convention planners and their suppliers. Specializes in the health, science, education, and engineering industries.

Society of Company Meeting Planners
2600 Garden Rd., Suite 208
Monterey, CA 93940
For company meeting planners and their suppliers.

ASSOCIATIONS FOR CONSULTANTS

American Association of Professional Consultants
9140 Ward Parkway
Kansas City, MO 64114

American Society of Trial Consultants
Towson State University
Towson, MD 21204

Association of Management Consultants
500 N. Michigan Ave.
Chicago, IL 60611

Association of Management Consulting Firms
230 Park Ave.
New York, NY 10169

Council of Management Consulting Organizations
230 Park Ave.
New York, NY 10169

Institute of Management Consultants
19 W. 44th St.
New York, NY 10036

ASSOCIATIONS FOR WRITERS

Newsletter Association
1341 G St., N.W., Suite 700
Washington, DC 20045

ASSOCIATIONS FOR OTHER SPEAKER-RELATED INDUSTRIES

International Group of Agents and Bureaus (IGAB)
P.O. Box 1120
Glendora, CA 91740
Association for those who handle multiple bookings of professional
speakers.

International Laughter Society
16000 Glen Una Dr.
Los Gatos, CA 95030
An organization for speakers interested in the study of humor and laughter and how to better apply them.

PUBLICATIONS FOR MEETING PLANNERS

Association Management
c/o American Society of Association Executives
1575 Eye St., N.W.
Washington, DC 20005

Association Trends Newsletter
4948 St. Elmo Ave., Suite 306
Bethesda, MD 20814

Convention World Magazine
500 Summer St., 4th Floor
Stamford, CT 06901

Medical Meetings Magazine
63 Great Rd.
Maynard, MA 01754-2025

Meeting Manager
c/o Meeting Planners International
1950 Stemmons Freeway
Dallas, TX 75207-3109

Meeting News
1515 Broadway
New York, NY 10036

Meeting Planners Alert
10 Midland Ave.
Newton, MA 02158-1021

Meeting Planner's Guide Book
6 Morton Court, Suite C
Mill Valley, CA 94941

Meetings and Conventions
One Park Ave.
New York, NY 10016

Successful Meetings
633 Third Ave.
New York, NY 10017

Tradeshow Week
12233 W. Olympic Blvd., Suite 236
Los Angeles, CA 90064

Western Association News
1516 S. Pontius Ave.
Los Angeles, CA 90025

PUBLICATIONS FOR SPEAKERS

Executive Speaker Magazine
P.O. Box 2094
Dayton, OH 45429

Humor Newsletter, Corporate Comedy
P.O. Box 9061
Downers Grove, IL 60515

Inside Talk Newsletter
Box 103
Auburndale, MA 02166

Laughing Matters Newsletter
110 Spring St.
Saratoga Springs, NY 12866

NSA Speak Out
4747 N. 7th St., Suite 310
Phoenix, AZ 85014

Sharing Ideas Newsmagazine
P.O. Box 1120
Glendora, CA 91740

Toastmasters Magazine
2200 N. Grand Ave.
Santa Ana, CA 92711

WHIM Newsletter
Arizona State University
Tempe, AZ 85287

PUBLICATIONS FOR CONSULTANTS

The Consultant's Voice
American Association of Professional Consultants
9140 Ward Parkway
Kansas City, MO 74114

Consulting Opportunities Journal
5000 Kaetzel Rd.
Gapland, MD 21736

Professional Consultant and Seminar Business Report
20750 Ventura Blvd., Suite 206
Woodland Hills, CA 91364

Watkins Report, Consultants Marketing
16 Haverhill St.
P.O. Box 216
Andover, MA 01810

PUBLICATIONS FOR WRITERS

American Bookdealers Exchange
P.O. Box 2525
LaMesa, CA 92041

Circulation Management
320 N. A St.
P.O. Box 50
Springfield, OR 97477

Editor's Desk
P.O. Box 6055
Altadena, CA 91001

Poet's Review
301 Plymouth Dr. NE
Dalton, GA 30720

Publishers Marketing Association Newsletter
2401 Pacific Coast Hwy., Suite 206
Hermosa Beach, CA 90254

Towers Club Newsletter
P.O. Box 2038
Vancouver, WA 98668-2038

Writer's Digest
1507 Dana Ave.
Cincinnati, OH 45207

Writer's Journal
P.O. Box 65798
St. Paul, MN 55165

Writer's Nook News
10957 Chardon Rd.
Chardon, OH 44024

PUBLICATIONS—SPEAKER INDUSTRY-RELATED

Business Opportunities Digest
301 Plymouth Dr. NE
Dalton, GA 30720

Communication Briefings
806 Westminster Blvd.
Blackwood, NJ 08012

Human Potential
P.O. Box 1666
Dover, NJ 07801

Legal Information Review
1474 Eye St., N.W., Suite 1200
Washington, DC 20005

Networking News
9903 Santa Monica Blvd., Suite 183
Beverly Hills, CA 90210

Opportunity Connection Magazine
P.O. Box 57723
Webster, TX 77289

DIRECTORIES OF MEETING PLANNERS, ASSOCIATIONS, AND MEETINGS

Corporate Meeting Planners Directory
1140 Broadway
New York, NY 10001

Directory of Conventions
633 Third Ave.
New York, NY 10017

Encyclopedia of Associations
Book Tower
Detroit, MI 48226

Exhibits Schedule: Directory of Trade and Industry Shows
c/o Successful Meetings
633 Third Ave.
New York, NY 10017

Hotel and Travel Index
P.O. Box 5820
Cherry Hill, NJ 08034

International Association of Conference Centers Directory
45 Progress Parkway
Maryland Heights, MO 63043

National Trade and Professional Associations of U.S.
1350 New York Ave., N.W.
Washington, DC 20005

Nationwide Directory of Association Meeting Planners
1140 Broadway
New York, NY 10001

Nationwide Directory of Corporate Meeting Planners
1140 Broadway
New York, NY 10001

Travel Industry Publications, Inc.
3420 Quentin Rd.
Brooklyn, NY 11234

U.S. Industrial Directory
44 Cook St.
Denver, CO 80206

Who's Who in Association Management
c/o American Society of Association Executives
1575 Eye St., N.W.
Washington, DC 20005
ASAE membership directory.

World Meetings
Front and Brown Streets
Riverside, NJ 08075

Yearbook of International Organizations
175 Fifth Ave.
New York, NY 10010

DIRECTORIES OF SPEAKERS, SITES, AND SERVICES FOR MEETING PLANNERS

America's Meeting Places
460 Park Ave. So.
New York, NY 10016
Meeting sites.

ASAE Directory
c/o American Society of Association Executives
1575 Eye St., N.W.
Washington, DC 20005
Speakers, sites, and services.

Association Meeting Directory
1726 M St., N.W., Suite 1002
Washington, DC 20036
Speakers, sites, and services.

Association Meeting Planner's Directory
1140 Broadway
New York, NY 10117-0130
Speakers, sites, and services.

Association Planner's Guide
500 Summer St.
Stamford, CT 06905
Speakers, sites, and services.

Conference Services Directory
101 Curl Dr.
Columbus, OH 43210-1195
Speakers, sites, and services directory.

Conventions and Meetings Canada
72 Wellington St., W., Suite 207
Markham, ONT L3P 1A8
Canada
Speakers, sites, and services.

Directory of Conference Facilities and Services
1623 Anderson Ave.
Manhattan, KS 66502
Speakers, sites, and services.

Directory of Incentive Travel International
747 Third Ave.
New York, NY 10017
Sites and services.

Gavel Annual International Directory
P.O. Box 5870
Cherry Hill, NJ 08034
Speakers, sites, and services directory.

Gerosota Publications
3530 Pine Valley Dr.
Sarasota, FL 33579
Speakers' directory.

Key Seminars
5912 Newton Ave. So., Suite 5000
Minneapolis, MN 55419
Speakers' directory.

Meeting and Event Planning Guide
2811 Wilshire Blvd., Suite 430
Santa Monica, CA 90403
Speakers, sites, and services.

Meeting News Directory
1515 Broadway
New York, NY 10036
Speakers, sites, and services.

DIRECTORIES OF SPEAKERS, SITES, AND SERVICES FOR MEETING PLANNERS

Meeting Planners Guidebook
180 Harbor Dr., Suite 112
Sausalito, CA 94965
Speakers, sites, and services.

Meeting Planners International Buyer's Guide
1920 Stemmons Freeway
Dallas, TX 75207
Speakers, sites, and services.

Ron Fellows Speakers Directory
2014 Siegle Dr.
Lemon Grove, CA 92045
Speakers' directory.

Select Guide to Seminars
44 Forster Ave
Mount Vernon, NY 10552
Directory of seminars.

Seminar Information Service Workbook
17752 Skylark Circle, Suite 210
Irvine, CA 92714
Directory of seminars.

Talk Show Guest Directory
2500 Wisconsin Ave., N.W.
Washington, DC 20007-4570
Media guest directory.

Tradeshow and Convention Guide
Box 24970
Nashville, TN 37202
Speakers, sites, and services.

Who's Who in Professional Speaking
c/o National Speakers Association
4747 N. Seventh St., Suite 310
Phoenix, AZ 85014
National Speakers Association membership directory.

TRAINING FOR SPEAKERS

Constance Dean Yambert
1485 Locust St., Suite 3
Pasadena, CA 91106
Speaking coach.

Dottie Walters—Enter the World of Paid Speaking
P.O. Box 1120
Glendora, CA 91740
Seminars, products, and consulting services for professional speakers.

Elizabeth Sabine
11857 Addison
North Hollywood, CA 91607
Voice coach.

Dr. Evelyn Bowling
7806 Madison Ave., Suite 107 D
Fair Oaks, CA 95628
Speech and voice coach.

Executive Television Workshop
1271 National Press Bldg.
Washington, DC 20045
Training for those who appear on television.

Rou de Gravelles Workshops
225 Carnation Ave.
Corona del Mar, CA 92625
Presentation skills and platform showmanship; coaching with video

Steve Whiteford
2455 Silverlake Blvd., #D
Los Angeles, CA 90029
Speech and voice coach.

Dallas Speakers Bureau
P.O. Box 140071
Dallas, TX 75214

International Platform Association
2564 Berkshire Rd.
Cleveland Heights, OH 44106

TRB Showcases for Black and Ethnic Speakers
904 Silver Spur Rd., #228
Rolling Hills Estates, CA 90274

National Association for Campus Activities, NACA
3700 Forest Dr.
Columbia, SC 29204

Ron Fellows Professional Speakers Showcase
2014 Siegle Dr.
Lemon Grove, CA 92046

Speakers Bureau International
961 Eglinton Ave. East, Suite 200
Toronto, Ont M4G 4B5
Canada

Business and Professional Research Institute
1700 Post Rd.
Fairfield, CT 06430

SEMINAR COMPANIES

Careertrack Seminars Inc.
5370 Manhattan Circle, Suite 205
Boulder, CO 80303

Dun and Bradstreet Business Education Services
P.O. Box 803
Church St. Station
New York, NY 10008

Fred Pryor Seminars
2000 Johnson Dr.
P.O. Box 8279
Shawnee Mission, KS 66201

Keye Productivity Center
P.O. Box 27-480
Kansas City, MO 64180

Padgett-Thompson Inc.
P.O. Box 8279
Shawnee Mission, KS 66208

Seminar and Conference Management Network
P.O. Box 582
Edison, NJ 08818-0582

Seminars International
15910 Ventura Blvd., Suite 1207
Encino, CA 91436

Index